Still The Soul
Survives

Pamela Goldstein

Still The Soul Survives

*A Journey of
Compassion,
Memory
and Self-Discovery*

Pamela Goldstein

This book was written by memory, and mine is imperfect. I've done my best to be faithful to my experiences, and when possible, have consulted others who were also present during that time. To the best of my ability, I have re-created locales, people, and organizations in order to maintain the anonymity of others. I have also changed some identifying characteristics, such as physical descriptions, occupations, and places of residence.

Published by Unbreakable Bindings

ISBN (paperback): 978-1-7383512-0-6
ISBN (ebook): 978-1-7383512-1-3

Editing by Carol Rehme
Book design and production by www.AuthorSuccess.com

Printed in the United States of America

Still The Soul Survives is dedicated to people everywhere trying to repair the world one good deed at a time. —Tikkun Olam

Foreword

By John Cappucci

Teaching the Holocaust to university students has been one of the most challenging tasks in my academic career. As the course progresses, the content becomes increasingly disturbing, traumatic, and difficult to discuss, let alone attempt to explain. After I have nearly completed the course, I ask the students a perplexing question: is the Holocaust over? The students are puzzled, given that they just learned about the liberation of the camps and the defeat of Nazism. However, I ask them, what of the survivors? The physical scars. The psychological damage. The spiritual confusion. All these forms of harm did not disappear after 1945. Pamela Goldstein's *Still The Soul Survives* provides an answer to my question by showcasing the effects the Holocaust has had on survivors in their twilight years.

For a book about the Holocaust, the setting is unique. The memoir does not take place in a concentration camp in Eastern Europe, in a remote Belarussian forest involving partisans, in a dilapidated ghetto in Warsaw. Instead, the setting is primarily within a Canadian hospital in a medium-size rust bucket town. Pam becomes the caregiver, confidant, and consoler of Holocaust survivors who are patients in a hospital in the Windsor/Detroit area. *Still The Soul Survives* explores the relationship Pam cultivates with the survivors and the knowledge the survivors impart to her. Throughout the book, Pam runs to the library as she learns about aspects of the Holocaust and events in

Jewish history. In a sense, *Still The Soul Survives* might be classified as a *Bildungsroman*, as it chronicles the protagonist's educational journey from knowing little about the Holocaust to experiencing its devasting effects on those in her care. Pam sees first-hand the damage the Holocaust has done to the survivors. Why would the smell of charred flesh in the burn unit cause someone to become hysterical? Why would a patient want to be covered in his own bodily fluids rather than allow anyone to touch him? Why would a palliative patient hold a knife to a nurse's throat? These types of instances are what makes *Still The Soul Survives* approach to the Holocaust impactful.

Behind the shadow of the Holocaust, the memoir is also a journey to Judaism for a young woman. She was raised in the Christian tradition, but later discovered her Jewish heritage was concealed from her. It not only explores her path toward discovering her Jewish identity and faith, but also discusses the challenges she had in fitting in with the community, experiencing antisemitism, and building a life for herself and her family. Her importance among the survivors leads to her being asked to perform a sacred and personal task. This task opens *Still The Soul Survives* and will remain with the reader.

As there are only a few remaining survivors left, I wonder if future generations of students will truly grasp the gravity of the Holocaust? Will they recognize that it was not just another catastrophic event that took place on another continent long ago? *Still The Soul Survives* ensures that the suffering endured by Holocaust survivors will not be remembered as an inconspicuous drop of silence, but rather as a formidable tide of truth.

John Cappucci, Ph.D.
Principal and Vice-Chancellor
Stephen A. Jarislowsky Chair in Religion and Conflict
Associate Professor
Assumption University

Where Can I Go?

Tell me, where can I go?
There's no place I can see.
Where to go, where to go?
Every door is closed for me.

To the left, to the right,
It's the same in every land.
There is nowhere to go
And it's me who should know,
Won't you please understand?

Now I know where to go,
Where my folk proudly stand.
Let me go, let me go
To that precious promised land.

No more left, no more right,
Lift your head and see the light.
I am proud, can't you see,
For at last I am free:
No more wandering for me.

Now I know where to go,
Where my folk proudly stand.
Let me go, let me go
To that precious promised land.

No more left, no more right,
Lift your head and see the light.
I am proud, can't you see,
For at last I am free:
No more wandering for me.

1

The noblest of deeds is that of burying your fellow brethren.
It is the one mitzvah that cannot be repaid.
(613 Mitzvot)

Windsor, 1993

Twenty years is a long time to work hand-in-hand with death. I never wanted this, but I made a promise and I could never turn my back and walk away. Too many people had already done that.

I pulled into the lot of the Rachel Kaplan Memorial Chapel and parked next to the cars already there. Across the street stood a neat row of brown brick homes with white painted porches, all of them sitting on postage stamp-sized lots. They looked exactly the same as they did in the twenties and thirties when they were first built. The only difference was the people who resided there. Once the old neighborhood of Windsor's Jewish community, new refugees and immigrants, traumatized by their war-torn countries, occupied the old, dilapidated houses now. New refugees, new country, new traumas—same sense of family—same sense of not belonging, of not being home.

I waved at the police patrol car slowly driving down the street. I recognized the men from when I worked in the ER of our local hospital.

The window rolled down. "Evening, Mrs. Goldstein. How long are you ladies going to be tonight?"

I glanced over at young kids playing street hockey in the cul-de-sac. "An hour at the most. The neighborhood looks quiet today."

"It is. One of the safest parts of town, these days." He nodded his head. "Have a good night, now."

I entered the unadorned brown box of a building with my emotional armor in place. People who weren't Jewish didn't know the heartache and pain felt in this place nearly every day. Only the Hebrew words on the front of the building explained what happened inside. It was a funeral home, a place where bodies were prepared for burial, where even with the funeral taking place, a new life begins for the bereaved—a life without their loved one.

A team of women known as the *Chevra Kadisha,* a group of committed Jews who prepare the body for burial, greeted me at the door. Without saying a word, we headed down the stairs into the room where we performed *taharas,* the ritual purification for deceased Jewish bodies.

Debbie, a social worker and friend who helped me establish the *Chevra Kadisha* for women, grimaced after we entered. "I wish this room had windows. It always reeks of Death in here."

Debbie was right. Windows would have made a welcome breeze. I thought the room emitted the stench of day-old meat with discarded layers of fat sitting in blood.

Debbie and I exchanged glances, both of us sinking into a state of depression. The smell clung to my skin. When I inhaled, it coated my mouth and stayed there.

"Every time," whispered Debbie. "Every time I inhale that smell I'm right there with them."

"I know," I replied.

An industrial steel sink and counter ran along one musty, chilly wall. A plain pine casket waited in one corner, opposite a walk-in refrigeration unit. No one had painted the dingy, beige walls in years.

Stained glass windows, detritus from the earliest synagogue in Windsor, languished against the other wall. They were stored here in the fifties when a new synagogue replaced the original. I always wondered why such beauty that had adorned that synagogue, was laid to rest in this ugly room of Death instead of being used again. No one had an answer.

We opened the refrigerator door and rolled the corpse cart into the harsh light of the room, directly over a drain. *Taharas* may have been the noblest *mitzvot,* good deeds, to perform, but for me it was the most difficult. I usually coped by compartmentalizing, putting my feelings on the back burner until I could deal with them at another time, at home. That did not work this time. I was too emotionally attached to this deceased soul, Ellie. Tears already filled my eyes.

Each member of our team stepped into position. With two stationed on each side of the table and one at each end, we removed the clothing from the body. An intravenous catheter remained in the left forearm, just below numbers the Nazis tattooed on Ellie shortly after her sixteenth birthday. Had the nurse who started the IV understood the significance of that tattoo? Doubtful. Tattoos were not discussed in history classes, if the Holocaust was mentioned at all.

Being the lone nurse on the team, I removed the catheter and placed it on the counter behind me. "Let's begin."

We filled two buckets with warm soapy water and cleansed the body from head to toe, each woman moving in the same rhythm, with the utmost care, gentleness, respect.

One member recited the prayers that accompanied each step of the tradition. *V'kaper adomati amo . . .* and God's earth shall atone for God's people.

I cracked an egg into one pail and filled it with water, making sure the egg frothed. The egg signified the completed cycle of life. I filled two more pails with only water.

After knowing Ellie for so many years, I understood how being cold triggered her memories of Auschwitz and Mauthausen and that cold terrified her. I made certain the water felt warm to the touch, an illogical thing to do, but I did it for Ellie.

Debbie tested the water. "Pam." She glanced up at me. "Thank God you did that. Cold water always—" She stopped, unable to finish her thought.

Tears continued down my cheeks as I lifted a pail and poured a steady stream over the body. To ensure a continuous flow, another team member poured the next pail; a third poured the last, the one with the egg. The room remained silent except for the splashing water gurgling down the drain.

V'al shadai v'tain lekhem rakhamim . . . and God Almighty give you mercy.

My eyes lifted to Ellie's mouth. It curved into a slight, contented smile. The past no longer haunted her. She had peace.

Working as a team, we dressed Ellie in a tunic and pants—her shrouds. I wrapped a long, thin strip of linen around her waist and twisted together the end pieces seven times before shaping it into the Hebrew letter, *shin,* the first letter of the word of God. Three loops. The *shin* reminded me of an angel. I proceeded to tie two more strips below the knees and formed a *shin* on each side.

After gently brushing the curls off Ellie's face, I settled the shroud bonnet over them, and tied it neatly under her chin. Ellie always reminded me of my grandmother. She had the same care-worn face, one carved with lines created by years of tragedy and grief. After a moment, I coaxed a single silver curl onto her brow. In life, that curl refused to stay anywhere but on her forehead. I couldn't imagine her without it.

We covered her body with a linen sheet after placing shards of ceramic on her eyes and mouth, the symbol that this soul is now broken. Gone.

V'brechu adonai v'sharekha ... May God bless you and protect you. May God's face shine unto you and be gracious to you. May God's countenance be lifted unto you and give you peace.

With that prayer, the *tahara* was complete.

According to rabbis, this ritual prepared a Jewish body to meet God. I didn't believe them. I had stood by this woman's death bed five hours earlier, when she told me she loved me for the final time. She took her last quiet breath while I held her hand and kissed her cheek. "I love you too, Ellie."

Ellie's soul left its human form in that hospital room, in the still silence of serenity. *Hashem,* God had already welcomed her Home. Before the *tahara* began.

"Ellie Lieber ..." My voice caught in my throat and I paused until I could steady myself. "Forgive us for any indignity you may have suffered at our hands in our efforts to usher you from this world to the next. We acted in good faith and did this for the sake of all that is Holy."

"*Amein,*" whispered Debbie. She impulsively hugged me while bursting into tears. "That's it. It's over. She was the first one that asked, and ended up being almost the very last to die."

I wanted to cry as well. I wanted to cry out in rage for what this woman had endured at the hands of fellow humans, but Ellie deserved dignity during her final moments on earth. I bit the inside of my cheek as I fought to remain calm.

After returning Ellie to the refrigeration unit, we climbed the stairs. Debbie opened the door to the outside. "We have officially performed *taharas* on all but four of the Holocaust survivors in this town, like you promised them."

"And I think those four women are going to outlast us all."

Debbie nudged me with her elbow. "No doubt, no doubt."

We walked into the parking lot and gulped in air as if we had been strangled and could only now gasp for breath.

Debbie lifted her face towards the sky in the west. Her raven curls bumbled across her cheeks just as a lone red-tailed hawk flew over her head. "Thank heaven for spring flowers," she said, not noticing the giant bird soaring above.

I plucked a few purple pungent blossoms from a nearby lilac bush while still watching the bird in flight. "Well, these clear out the stench of the room a bit."

Debbie took the offered lilacs from my hand. "Do you realize we've performed over seventy *taharas* together? Forty-six survivors plus the others in the community who died during this time."

"You kept track?"

"Yes, and I'm not performing another one ever again. I can't do it anymore." Debbie held up her hand. "Don't get me wrong. I understand they gave me an incredible honor by asking, believe me. I'm just . . . done. I want to sleep in peace at night without thinking of these women and their stories."

When I lifted a speculative eyebrow, she grimaced. "That's not gonna happen, is it?"

"Probably not. They'll haunt me for the rest of my life."

"I know. Oh, I made another decision. I'm not going to *shul*, synagogue, this Saturday to say the Mourner's *Kaddish*, for them. Just not doing it anymore, sitting in that big mausoleum of a synagogue, pretending I'm comforted by the words of a prayer I don't understand. In fact, you know what? I don't want to be Jewish anymore. I'm walking away for a good long while. Forgive me?"

I kissed her cheek with affection. Deb and I had been through a lot of life together. "There's nothing to forgive. I'd feel as if I'm betraying every Jew that came before us if I walk away. There's no one left from their families to say *Kaddish*."

Debbie's shoulders sagged. "I know, but we've done what we needed to do for them. They're all dead, Pam. Saying Kaddish serves no purpose."

"Kaddish puts closure on our promise to never forget. It's why the entire congregation stands at Kaddish, so we can't forget." It was my turn to nudge her. "And I'm not obsessed. I did get married and have three children."

"Each with names of a Holocaust survivor."

"*Oyyyy!* Yours, too."

"Don't remind me. After all these years, I still can't get my head around the world allowing the Holocaust to happen." She pulled out her car keys from her purse. "Never in a million years did I think our friendship would bring us to this point. When I think of all we've done together, and almost all of it for them."

She tried to distance herself so she could say goodbye. "Okay, my friend." I could hear the finality in her voice. "I'm out of here. I'm going back to being a wife, a mom, and a social worker. It's enough for me. Have a good life."

I gave her a quick, fierce hug. "I sure will miss you. *Shalom.*"

I rarely used the Hebrew word, but it felt appropriate in this moment. Shalom means not only hello and goodbye, but also peace. I prayed Debbie would find some measure of peace in her life.

Heading down the main drag of the city, I did my usual; pulled into Wendy's and ordered a spicy chicken sandwich. The spices killed what the smell of that room left in my mouth.

After the sandwich mollified my taste buds and the smell disappeared, I headed home to a long, hot shower and bed. My thoughtful husband had a glass of wine waiting on my bedside table.

"You okay?"

I plopped on the bed beside him. "Sure, why wouldn't I be?"

"Because Ellie was your favorite, and the first one to ask you to do it."

"I'm all right. You act as if I'm going to get hysterical because a little old lady died. I'm not going to do that and you know it." I promptly burst into tears.

Will pulled me close and kissed the top of my head. "Yup, I know it. She wasn't that old, you know—barely in her sixties."

"Oh God, you're right." I took the tissue William offered me and blew my nose. "How could I forget that? She certainly looked a lot older."

"Yeah, guess that's what surviving hell does to you." Will tucked the blankets around my shoulders. "Go to sleep. I've got you, now."

Even Will holding me did not stop the nightmares about the Holocaust. No matter how the dreams began, they always ended with a stormy sky and clouds of soaring predatory hawks darkening the horizon, glaring at me, returning me to 1973 and my first patient who was a Holocaust survivor—Jacob Masinsky.

2

*Embracing a healing presence requires you
to just be in the moment together.*
(Nancy L. Kriseman)

Everybody has pivotal moments in their lives—the ones where meeting someone totally alters who you are as a person and what you believe. Mine happened in 1973.

It took a single second for me to realize Jacob Masinsky would change my life forever. He arrived on my hospital ward, Two East, during an ugly gray, rainy day in January. The sky had been in confusion for two days, trying to decide if the rain should turn into snow. Some people called it a widow's sky, dark and weeping. I was twenty-one and had been a nurse for all of six months, thinking I knew everything about life and the world. I didn't even think about that ominous sky.

"Ah, such a *sheyne meydl*," Jacob exclaimed when we met. His bright blue eyes appeared even more vivid atop his sunken cheeks. "Do you know what that means?"

"Pretty girl?" My grandfather called me *sheyne meydl*. I thought it was German.

"Close enough my darling. Take me to my room." He took my arm. The hump in Jacob's back made him look shorter than his five-foot-four frame. He barely came up to my shoulder when we stood side by side. "I won't need that wheelchair while walking with you, *meine herlikh meydl.* I feel thirty years younger already. Are you Jewish?"

"Pretty sure I'm not, Mr. Masinsky."

"Well, nobody's perfect."

Jacob didn't walk, he shuffled down the hall while letting out a little "*oomph*" after every other step.

"Do you use a walker all the time, Mr. Masinsky?"

"Not when I have such a beauty to hold onto," he joked.

Jacob needed to gain weight. His limbs stuck out at unusual angles from his body as if they were thin tree branches that even a gentle breeze could snap. I made a mental note to add protein drinks for his snack time.

He seemed so happy-go-lucky, always cracking jokes, but something was amiss. If a nurse or attendant helped him, he insisted on giving the person money. That's not something patients needed to do. I later learned from his wife, Sarah, that he had to give "bribes" during the war, in order to survive. Need a loaf of bread? Bribe. Need to cross the street to get to the bread? Bribe the Nazis standing in your way. Need a doctor? Forget it. You're a Jew. Find a Jewish doctor if they were still allowed to practice. Need medicine? Bribe.

I never knew people bribed the Nazis for such a trivial thing like crossing the street, or that those soldiers refused Jews permission to do so on their whim. That fact was the first of many revelations I would face because of Jacob. The second revelation? I knew absolutely nothing about World War II. When it came to learning about that war in high school, our teacher chose to teach us about the Six Day War instead. He said it was history in the making and we needed to understand that even more.

My head nurse, Mrs. McAvoy, made sure staff members put any money they received from Jacob in a jar at the nurses' desk before the end of day. Each morning Sarah returned it to her husband. Mrs. M. gave derisive glares to anyone not understanding why we did that—mainly nurses like me, under the age of twenty-two. She barely spoke to us "clueless babies."

One of Windsor's most distinguished doctors, Ben Luborsky, placed his hand on my shoulder in an endearing, father-like way after hearing one of her tirades about intolerable, stupid young whips.

"Don't take it to heart, Miss Kilborn. Her father freed a concentration camp during the war. He was never the same after that."

When Ben spoke, his baritone voice caressed a person like velvet and he had the patience of Job when dealing with me and the other young nurses. I adored him.

"A concentration camp, sir?" I said.

Ben wrote names on a piece of paper. "Look up Auschwitz and Mauthausen. That's where they incarcerated Jacob, and why he's a patient now."

I headed to my local library branch after work.

Apparently, I only knew weird facts about wars back then. For example, after World War I, the poppy flourished in France and Belgium because lime from the war's rubble, and nitrogen from soldiers' blood seeping into the ground had enriched the soil. I didn't know about concentration camps during World War II, but why poppies grew on battlefields I could recite fact after fact about that.

On this day in the library, I learned new words and facts—Holocaust, Final Solution to the Jewish Question. Six million Jews murdered in concentration camps by the Third Reich. Medical experiments.

My stomach roiled. Jacob's stays in the hospital were the result of medical experiments he endured at Mauthausen. His doctor, Windsor's leading urologist, did not go into details about Jacob's wounds, leaving a young nurse's imagination to run wild. A permanent Foley catheter had been in Jacob's bladder since the war. The rubber tube caused constant infections and pain.

Over the course of six months, Jacob stayed on the unit several times while the urologist tried to repair some of the damage done in the camps. Jacob always became depressed when the surgery failed yet again. I tried to cheer him up with a cup of tea and homemade cookies.

He squeezed my hand one day. "Thank you, *sheyne meydl*." A melancholy smile crossed his face. "One of the reasons I keep coming back for more treatments instead of giving up is because I get to spend time with you."

My heart melted into a puddle. I loved this sweet man. How could anybody hate him, let alone try to destroy him?

During his hospital stays, Jacob and I spent more and more time with each other. I enjoyed listening to his old-fashioned jokes and his chortles of delight when he made me laugh.

I also spent more and more time in my library taking a personal crash course in World War II.

"You remind me of someone," Jacob insisted one day.

"Who?"

"The daughter I always wanted." His periwinkle eyes twinkled. He would have been such a great father.

Jacob and I loved cookies, especially shortbreads. We also enjoyed tea and reading books. Most afternoons, after my shift ended, I brought him tea and cookies and read Harlequin Romances. Jacob enjoyed the fluffy love stories, delighted to listen as I plowed through page after page. Every day he spent on the unit, became that much brighter for me.

Due to a rash of various household and boat fires in Windsor that spring, the hospital admitted several burn victims to my floor, the Isolation Unit. This unit was small compared to other floors in the hospital, twenty-six beds as opposed to thirty-six. We tended to six severely burned victims simultaneously. The smell of charred flesh permeated every corner of our little unit.

Treatment consisted of debriding, or scraping away burnt flesh while patients soaked in a large tub of a Betadine based solution in the Physio department. The room, barely large enough for two people to work on either side of the giant tub, contained a stainless-steel counter with a large sink at one end. A mechanical hoist used to transfer the patient from the stretcher to the tub, poised on the other end. A person didn't survive if he suffered from claustrophobia.

The arduous two-hour debridement took place every day. We removed each piece of loosened, charred tissue by painstakingly snipping it away from the new tissue growing underneath. The patients cried out in agony.

Because debriding required so many staff members, an edict came down from the Nursing Director's office. All single nurses had to work overtime until the hospital decided what to do about the situation. One of those singles, I put in twelve- and eighteen-hour days.

By week two, all six patients had developed a staphylococcal infection. The smell of charred flesh had a new dimension to it—rotting human tissue. Dead skunk has a similar odious smell, but this was worse.

The two-hour routine in the Physio room became torture for patients and staff. With no way to vent out the stench, it permeated our skin pores, embedded itself into our mouths and noses. Food tasted like that smell. I couldn't bear to eat, not even pizza. Two East nurses applied for transfers off the unit in droves.

By the end of eight weeks, I dropped from 130 pounds to ninety-eight.

During the ninth week of burn victims and horrific smells, an orderly wheeled Jacob Masinsky to the unit for his routine admission. As Admitting Nurse for that day, I greeted him at the end of the hall. He stared at me strangely. His face paled. "What has happened to you?" he cried.

Within seconds, his eyes bulged with terror and he screamed. *"Nein! Ich ken dos nisht ton no khamole makh mir nisht!"*

"Jacob, what's wrong?" I felt his pulse rocket to one hundred and eighty.

Jacob shook his head from side to side screaming, *"Nein, nein, nein!"*

I did not put two and two together. Maybe if I had known more about the history of World War II I might have done that. Instead, I followed my instinct that told me something on the unit caused this reaction and spun the wheelchair around. I brought him into a sitting area on the next unit. After putting my arms around him, I kept him close. "Jacob, it's all right. You're safe."

Jacob openly wept and clung to me. My own panic surfaced when I realized no phone existed there. I could not leave him in this state, but I had no way to get help.

Relief flooded over me when I heard Dr. Luborsky running down the hall, calling for Jacob. "Over here, Dr. Luborsky," I called.

Ben knelt in front of Jacob while speaking rapidly in a foreign language, Yiddish.

"I-I didn't know what to do," I explained, feeling like a prized fool, "so I moved him off the unit. He's terrified."

"And justly so, I'm afraid." Ben rose to his feet and took the wheelchair. "You did the right thing, Pamela. I'll deal with this now. Go back to work."

"But what happened?"

"The smell."

I headed to Jacob's new room on another floor at the end of my shift, hoping he felt better. When I saw him sitting in a chair by his bed, I barely stopped myself from crying out. His face looked inhumanly white, as if all the blood had been drained from his body. His eyes had become rheumy, deadened, vacant.

Dear God, what do I say?

His *tallis*, prayer shawl, draped across his shoulders while he stared at a small black prayer book, a *siddur*. He didn't read the words. He recited them by rote.

14

Sarah gently adjusted the *yarmulka*, skull cap, her husband kept on his head. "He's been like this since they brought him here from your floor."

I could never pull Jacob back from where his memories had taken him. All his pain and fear, all the horrors he had desperately tried to forget, had been rudely re-awakened by a single putrid smell.

I knelt in front of Jacob and put my hand on his arm. "Hi Mr. Masinsky. How are you doing, now? A little better?"

Obviously not.

In my young mind, hopes and dreams were why people lived. With each one shattered, the heart shed them like leaves, until one day there were none left. Jacob had no more dreams, no more hope. The smell had made sure of that.

He looked up from his *siddur* when he heard my voice and placed his trembling hands on my cheeks. "*Meine sheyne medyl*, I never wanted you to know any of my life. But here you are, so thin, as if you had been there with me, and knowing that horrible, horrible smell."

I gently ran my fingers across the tattoo on his forearm. "Can you tell me what happened?"

Sarah wiped her eyes. "She's stronger than you think, Jacob."

Jacob nodded at Sarah's words. He held my hands tight. "The Nazis destroyed my father's bookstore on the night of Kristallnacht, in 1938. They beat him and left him for dead. I found my papa the next day in front of the store, beside the burning rubble of books. He was nearly frozen and unconscious." Jacob held my hands to his heart. "He died that afternoon. Immediately after his funeral, Sarah and I escaped to Poland." He inhaled deeply and exhaled with the words, "but I've said Kaddish for him every single day since then."

I had no idea what Kristallnacht entailed, but I didn't dare interrupt Jacob.

"The Nazis took us Jews by surprise when they attacked Poland a year later. We didn't see it coming and we should have. Shame on us. Many of us ran into the forests with only the clothes on our backs. Sarah and I became partisans. Eventually, the Nazis caught most of us and sent us to Auschwitz."

He released my hands and stared down at the pages of his beloved book.

"I did terrible, back-breaking labor. My fingers and hands became raw to the bone and bled. Blisters formed every day." He held one shaky hand up to see the scars that still covered it after so many years. The fluorescent lighting of the room shone through his fingers, making them almost translucent, highlighting the scar tissue even more.

"They sent Sarah to one of the women's buildings. I saw how the officers looked at my Sarah and I knew they would make it bad for her."

Sarah whimpered at his words. "An officers' relaxation quarters stood at the gate of the camp. I thought it belonged at a university the way ivy covered it. The Nazis raped Jewish prisoners there, the most beautiful ones. If a boy or girl was a virgin, they found it even more exciting." She swiped tears from her eyes. "I became a favorite."

Jacob put my hands to his face. I felt his jaw muscles trembling, his cheeks rising and falling with every near-hysterical breath he took. I wanted to pull away. I did not want to feel his terror, but he needed me close, and I could not move.

"One wretchedly, frigid morning, they shipped the men in my barracks to another camp—Mauthausen. My first day there, the Nazis forced us to stand in the Centre Square. We watched as they brought in fifty Jews. They claimed these men had not made their quota for the day. Those bastards—those, those monsters forced them to strip and lie face down, then sprayed them with water."

Jacob shuddered, the look of horror on his face surely a mirror of what appeared on mine. I quickly placed a blanket around his shoulders, trying hard not to gag at the gruesome picture he painted.

"The Nazis kept spraying water until all of them had frozen in ice. And they left them there. I remember hearing one officer exclaim what a shame he didn't have his ice skates."

A huge sob escaped his lips. "May Hashem forgive me, but I stole one of those jackets in that pile next to the frozen men."

The ugliness of a war I still knew little about had exploded my universe into a million irretrievable fragments. I wanted to cover my ears and run back to my safe, innocent world where no monsters existed. But I couldn't. My innocence disappeared that night, with Jacob's memories. The Holocaust showed me how ugly and dirty and cruel life could get.

"There were underground tunnels and rooms," continued Jacob, "where I met Doctor Aribert Heim. *Baruch Hashem*, blessed is God, he stayed there only a short time to carry out his experiments."

Jacob took my hands from his face and held them tight again. "He did experiments on us. With my own eyes I saw him cut open a healthy person. That man screamed so loud, it hurt my ears. He didn't die until Heim carved out his heart. And all that monster said while removing each organ was how intriguing it all seemed."

Jacob became even more distraught. "He performed experiments on men . . . on me. He removed my left testicle without anesthetic, wanting to see my reaction to the pain. I would be damned to Hell before I would let that devil hear me scream. I nearly bit off my tongue. Then Heim removed my right one. When I still didn't scream, he decided he would remove the one sign that signified me as a Jew. He removed part of me, trying to make a foreskin again. He said he did it as a favor. Only it didn't work. It—"

"All right, Jacob, I think our young nurse has heard enough." Dr. Luborsky had entered the room and stood behind me. He placed his hand on my back. I know he felt my body trembling.

Jacob looked up. "She understands." He kissed my hands. "That smell that made you so thin is the smell of Auschwitz. Burnt, rotten flesh. Greasy flakes poured out of the chimneys of the incinerators twenty-four hours a day and covered the buildings and ground like snow. Only they didn't brush off like regular snow. They smeared, and the flakes were gray."

I cleared my throat and tried to speak in a calm voice. "I figured as much. Everything I eat or drink tastes like that."

"Yes. Now you know a little of what it felt like. No one should have to know." He cried even harder. "I thought it didn't matter if they destroyed me, so long as I could still stand and face them. Then I had won. But . . ."

Ben gently pushed me to the side and leaned over so Jacob could only focus on him. "Of course, you've won, Jacob. The Jews won. And we have Israel, now. We have a place where we can go if, God forbid, another Hitler rises again. Our home."

Jacob closed his eyes. He still held my hands. "*Chavela*, I need you to promise me you will get away from there. I need for you to promise me to do this. Do this for me, *hertzelah*, little heart."

"I promise. I'll apply for a transfer."

"*Gutte*. Now help me to my bed. You should fix for me the pillows the way I like."

Once Dr. Luborsky and I had Jacob safely in bed and I fluffed his pillows the way he liked, he grabbed my hand again. "You have a *gutte neshuma*, my girl, a good soul. If I had been blessed to have a child, I would want to have a girl like you. I would have called you Chava, my life, my little bird."

"I would have been honored to have you for a father." I kissed his cheek. "Good night."

"*Gutte nachte, meine Chavele.*" Shock from the day's ordeal made him fall asleep with unnatural speed.

I left the room and ran for the outside doors. Once in the fresh air, I turned to the nearest garbage bin against a wall and vomited.

I could barely stand. "You let this happen to him? Why? Dear God, why? You're supposed to be the good guy and save people."

My heart felt like birds' wings when they flap in a panic after being trapped. I could find no escape from this awfulness. I drove to the Detroit River and walked along its banks, hoping to calm down. I had always found comfort by the water when it gently lapped the shore. Not this time. The muddy river looked different to me now—dark, menacing.

I pulled my coat tighter around me. Birds had disappeared and were silent. A storm was about to arrive. After a while, I sat on a nearby bench wondering how to even begin to understand what Jacob had told me. I finally allowed myself to cry.

I lost track of time while watching churlish clouds writhe and coil in their vengeful approach. The wind had whipped into a frenzy, a shrieking, keening omen of the carnage I would soon learn about. Waves no longer lapped, but furiously crashed, wild and indiscriminate, wanting to destroy everything in their path, as if they had always known what I discovered in Jacob's room—and demanded revenge. Rain pelted my face and arms like steel needles raging down in a biblical deluge. I didn't move. Within seconds the greasy pavement around me drowned in giant puddles. I stood and faced the pain of the rain.

"Are you mocking me God?" I pointed to the sky, accusing Him. "All right, I should have known. I should have known what to say."

My eyes hurt from being opened so wide. I seemed to be able to see through everything now—and all that remained was a never-ending layer of harsh cruelty. My grandmother had tried to protect me from such horror by forbidding discussions of politics and history around me.

"I get it now, Grandma. You should have explained."

After several more minutes, I finally felt numb and returned to the parking lot. I stopped moving when I reached my car. A lone bald eagle sat in the tree not even ten feet away, staring at me. He flapped his enormous wings once. I had never seen an eagle in downtown Windsor, and I didn't dare move. Was he injured?

The storm subsided as quickly as it began. As the silence settled like a shroud, the eagle tilted his head at me and took off, soaring over the river.

"What was that about?" I said aloud, expecting no one to answer, and got into my car to head home.

My mother had waited for me in the kitchen. "You worked a long shift."

"Yeah, an emergency with one of the patients."

"If you were a secretary, nothing like this would happen. You should reconsider being a nurse."

After taking my rain-soaked shoes off at the door, I padded to my room, thinking I needed to get a place of my own. "Talk later."

The following morning Dr. Luborsky ordered that Jacob could no longer be a patient on Two East.

3

The Jewish people are recognized by three qualities:
They are compassionate, they are modest,
and they perform acts of loving kindness.
(Y'vanot 79a)

As soon as I arrived at work the next day, I did as Jacob requested; I put in for a transfer to another unit. Unfortunately, I would have to wait six to twelve months, not that it would have made much difference. I knew the smell and understood its significance.

Throughout the day, I wondered what was worse—being the evil perpetrator doing the maiming, killing and destruction, or being the apathetic *schmuck* watching the evil and not caring enough to do something about it. With more despair in my soul than I could handle, I realized Jacob and his history would never leave me. And his story was only one of millions. Now that I knew what had happened, how could I ever forget?

I concluded that if the Holocaust had been allowed to happen nobody in society cared about anything except what mattered to them. Tolerance and acceptance of one another had vanished—if it had ever even been there. The haters of our society murdered people who dared to dream of a better way to live. They gunned the men down who gave the world the blueprint to follow in order to make that dream come true. One glaring truth stood out in all of this awfulness—Jews didn't count in any way unless they were dead. Why?

I didn't think my depression showed, but Dr. Luborsky sought me out several times after that night with Jacob. Ben was one of those men who exuded an air of calm and wisdom through his thoughtful and practical nature. He seemed to always have answers for a young nurse's naive questions. However, this time, when I desperately needed answers about the Holocaust, Ben didn't have any.

"Why does anybody do bad things to good people, Pamela? Who knows? Maybe it's in man's nature. I go on as best I can."

He went on as best he could? I'm not sure what I expected, maybe a little brilliant insight like Martin Luther King, Jr. or Robert Kennedy, but not this.

"You dissociate when something like this happens?" I said.

Ben looked surprised. "Maybe. Maybe more a compartmentalization. I think most doctors and nurses do that. We all suppress our emotions. We shut down emotionally and do the task at hand. But, at some point we have to stop and deal with whatever it is that we found too horrible to face."

He searched my eyes, hoping I'd open up and tell him what I felt. Trust him. He knew I wasn't coping and so did I, but I would never admit it. I had learned well from my mother's side of the family, the Pilch clan. They found any demonstration of emotion worse than the plague. Trusting someone was akin to a heinous sin. I couldn't do it, not now.

My family on my mother's side were loud and boisterous. They constantly joked and studied each other, measuring each other's qualities and knowledge, ensuring they lived up to Grandmother Pilch's moral standards. Most important—they were *never* there for each other. My mother didn't trust any of them. She didn't trust my father either. And she raised me to be the same as her. Can people change and trust after that kind of upbringing?

"I can tell you're already compartmentalizing," exclaimed Ben, interrupting my inner turmoil on trust. "When do you stop and begin to deal with all of the bad stuff, Miss Kilborn?"

I looked up at him, shocked. He never referred to me by my last name. "I haven't figured that out yet, sir."

"Well, there are consequences to ignoring your feelings."

Ben must have been able to see inside my brain. My mind overflowed with containers of painful and trivial embarrassments, and piles and piles of mistakes I'd already made.

"Digest it a little at a time if you must, Pamela, baby steps, but learning how to cope with the Jacobs of the world is as difficult as this work gets. And you need those skills if you are to survive. I am here if you need me."

Ben observed my face with a wistful smile. "You have the most beautiful hair, my dear. Such an unusual shade of chestnut red. I only ever knew one other family with that color. They came from a northern area in Germany, Holstein County."

"That's where my grandmother came from."

"It couldn't be the same family, though. They were all Jewish."

"Well, then, that definitely isn't me and my family. My mother is Lutheran and my dad's Irish."

Mrs. Smith, my local librarian, actually gave me part of my needed solution to handling my aching brain when I arrived at the library that day. "You know Ben's right, Pamela." She spoke crisply, almost in military manner. "Maybe you should think of your brain as a library filled to the sky with old books that have started to rot. You need to get rid of these old books before their decay moves to the new books. We only have so many shelves."

I understood Mrs. Smith's sentiment, although I feared it was easier said than done.

After continuing my reading about the war and the people who survived, I decided my first baby step needed to be finding compassion and understanding for my own family, and accepting who they were, warts and all. The Pilchs weren't bad, just the opposite. They filled their days being compassionate to the people around them. I remember walking with my grandmother, Alvina Pilch, to take chicken soup to an ailing neighbor. Grandma also fostered children, mostly teenagers. Having six of her own didn't stop her from giving these kids love and stability. She was a good soul who died too soon. I was eight when she passed away.

My Aunt Tootsie, who moved around the world every two years with her husband, an American air-force man, taught children and adults how to read English wherever she went. Willard became a high school teacher and guidance counselor.

If I thought about it, every member of the Pilch clan did a lot of good. They understood their civic duties meant volunteering in their communities. Almost all of them had served in the armed forces. My harsh reality? I didn't think I lived up to their expectations of what a good human should be. I felt baffled by their lofty behavior, completely bored by their political rants which I truly regret not paying attention to now. They scolded, silenced—and shut me out. The sad fact is I never understood why I was a failure in their eyes. And I never bothered to ask. I think I was too afraid to hear the answer.

However, I did make a list of questions I wanted to ask my family when I could muster up the courage to face them. My mother used to call me the drama queen of list making, a habit I began in grade school when I wrote down every book I read. Those lists covered a lot more categories than books as I got older—lists with titles—the meaning of new words lists, what-if lists, lists grounded in my fears like flying, and with my recently found knowledge, what would happen if a resurgence of the Holocaust occurred. I made shopping lists for holidays, food lists, lists of people I needed to confront, people I needed to thank. Lists of my inadequacies and how I could fix them. Lists of the lists I had made.

My family's attitudes were never going to change. I needed to amend *my* attitude. I told myself that I'd eventually do that and ask those questions—just not yet. They weren't a priority at the moment.

Second baby step—I needed to really study World War II and the Holocaust in order to anticipate what my patients would tell me. It served no good purpose to practically have a nervous breakdown every time I heard one of their stories.

I returned to the library again, on my day off, and told Mrs. Smith my study plan and showed her my list of topics I thought needed to be covered. She laughed at my page and a half of titles. "You're funny. I forgot you made so many lists. Follow me."

She knew exactly what books to give me to read. "War is war, so all of the battles aren't what you need to study. Start with what's bothering you the most about World War II, the Holocaust. If you get overwhelmed, talk to me. I can help."

The first book I read described Dachau, the first of the camps. Page after page contained pictures with images too obscene for my mind to even absorb, let alone accept and comprehend. I quickly shut the book and headed for home.

After a sleepless night, I returned to the library. This time I looked up Auschwitz.

"You doing okay?" said Mrs. Smith when she passed the desk I sat at. My brow had creased into worry lines. I could feel them. A look of horror must have etched itself onto my face as well. I found myself with my mouth agape several times.

"I don't understand how anyone who survived is not insane. How are the soldiers not insane? I look at this history and the pictures, and then I look at people around me, wondering if they knew about it, and I hate them. I hate all of them because they did know." Mrs. Smith placed her hand on mine in an awkward manner. Inanity like the infamous Pilch family pat. If someone in the family should ever need consoling they were given a half-hearted pat on the back with a "There, there, now leave me alone." I vaguely wondered if maybe Mrs. Smith and I were distantly related.

"Not all of them, Pamela. The news about the Holocaust came out in fragments and a lot of the newspapers in the world didn't even bother to report it. We can't hate everyone. In fact, we can't hate anyone. Not even the Nazis. Were they sick monsters? Many say they were. But, if they're sick—"

She frowned in consternation when she saw I didn't buy any of what she claimed. "We have to remember there were a lot of people who fought against the Nazis and tried to help the Jews. Our job is to look for the good. Look for the people who tried to help. There's where our inspiration and hope come from." After reading two more books, I still could not find the helpers Mrs. Smith described. I couldn't stand the distance between me and the reality of this world she claimed had good people. They were too few and too far between for me to see. I fell into an even deeper depression.

4

Worry yourself not about tomorrow, lest there be no tomorrow.
And it turns out you are worried about a world that is not yours.
(Sanhedrin 100b)

Spring, 1973

Once my search for good people began, I recognized those good people Mrs. Smith talked about in less than a week. The director of the hospital's makeshift burn unit, Dr. Chosen Lau, believed in the goodness of humanity. With a voice as gentle as a lullaby, Chosen called staff members his family, his team. He was by anyone's standards, a good man. And then there was Ben Luborsky, another good man. How had I missed seeing these men for who they were? They were cut from the same cloth–both pillars of courage, morality, and reason.

Chosen included the staff in determining how to care for our patients. He sent us to as many workshops and in-services as possible, in Detroit and elsewhere. After weeks of daily debriding baths, massive doses of antibiotics, and a few amputations of gangrenous body parts, the ghastly smell faded from our patients. Not from the walls of the unit or physiotherapy rooms—that would necessitate a major washing and new paint—but definitely from the patients themselves. My weight went up to 103 pounds. A hefty size two.

Eventually, several burn victims became healthy enough to go home. We had a *bon voyage* party for each of them with balloons and cake and champagne. I'm not sure which staff decided to make singing "So Long, Farewell" from the musical *Sound of Music* a tradition, might have been me, including all the dance steps and movements. With the success of our patients, Two East began its slow return to normal. Single nurses only had to work ten hours a day. Mrs. M. finally allowed staff to take vacations.

Dr. Lau insisted that my friend Rose, a fellow nurse, and I take two weeks off. "Go be young girls and have fun. Forget about this place and gain weight. Do things girls your age do. Fall in love."

Rose and I took Dr. Lau up on his suggestion. Two weeks of not dealing with so much stress and trauma would feel rejuvenating, like a shot of vitamin B-12. We eagerly headed to Montreal, a city entirely different from Windsor. According to travel guides, Montreal possessed a European, cosmopolitan ambiance.

Montreal, *c'est si bon*. This French-speaking capital of Canada reeked of culture, but at twenty-two, I didn't care about culture, language, or geography. In fact, I had failed geography. I adored the *haute couture* dress shops. I also loved the food—maple crepes and madeleines.

After browsing through spring sales on Bishop Street, home of those fashion boutiques famous people like Cher visited, Rose and I donned our new purchases and went off to Chateau Champlain Hotel's Le Caf' Conc to see a tribute show to Edith Piaf, France's famous chanteuse.

We both marveled at the enormous white hotel as we walked up to it. "It's like a gargantuan spaceship landed in the middle of all these historical buildings," Rose said with awe. "It's so out of place."

"It's fantastic. Circles upon circles, even the windows are half-moons."

In order to reach Le Caf'Conc, we climbed a giant spiral staircase in the middle of the lobby, through a massive chandelier of hanging crystal orbs sparkling and twinkling like stars. Leave it to the French Canadians to master creating a magical ambiance of love in a lobby.

A maitre d' dressed in a tuxedo with tails approached us. "*Bon soir, madelles.* Table for two?"

"*Oui, merci,*" I replied. He gave us the once over before showing us a table, I suspected sizing us up to make sure we fit in with Montreal's elite.

He sat us at one of the window tables, one of the best seats in the club. Rose watched him return to his post. "He flirted with you, Pam. It's why we got this table."

"Give over, he did no such thing."

"They have escargot," Rose exclaimed with hushed excitement when she opened the menu. The maitre d' with the penguin suit was already forgotten.

"Okay, but do they have something that's normal, like a hamburger?"

"Oysters."

"Ew, I'll settle for a steak." I looked away towards the bar.

And that is when I saw him.

Tall, broad-shouldered, dark curly hair, and the most beautiful green eyes that ever graced this earth. "Oh my God, Rose, look at that."

When she saw him, she made a *squee* sound. "The perfect male specimen. Look at those full lips with a Pepsodent-white grin. His teeth are sparkling, aren't they? Tell me they're sparkling."

He definitely smiled–and maybe sparkled—at *moi.*

A waiter stopped at our table with a magnum of pink champagne. "From the gentleman at the table by the bar." He nodded in Green

Eyes' direction. "He has a message for you, Mademoiselle. It's from *Shir ha Shirim*, Solomon's Song of Songs." The waiter began to recite the poem in Hebrew, a language neither Rose nor I recognized.

As we puzzled over the foreign words, Mr. Green Eyes walked over to the table, translating into English: "My beloved spoke and said to me, rise up, my love, my beautiful one, and come away."

My heart skipped beats. Breathing suddenly became impossible. I felt faint when the spicy smell of his cologne wafted my way—musky cinnamon and cloves—heady and delicious.

"For, behold, the winter is past. The rain is over and gone. The flowers appear on the earth." He leaned in closer to me and I could feel the warmth emanating from his body. "Arise, my love, my beautiful one, and come away."

I sat there speechless, unable to turn away from him.

Rose on the other hand, gave him the key to our room. "I'll walk the streets all night."

My cheeks burned with mortification as I kicked her under the table. "Rose, what are you saying?"

He laughed and placed his hand on her shoulder, keeping her in place. "Not necessary." He turned back to me. "I'm Arik, and besides being the most beautiful girl I have ever dreamed of seeing, who are you?"

Arik.

I still sat speechless, but not Rose. "She's Pam from Windsor, twenty-two, and a nurse."

Arik took my hand in his and my body shivered. His skin felt so hot against mine. This had to be how two stars felt when they collided. Or menopausal hot flashes.

"Thank you," said Arik. "And you are?"

"Rose. We work together in an Isolation unit, but right now it's a makeshift burn unit."

Oh my God, girl, shut up.

"Good to meet you Rose." He looked back at me. "*Boay.* Come, dance with me."

Rose had an idiotic grin on her face. "I'll order us some food. They have steaks." I glared at her.

The haunting song, *La Boheme,* by Charles Aznavour, played, enveloping us in our own private starlit cloud. *La bohème, la bohème. On était jeunes, on était fous,* we were young, we were foolish.

When Arik put his arm around me and pulled me close to his body, I lost all sense of reality. He was so solidly built, so strong. So safe. Heat emanated from his chest and beamed into mine. It connected us. In that single second, I fell in mad, delirious, obsessive, hungry love. I stumbled over the realization.

"I don't know why, but from the moment I saw you, I knew we would be together. You're my *besheret,* my destiny. You'll bring me peace of mind."

"You write poetry, don't you?" I managed to squeak out.

Arik leaned down until we were only an inch apart, making me gasp for air again. I would need an oxygen tank before this dance ended.

"If I'm speaking like a poet, it's because you bring it out in me." He pulled me tighter to him. "What are you doing to me?" he whispered and brushed his hand against my cheek.

Amazingly for me, the diva of obtuseness when it comes to men, I knew he was going to kiss me. I felt a rush of helplessness. A tide of warmth left me limp at the very thought of his lips on mine. He kissed me softly at first. Everything blurred. As he kissed me with more and more passion, I found myself clinging to him, feeling his searing kiss to my core. He became the only solid thing in my bizarre, dizzy world of nursing, my crazy family, and Jacobs. I opened my mouth for him. Before I knew it, I kissed him back with as much passion and desire as he had.

He pulled away a little when the music stopped, a look of surprise on his face. "Oh my God," he whispered. His hand shook as he gently touched my lips. "You don't play fair, Pamela. I'll never be able to let you go now."

Arik cleared his throat and straightened his shoulders when he finally realized we were still in the middle of the dance floor. "Wow." He took my hand. "I need to sit and catch my breath."

"Oh, good," I said, still feeling stunned from the kiss. Had we even danced or did we just stand there? "I thought it was only me having trouble breathing."

Rose and I spent the rest of the evening with Arik and his friends in the nightclub district, La Place de la Jacques Cartier, at a Klezmer/Finjan music bar owned by another Israeli. The band playing that night came from New York. I barely noticed. Something inside urged me to memorize every minute detail of Arik's face instead.

Rose and I learned how to dance the Hora and listened to a lot of Hebrew and joyous music. I loved watching Arik and his friends together—teasing, laughing, joking. This kind of camaraderie and love I desperately longed for and needed. Arik let me become a part of his wonderful world that night.

At one point he leaned over and caressed my cheek. "You are joy to me." He had such a radiant, loving smile. "I'm not kissing you anymore tonight, or else I am afraid poor Rose really will end up walking the streets."

Rose jumped to her feet. "I still could." Everybody laughed, including me.

Each time we met during those first days Arik presented me with a long-stemmed yellow rose.

"Why a yellow rose, Arik?"

"A single yellow rose without thorns means our love is pure and true and will last forever." He kissed me, sweetly, sensually. "If I don't give you a yellow rose, you will know I am unhappy. Okay?"

"Wait, but what if the florists don't have any yellow roses?"

"Don't worry. I'll think of something else."

While I fell in love with Arik, Rose had become smitten with one of his friends, Kaito, and spent almost all her time with him. He came from Japan to study medicine at Weizmann Institute in Tel Aviv, fell in love with Israel and its people, and decided to stay. He worked at the hotel with Arik for the summer.

Every pore in Arik's being exuded a passion for living, and it rubbed off on me. With him at my side, I saw objects and their shadows standing out in sharper and more brilliant detail—the colors of streets, buildings, flowers and trees—all of them screamed out for me to be impressed with where they appeared on Montreal's spectrum of life. God had created a magnificent atmosphere for us.

Once I realized I could trust Arik, a real first for me, I told him anything and everything he wanted to know. I talked about my childhood, my grandmother, Tootsie being in the US Air Force. I even told him about my old dog Snooper. Discussing secret details of my life seemed to be the only thing I could do with Arik. I couldn't shut up. Within those two weeks, Arik learned more about me than anyone else ever had.

Arik trusted me, too—such an incredible, humbling feeling to have someone trust me with their soul. I learned about his family, his kibbutz, his friends, his passion for photography, wanting to own a vineyard, his training to be a fighter pilot, being in the Six Day War—I just never learned his last name. It didn't seem important.

One night, we went across the street from his uncle's hotel, to a park where we enjoyed a picnic dinner and wine. I told Arik about my history teacher throwing away the curriculum in 1967 and teaching us about the Six Day War.

Arik pulled out an ethereal dessert made from meringues called Pavlova while listening. "That war still isn't enough for today's political arena, Pamela. Jews have always lived in Israel and Jerusalem since King David. They went into hiding and changed their names, but they never left the country. Thousands of artifacts from that time are dug up daily. It doesn't matter though. Those are dead Jews. The world loves dead Jews, but we living Jews don't count, no matter where we live. My question is, what's the point of caring so much about dead Jews, including Holocaust survivors, if you don't give a damn about the Jews that are living and building their land back up while being constantly attacked?"

I nearly choked on his words. He knew the world only loved dead Jews. It wasn't only me who thought that. So then, what *was* the point? None of it made sense.

"There is only one answer, Pamela. Antisemitism. I think the world is perverse in how it is so maniacally obsessed with dead Jews. People, especially Christians, wear that obsession like a cloak of righteous goodwill, when in fact there is not a single piece of goodwill for us."

He fed me another spoonful of the Pavlova. "I want to meet that teacher and thank him for teaching you about the war. He even made you a Zionist."

"What's a Zionist?"

Arik laughed. "Okay, so maybe he didn't do such a good job. A Zionist believes that Israel is Jewish and we Jews can live there under our own democratic government."

"Well, of course you can do that."

"A great many disagree, as a matter of fact. Part of that worldly perversion. Egypt and Syria are plotting to wage another war against us yet again, and we won't know when it will begin, so we have to be constantly ready to go to battle."

My heart fluttered with fear. "You actually might be in another war?"

Arik poured us each another glass of wine, something we drank frequently. He wanted to taste as many wines from vineyards across Canada as he could. "*Khen*, yes. I've trained for years to do this. The only real danger would be if we were taken by surprise and weren't in the air already."

He gently tugged my hair. "Stop frowning. I'm a good pilot. Things will be fine."

After hearing of my family's Christian background, Arik needed to know if I would consider converting to Judaism, which led to a discussion about our future together. He had worked at his uncle's hotel to become fluent in English, but eventually he wanted to live in Israel. Would I convert and live in Israel with him?

In a heartbeat.

As long as I live, I will never forget that night—a lifetime in a moment. Arik had become the chimerical embodiment of every desire I had ever owned. His love completely unraveled my small-town mind and left me with no coherent thought other than I loved him. I didn't even think how my leaving Canada would affect my mother. She considered me her only confidant.

On the last night of my two-week vacation, we took a horse-drawn carriage to the top of the triple-peaked mountain located in the heart of the city. *Mont Royal.* After enjoying yet another picnic and wine, we laid back and looked at the sky.

"What's it like being in one of those little planes, Mr. Israeli Fighter Pilot?"

Arik's shoulders shook as he tried to suppress his laughter. "Those little planes are over fifty feet long and weigh almost 15,000 pounds. I can fly over a thousand miles per hour."

I stared at him. "That's incredible. I can't imagine flying, let alone that fast. Does your plane have a name?"

"It's a *Nesher* which means hawk or vulture. I think in English they're known as sky-hawks. I can soar so high I can see for hundreds of miles at a time. And sometimes I can see *Hashem*."

"Are you alone when you fly?"

"*Khen*, yes. You realize how alone you are in the world when you are up there."

I leaned over him and gave him a sassy smile. "Well, now that you have me, you won't feel like that anymore, because I'll be waiting for you when you return."

Arik didn't return the smile. "Yes, you will. You are a gift from Hashem and I am in love with you. I want you to marry me and move to Israel in the fall."

My arms gave out and I fell on top of him. "Marry you?"

"Yes, marry me. I love you and you know I do."

"I love you too." The words glided from my lips with such ease. "Okay, yes. I'll marry you."

After several more kisses, he said, "good, so we're engaged."

Arik sat up and put his arm around me. "I do have one question I want to ask, but I worry what your answer will be."

"You've changed your mind already?"

"Oh, no, no." He kissed me. It was a different kiss from before I agreed to marry him, more powerful and possessive. I was his. "I am very serious about us marrying," he said with determination.

"Okay, so ask me then."

"When were you raped and who did it?"

I nearly jumped off the blanket. I didn't know what to do or say. No one had ever guessed before. "How did you know?"

He took my hand in his and I'm not sure if he did it to keep me steady or prevent me from running away. "Pretty hard not to. If I approach you from certain angles, you almost jump out of your skin. He attacked you from the front and knocked you backwards."

Arik nailed it. That was exactly what had happened. "I'm sorry. I didn't realize I did that."

"Don't apologize." He brushed the hair off my face. "Tell me about it."

I flopped back on the blanket and put my arm over my eyes, thinking this might become an epic disaster. What could I possibly say that wouldn't make him think of me without disgust and revulsion?

"It happened a while ago," I finally managed to get out.

"How old were you?"

"Eighteen, my first year in nursing school." My cheeks burned with humiliation. "A member of my high school's football team asked me to be his girl. My friends thought it was a huge accomplishment, so, I agreed, but we had nothing at all in common and I ended the relationship when I entered nursing school. Having never been rejected before, it didn't sit well with him."

I'm not sure what emotions showed on my face, but Arik put both of his arms around me and kissed my forehead. "It's all right. Tell me."

"He begged me to go to his college prom with him, for his graduation. One last favor for old times' sake. Please."

"So, you agreed."

I nodded. "We went to his frat party afterwards and he got high on cocaine and something called window-pane. He decided our going to bed would be a great graduation present. I disagreed. He went into a rage when I tried to leave and threw me down a flight of stairs to the basement. Something snapped at the base of my spine when I landed on the concrete floor and I couldn't move."

Arik held me tighter when I gasped. I didn't want to discuss this, not on such a perfect evening. Arik had just proposed to me. I turned to tell him that, but his face showed so much understanding and compassion.

"There's not much more to say. He finally collapsed from the drugs and booze and I crawled out from under him. I made it out the door and down the street. A milkman saw me and gave me a ride back to the student nurses residence. End of story."

"I'll kill the bastard," muttered Arik. I could feel his chest shudder with rage. That made me feel even worse. I didn't want Arik to be upset about anything, especially my past.

"It was my fault, I guess. I should have known he'd do something like that. He was always drunk and high on drugs."

"That's not an excuse." He tilted my face up so I could see his eyes. "And no, it was not your fault." Arik seemed so large and safe when I looked at him. "I wanted to make love to you tonight, but we've only got a few weeks until we get married. I think we should wait until then."

"Why?"

"It'll make you feel safer."

Truth be told, it did. The thought of letting someone become so intimate with me practically destroyed me. Because he recognized that and offered to delay until we married made me trust him more.

"You've suspected I was raped for a while now. Is that why you didn't try to make love to me?"

Arik had laid down and pulled me beside him. "Yes. Enemies raped my sister a few years ago. She's had a really hard time getting over it." He snorted. "She still won't go outside alone."

"I could never be afraid of you, Arik. I think you're wonderful."

Arik knocked the air out of me with his next kiss. "I think you're amazing too. And very brave. My sister hasn't let a man near her since her rape." He ran his hand down my side, making it impossible for me to not moan with desire. "Israel is going to love you."

I made the ten-hour drive to Montreal a few times those last few weeks, so Arik and I might spend as much time together as possible before he headed back to Israel for the High Holidays. I had fallen for him, so fast and so hard. Arik had become fiercely protective after that night on Mont Royal, gentler, and more loving. And he had a lot more resolve than I did when it came to his decision about making love. I counted the days until we married.

"I feel as if we have been in love many times before, in past centuries and worlds," he said one night.

I understood what he meant. Whenever Arik kissed me, I felt as if I had fallen through time and space and stars and sky and galaxies—and every celestial being in between. I even fell through my own lifetime, passing across other lifetimes of lovers to merge with his. It had been less than sixteen weeks, four short months, since we had met, but I *knew* him and he knew me.

Arik had a plan—return to Montreal after going to Israel for the High Holidays, and marry me on Tuesday the ninth of October. Tuesdays were considered good luck in Israel. It was the day God said it was good twice. We applied for a marriage license. Stupidly, I never bothered to read his last name. I figured I would have that name for the rest of my life, I didn't need to know it then. Once married, we would visit my parents and pack my belongings, then both of us would fly back to live in Israel, an entirely new, otherworldly perfect Paradise for me.

Other than Rose, I didn't discuss our plans with anyone. I didn't want to share Arik. He was too perfect, too precious. And he was mine.

On October the sixth, I awoke with a start. My chest hurt all day and I couldn't catch my breath. Rose and I worked the afternoon shift that evening. I still had difficulty breathing while at work and my pulse pounded in my head. Had I come down with a cold? That would be a disaster. Arik was returning to Canada the next day.

"Pam," called Rose from her patient's room. "You have to see this."

A Breaking News Alert had interrupted regular programming and an anchorman looked at the camera with a somber look. "At two pm, Israeli time, on Yom Kippur, the holiest day in the Jewish calendar—during the Muslim holy month of Ramadan—Egypt and Syria launched a coordinated surprise attack against Israel."

I collapsed against the wall behind me. "No," I whispered in horror. "No!"

He continued. "As Israeli Sky-hawks winged towards the front line, Egyptian missiles hiding on the ground shot them down. So far, an estimated 1,000 soldiers and thirty-four planes are lost. With me now, from Israel is . . ."

I ran into the utility room of our unit and fell to my knees. "Please God," I begged. "Please let him be alive. Please."

In the days that followed, newscasters informed me Israel had lost nearly 3,000 soldiers and 103 pilots in the Yom Kippur War. It became known as the bloodiest military confrontation between Israel and its Arab neighbors, totaling nearly 53,500 casualties on all sides involved.

"One must wonder how religious the Muslim faith truly is," said one news commentator, "to orchestrate a war on one of the Muslims' holiest holidays. It's beyond the Pale, isn't it? And last year, it was the murder of a dozen Israeli Olympic participants . . ."

My chest felt as if an anvil sat on it. The Israeli planes had been on the ground when the enemy struck.

I didn't need to hear any more news.

Rose tried to reassure me. "Surely, we would have heard something by now, Pam. Have some hope."

Hope?

Arik had mentioned the title of the Israeli national anthem meant hope. *Ha'Tikvah.*

I had none.

5

Ask not for a lighter burden but broader shoulders.
(Tanach)

October 1973

I called Tootsie the next morning. "You know those premonitions we Pilchs all get before someone we love dies?"

"Why," gasped Tootsie with dread in her voice, "who did you have one about?"

A sob escaped my lips. "My fiancé, Arik, an Israeli fighter pilot."

"Oh God. That war they're talking about."

After an hour of telling her about Arik and our plans to marry, Tootsie took a deep breath. "And you think he died in this Yom Kippur war."

"Yes."

"Aw, my darling girl, I wish I could be there for you." She cleared her throat. "You do realize you have to go to Montreal. You need to know for sure."

"Do you think he's dead?"

"I'm not sure, Pam. Be prepared. Call me when you find out."

The flag flew at half-mast when I pulled up to the hotel owned by Arik's uncle. "Please, God," I prayed when I saw the lowered flag, "please no."

I still hadn't prepared myself for the possibility of Arik being dead. I'd had these sensations before and they always ended up being an elderly person's death, but . . . this premonition had been too strong, too terrifying. Every time it washed over me, I nearly passed out. That had never happened before. I should have known better than to pretend it couldn't be him.

After sucking in a deep breath, I squared my shoulders and forced myself to enter the hotel. I left my suitcase in the car. I wouldn't be staying.

The receptionist, Arik's cousin, burst into tears when she saw me enter the hotel. "Arik's missing in action and presumed dead," she blurted out.

I froze. "I-I beg your pardon?" Arik's voice drowned out the rest of her words. *The only real danger would be if we were taken by surprise and weren't in the air already.*

"They're sure Arik's plane was one of the first ones shot down from what he said before the radio died."

I clutched the desk when my knees almost buckled. My heart could barely beat. This is a mistake, God. We're getting married this week, on the ninth. I have a dress.

"My mother says that there isn't a single family in Israel that the war didn't affect . . ."

But I love him, God. I trust him. I–I trust him. I . . . trusted him.

"Almost all of our friends are dead too," the girl continued.

All his friends.

"His *Eema* is devastated. His *Abba* stares ahead at nothing. Arik was their favorite son."

"Thank you," I murmured. "I won't be staying after all."

"No, Pam. Please stay."

42

I tore out of the hotel. The once beloved city of my dreams, full of romance and love, had turned into an abyss of horrible, black pain.

With one last dram of hope, I drove to the Finjan bar. Maybe someone there would tell me they had found Arik, and this war had been a cruel nightmare. A paper on the door said it would stay closed until further notice. The owner had died in the war.

"No, no, no, no, no," I whispered while staggering back to my car before collapsing in front of its open door.

I stared ahead into nothingness. How could my idyllic life suddenly turn into such a horrifying cataclysmic disaster?

I had to leave Montreal. After easing the car onto Highway 401, I began the ten-hour drive home. There was no real thought process, no focus, only a stabbing pain in my chest and the fear if I started to cry, I'd never stop.

Somehow, I managed to drive the three hours to Kingston, Ontario before stopping for gas. The truck driver of an eighteen-wheeler asked me if I felt okay. I impulsively told him about Arik.

"I know what you're going through," he said with brotherly compassion. "I'm a soldier. Lost my first fiancée to a bomb. We weren't even on active duty when it happened. We were on vacation."

"That's horrible." I had given him one of those practiced instinctive responses nurses give without any thought or feeling. At least I could do that.

"Tell you what," he said after observing me for another moment. "Follow behind me until London, so I can keep an eye on you and make sure you're safe. I have to turn off there, but at least that'll get you almost all the way home."

I nodded my head when I heard the word home. I needed to go home.

"Stay focused on the bumper of my truck. There's a picture of a dog on it."

We might have made another gas stop near Ingersoll, but I wasn't focused enough to remember. Finally, in London, over 400 miles and a day's drive from Montreal, I started to sob. I couldn't stop. What should have been less than a two-hour drive to Windsor, ended up taking me well over four. Seeing the road became an impossibility when my eyes veiled with so many tears.

With each mile I drove, a new guilty thought attacked me. *You should have begged him to stay with you. Why the hell did you not make love to him? He would have stayed.*

When the last service station of the highway appeared, I pulled over. Seventy miles to go. I went to the bathroom, got a burger, a large tea, and a giant box of donuts.

Simple things—go to the bathroom. I could do that. Eat a burger—sure, but it had no taste, no smell. Tea—easy, bring it to your mouth—my hand shook too hard and the tea spilled down my shirt.

After pulling back onto the highway, I turned on CKLW. With the volume of the radio on full blast, I shoved donuts in my mouth, crying the entire time. Icing and sugar dripped off my chin. I gasped when I saw I had eaten all twelve donuts.

By the time I reached my parent's house, I had been up nearly forty-eight hours.

My bedside alarm clock read 0400 hours. Four in the frickin' morning. My parents were asleep. I wrote a quick note: *I just got in and will be sleeping until late. Please, do not disturb.*

I collapsed on my bed. All of my thoughts revolved around Arik. *I should have begged you to return as soon as I got the premonition. Would you have come back to me then?*

I'd never know. Thoughts continued to circle in my head in what felt like an unending loop of guilt.

6

You kill yourself when you hate. It's the worst disease in the world.
(Jim Schiff)

I never called Tootsie to tell her about Arik and she never called me to find out. Like my mother had pointed out, I just hid in my room. I would not have answered the phone anyway.

I finally surfaced two days later, dressed for work, not even acknowledging my mother sitting at the kitchen table.

"Don't you think you owe me an explanation?" she said. "I understand you're an adult now, but you've been going away every day off since your birthday without any kind of an explanation. And this weekend you came home in the middle of the night in tears. You never even came out to eat or talk until today. You cried the entire time. What happened? Boy trouble?"

"Yeah, something like that." Don't ask me why I didn't tell her about Arik. I don't know. We had never shared inner thoughts about painful incidents in our lives.

"Did you have an abortion?"

I closed my eyes. What a wretched thought. If only we had made love and I was pregnant. There might have been some measure of solace in that.

"Drop it, Mom," I said. "My boyfriend left me, that's all. I'll be fine."

"Well, if you're okay . . ."

I opened the door. "I'm fine. See you tonight."

Every hope and dream I owned went down with Arik, and yet, despite that, I knew my soul had become irrevocably entwined with a little country I had never been to—Israel. But how? Neither God, nor Israel had instructions for me to follow.

I felt completely rejected in the fiercest and cruelest way when I remembered what one of Arik's friends had said. "You gotta understand something about Israel. You don't get to choose to live there. She chooses you. And it isn't easy."

My head hung in despair. "If you hated me, Israel, why didn't you say so instead of killing him? Why didn't you just leave me the hell alone?"

Two days was all I had after hearing of Arik's death to get my act together. I cried so much that my face had become raw from tissues swiping tears away. After parking my car, I stared at the hospital. I should have been married and on my honeymoon. The cold autumn wind against my face burned like a dermabrasion as I walked from the car to the hospital.

Of course, I told no one about Arik dying. I followed the old Pilch routine of showing no emotion, becoming Teflon. Old habits die hard.

Rose announced she and Kaito were having a baby and moving to Japan at the end of the month. He could not stay in Israel without Arik and his other friends. It hurt too much.

Rose's leaving Windsor became another devastating loss for me to face. Obviously, God didn't think I deserved Arik, Israel, or any close relationships. Had I been such a bad person? *Just tell me what I did wrong, God, so I can fix me.*

"How are you doing?" Rose said at lunch on her last day of work.

I closed my eyes. Sitting there seemed like such a horrible abom-
ination. I hated myself for having this conventional conversation
with Rose when I still felt so deprived and torn inside. "I'm okay.
It's like my grandmother always said, pie crust dreams, easily made,
easily broken."

"You can't possibly think that you've gotten over him already?
You loved Arik. I've never seen anyone so much in love. Even I'm
not in love that much."

"I'm fine, Rose." I pushed back my chair. "We need to get back
to work."

That afternoon we admitted Mr. C. to the unit. His cancer had
rendered him paralyzed from the neck down. He expressed his rage
about his condition in an endless gut-penetrating roar that made
the windows rattle.

Dr. Luborsky explained that for the last week, Mr. C. had refused
to allow anyone near him, not even his wife. Cancer had spread to
his lungs and he demanded to be left alone to rot and die.

Mr. C. reeked of body odor, urine, and feces. And vile smelling
phlegm. Dark green slime hung from his handlebar moustache
and ran down his chin. The more he bellowed, the more phlegm he
coughed up. He spat that phlegm over his chest.

I gulped after entering the room. His wife, a frail, mousy woman,
had taken a seat in the corner. When I said hello, she turned away.
Clearly, I'd be getting no help from her.

I moved next to my patient. "Hello Mr. C. I'm your admitting
nurse and I'm going to take your blood pressure." I grabbed a wash-
cloth, and wet it with soap and water to wipe the caked phlegm
stuck to his face. It smelled like rotten fish.

"Don't come near me or else I'll kill you."

I jumped back when I saw the hatred in his eyes.

"Leave me alone," he roared.

I ran to the nurses' desk in tears. "Why is he like that?"

Mrs. M. glared at me. "Stop your crying and get him cleaned up stat. We can smell him from here." She glanced at two male attendants who laughed at my distress. "You boys are helping her, so don't look so smug."

I groaned. Armed with washcloths, towels, a bar of Sunshine soap, and two attendants, I entered his room. "Mr. C. we're here to clean you up."

"The Hell you are. I'll kill you if you touch me."

The man looked crazed. Ready to exit the room, I noticed his forearm covered in sputum. On a hunch, I wiped it clean while he continued to bellow. He coughed up more phlegm and spit it at my chest, but I barely noticed. I had uncovered tattooed numbers on his forearm. I stared at them. "You were at a camp."

His roar mounted, but I sensed something different this time. I looked into his eyes, startled to see them swimming in tears.

"I swear I'll kill you if you touch me."

I try hard not to lose it but, thanks to my German—Irish on my father's side—Austrian-Dutch-Czechoslovakian heritage, I have a wicked temper. It had already been a very bad day—two debridements, Rose pushing me about Arik, and now this. I snapped.

"And how are you going to do that?" I practically sneered at the poor man. "From what I see, you're paralyzed from the neck down. How are you going to kill me?"

I backed away from his next explosion of expletives but quickly regained my wits. "Here's the bottom line, Mr. C. You stink to high heaven. I'm giving you a bath and cleaning you up."

"And I'll stop you."

"You and whose army?" I bellowed back. I gasped at my own anger. Oh, God, I had no right to yell at this poor soul. He only had days to live, if that. I should not have returned to work so soon.

I took a deep, calming breath and nodded at the two attendants.

"Get buckets from the utility room and fill them with soap and water." I'd never heard that kind of authoritarian voice come from me. Neither had the attendants and they rushed to do my bidding.

His wife sat in her corner.

I began cutting off Mr. C's filthy pajamas with my scissors. He opened his mouth to roar again. I held up the scissors. "Don't even start. You be quiet."

Mr. C.'s feet hung several inches over the bottom edge of the bed. He was well over six feet six inches tall. His paralysis made him dead weight, making it next to impossible to move him. It took over two hours for three of us to give Mr. C. a thorough cleansing, shampoo, shave, teeth brushing, and nail trimming. Two weeks' worth of excrement, urine, and phlegm did not come off easily. Huge infected ulcers caked in dried fecal matter covered his buttocks and it took time to clean them and put dressings on them.

Mr. C. never said a word. He stared at me as if I were the devil.

I put a makeshift bib around his neck to catch the continual phlegm. I could hear his chest rattle with congestion.

"Let's put him in a lounge chair so he's sitting up," I barked.

"Yes ma'am," said one of the attendants. Respectfully. I looked at him with surprise.

We needed four more staff to get Mr. C. in the chaise, but we managed.

I took his blood pressure and pulse in silence then returned to the nurses' station to finish the admission notes. Dr. Luborsky had written Mr. C.'s history. He had undergone injections into his spine in Mauthausen. Ben and the oncology team believed the injections had caused the cancer.

If only I knew this information before heading into that room, I might have been able to hold my temper. After that thought, I shook my head. No. My reaction would have been exactly the same. Fury flowed through my veins. I'm not sure when my grief had turned to rage, but I realized it was that hot anger forcing me out of bed and returning to work every morning. False courage to carry on.

I wiped the phlegm off my uniform and made tea for Mr. C. I also brought him a sandwich and ice cream. I just knew he wasn't a cookie man.

It shocked me at how much gunk he had coughed out in my short absence.

"That must feel good to get it all out," I said pleasantly as I changed the bib. I was determined to try again, to be nice, kind, caring, the way a nurse should be. The man smelled clean and no phlegm covered any part of his body. The awful odor completely disappeared after I sterilized the bed and put fresh linens on it.

He glared. I plastered a smile on my face that I am certain looked more like an angry grimace, and slid some ice cream in his mouth. He promptly spit it out.

"Egg salad sandwich then?" My voice dripped with sarcastic honey. What the heck? Why couldn't I be nice to this poor man?

"Why are you doing this to me?"

To him? His words took me aback. I didn't think I had committed any grievous act, and yet he felt assaulted. Other than him smelling so godawful and my head nurse telling me I had to, I could come up with no reason as to why I should not respect this dying man's wishes. He felt betrayed by God, something I could relate to, and he wanted to die smelling bad.

"In spite of what you think, Mr. C., you need to be treated with dignity."

My words hung between us as we stared at each other; his anger and hatred had become visceral.

"You lie," he snarled. "God has never treated me with any kind of dignity. It was bad enough when He allowed the Holocaust, but this? This? He betrayed me again when He caused *this* to happen.

How dare you stand there with that sanctimonious attitude and tell me I deserve respect. Leave me alone to rot the way I want."

I put my hand to my throat when I heard those words and forced my tone to soften. "Your doctor said you were in Mauthausen and the Nazis injected your spine with a chemical that caused these tumors to grow."

"*Shah*! You may bathe me, you're right, I can't stop you. But I will not talk about the Nazis!"

And I thought he might have confided in me about what he felt? Never in a million years. I insulted him by thinking he might. I was a kid. This man felt horrible misery—a misery that had consumed him from within. He would never be able to find peace before dying. I certainly couldn't help him. Nobody could.

I left the unit at the end of the day and cried all the way home. I didn't want this. I didn't want to be a nurse here, in Canada, facing the hostile, dying Mr. C.'s of this city. I wanted to be in Israel with Arik. "Why couldn't I have just had that?"

The rest of the week became torture for me. The head nurse put me in charge of Mr. C's care every day that I worked. He terrified the other nurses and they refused to go near him. It didn't occur to me that I could refuse as well.

His wife arrived daily with her eldest son in tow, and sat in that chair in the far corner of the room. Her son sat beside her, neither of them saying anything to Mr. C. He never spoke to them either.

He didn't have enough air to get any words out.

Mr. C.'s ominous chest rattle worsened with every passing hour. The x-rays showed the lungs had become so congested that Mr. C. could no longer cough out the phlegm. He was drowning. No doctor or nurse could do anything to ease this physical stress. His lips had become deeply cyanotic, almost purple. The rest of his face looked as if it had been carved out of dark gray stone.

"Is there nothing I can do for you?" I cringed at the tone of my voice. I sounded as if I begged him to let me help. "There must be something."

Mr. C.'s eyes closed. He wheezed with the effort to respond. "You're not a Jew and I hate you for that. Let me die the way I want to, alone."

I walked away, defeated.

Mr. C. died the next day. I felt useless. His son confessed he did too.

"Tell me about him," I pleaded.

"There's not much to say. He was a bitter, cold-hearted man. He never showed us kids any love. He didn't show my mother any affection either. They rarely spoke to one another. I'll never understand why she married him."

"Because he needed me," said his mother. "You don't understand because you didn't see how he was when he arrived here. He needed someone to take care of him. I did that. It was the least I could do after what he had gone through."

She sat in the chair in the corner of the room as always. Her son sat on the chair beside her while I collected his father's belongings and put them in a bag.

He rubbed his mother's back. "Dad went through the motions of living, including going to synagogue every day, but he never showed any emotion at all. He did try to control every part of my life. He demanded I become a lawyer. And he disowned me when I refused to marry the girl he chose."

"Don't speak ill of the dead," said Mrs. C. "He couldn't love again. The Nazis took that away from him when they murdered his first wife and children in front of him. He was broken."

Her son put his arm around her. "No, not broken. He was never alive after the war, Mum. Let's go home."

I turned to Dr. Luborsky when he arrived to sign off on Mr. C.'s chart. In his mentoring manner, he took me under his wing again and educated me about survivors and how they reacted to the Holocaust. He tried to answer the questions I didn't know how to ask.

"The Second-Generation syndrome, Pamela. Mr. C.'s children suffer from it." His jaw tightened with frustration and anger. He had displayed compassion for Jacob but no real emotion like this. "I'm afraid the Holocaust will affect Jews for generations to come."

My brows furrowed as I thought about that, so Ben plunged into a deeper explanation. "Many survivors like Mr. C. quickly entered into loveless marriages after the war, in their desire to rebuild their family life as quickly as possible. And these survivors remained married even though the marriages lacked emotional intimacy. Children were not nurtured enough to develop positive self-images."

He took a sip of the tea I had placed before him. "And sad to say, the war against Jews isn't over. Thank God, we have Israel. It helps us move forward with some sense of pride and dignity."

Israel again. Such a little country with such a big burden to bear. My need to go there had become all consuming. I thought I could actually taste the salty air of the Mediterranean Sea the way Arik had described it. If I could just see it with my own eyes, maybe I wouldn't feel so empty and black on the inside.

Ben took my hand and studied my face. "What has happened that's made you so distraught, Pamela? I want to help."

I shook my head as tears started to run down my cheeks. "I can't . . ." I gulped. "I can't."

Ben offered me his handkerchief. "All right. When you can talk about it, I will be here."

I don't know why, but I felt compelled after Arik's death to really understand what happened during the Holocaust, to know as many details as I could find. Why had the world finally woken up to the plight of the Jews, and "returned" their country to them, yet did nothing to help them survive could relate wars and attacks against them? In fact, the world condemned Israel every time it fought back and won. Antisemitism remained horribly, frighteningly alive.

I went to the library and looked up Mauthausen where Jacob had been tortured. Known as the toughest camp, designated for the *"incorrigible political enemies of the Reich,"* it exterminated the *intelligentsia*—the educated people and members of the higher social classes. Jacob had a Ph.D. in philosophy in his old community. He fit their description of intelligentsia. Of course, the Nazis sent him there.

Mr. C. had been one of the best mathematical geniuses at his university in the *old* country. According to Dr. Luborsky, not even Mrs. C. knew what had happened to him during the war. Dr. Heim "allowed" him to live in order to see if his injections had worked years later. The doctor had been that confident the Nazis would win. I shuddered at the thought.

I felt stunned and edgy after reading all of the grisly details about Mauthausen. "Well, congratulations Dr. Heim. Your experiments were more than successful. You bastard."

7

The Holy One Desires Heart.
Heart is the key to a complete, healed, and redeemed world.
(Sanhedrin 106b)

Almost a year had passed since Arik's death, and with every new Holocaust survivor I cared for, they numbered over twenty at this point, my obsession with World War II increased. Even Mrs. Smith commented on how much I read. Other than my initial reaction to Arik dying, I told myself I felt perfectly fine, but like turbulent waves crashing to shore in a storm, my grief engulfed me over and over again. I'd hear a song, reminding me of Arik, or a turn of phrase that sounded like his voice and I became an ocean of raw emotions. It hurt to breathe.

I still didn't talk about Arik's death to anyone, not even Dr. Luborsky. And Rose, the only person who knew Arik, who had shared the newness and joy of my love, had long since moved to Japan.

I slugged along.

A French phrase, *un pied en avant de l'autre*, one foot in front of another, described my attempts to function best. As I walked down the halls of the hospital that phrase kept haunting me—*however much we aim for the horizon, we only get there by putting one foot in front of the other*. I tried to move forward—failed miserably—but tried.

I came to another painful conclusion. Even though I still thought Israel had rejected me, I couldn't let go of the fact Arik had willingly died for this little country. If I loved Arik, I needed to come to terms with his choice. Israel had become all that remained of my shattered hopes and dreams of the future. At some point, I knew I needed to stop thinking of it as an enemy. I would have to learn how to love Israel as part of my healing. As part of my being.

I couldn't figure out how to do that yet.

The only motivation I had to keep going at this point was going to work every day. Two East returned to normal when Dr. Lau discharged our third burn victim. True to our "tradition," we brought in cake again and celebrated with the patient. I got really good at "So Long, Farewell, *auf Wiedersehen*, Goodbye;" even had a cute, little Tyrolean hat with a feather. The senior staff refused to participate, but there were enough of us younger ones who could do all the choreography to make it a happy send off.

My mother asked me once why we made such a big deal about our burn patients' victories, and I couldn't think of an answer. I just instinctively knew it was important—maybe like celebrating climbing to the top of a mountain.

Pain is a huge factor in the care of burn victims. Even as the burn heals, the pain can expand to other parts of the body and become worse. Most of our patients had second and third degree burns, which was beyond excruciating. Patients often became delusional until the agony began to abate.

Rochelle, a beautiful, middle-aged, Black woman came to our unit escorted by her pastor and half of the gospel choir from her church. People crowded by her bed, including her seven children and four foster kids, wanting to be by her side in her hours of need.

Dr. Lau sent them to our little lobby, even though it didn't have enough room for so many people. Still, everyone refused to leave the unit. They set up a twenty-four-hour prayer vigil.

Rochelle had become delusional. She couldn't hear her minister praying over her. Nor could she hear the choir at the end of the hall. Days turned into weeks and still Rochelle had no relief from her pain. She never settled, even with morphine.

"What will help, Rochelle?" I said one day.

"I want to yell at the top of my lungs."

"Then do it."

And that's how Rochelle finally managed, by yelling at the top of her lungs. If we interrupted her, she answered politely—then returned to yelling.

Weeks passed and Rochelle's caterwauling became more than any of us could stand. Out of desperation, I brought in an old record player from home, along with assorted albums. I hoped the music would distract Rochelle and magically ease her stress.

Broadway musicals didn't stop the yelling, nor did Glenn Miller, Vic Damone, or Frank Sinatra. Mahalia Jackson, one of my mother's favorites, was the last album I had.

Rochelle suddenly stopped yelling when she heard her. "Mahalia? Did I die? Oh, dearest Lord in Heaven, did I die and I'm about to enter Heaven?"

"No, no Rochelle," I said. "You're doing great. You're still in a lot of pain because your burns haven't healed completely, and we're keeping you in hospital until they do, that's all."

"Oh, thank you for explaining that." Her matter-of-fact tone sounded starkly normal in the sudden quiet. "Nobody ever does, you know."

I gave her a reassuring smile. "You forget. Dr. Lau visits you every day and tells you how you're doing. He's a good man." I felt thrilled to hear Rochelle attempting rational conversation. This was huge. "Your family tells me that you lead the gospel choir at the church at the end of the street."

"Yes ma'am, I do," said Rochelle. "Been doing that for over twenty years." Another lucid answer. "Am I allowed to sing?"

"Absolutely," I replied. Having lucid moments was such a giant step in Rochelle's progress.

Rochelle sang as loud as she could and in perfect pitch. Singing transformed her. She sang along with Mahalia when we brought the record player and album to the debridement bath. She sang when she had physio. Rochelle seemed almost euphoric. At one point, the entire staff knew the words to "Rock of Ages" and "How Great Thou Art," Rochelle's two favorites. She turned us into her very own gospel choir.

Another week passed and Dr. Lau proclaimed Rochelle well on the road to recovery.

"Hallelujah," said Rochelle and she began singing again. *When I get weak and I can't go on, I talk to my God and He gives me joy, joy in my soul.*

I had talked to God, too—a lot. He must not have heard me, because He sure didn't give me any joy. I was so bitter.

Because most of our burn victims had been discharged, our unit returned to a routine Medical-Surgical unit with occasional Isolation cases. We admitted Rabbi Dickerstein on a Sunday afternoon. For someone in his late seventies, he still stood over six feet tall, not frail at all, very robust. After he told me his wife had died several years earlier, I wondered if underneath all of that quiet dignity and radiance, I detected resignation.

His doctors believed he had a malignant tumor in his liver, small but with the potential to become deadly very quickly. They booked a liver biopsy and x-rays to take place in the next few days and, depending on the diagnosis, surgery, radiation, and chemotherapy.

Dickerstein had survived Treblinka concentration camp. Where I expected to see tattooed numbers on his arm, there were none. I asked why.

"Only the Jews who went through Auschwitz were tattooed. After their admission to Auschwitz, the Nazis transferred Jews anywhere they needed hard laborers, which is why your patients from Mauthausen had numbers. Treblinka was a death factory. The Nazis were desperate to complete their extermination of Jews, and Auschwitz didn't work fast enough. After getting off the train in Treblinka, the Nazis led almost all of the Jews directly into the gas chambers. No time for tattooing, no huts with wooden bunks, no lice, not even hard labor."

He looked down at his hands. "The few of us allowed to live were men strong enough to pull bodies out of the death showers and into the ovens."

Dickerstein told me the six killing facilities in the Euthanasia Program used gas chambers, disguised as shower facilities, to kill Jews with pure chemically manufactured carbon monoxide gas. Eventually, they switched to the pesticide, Zyklon B.

"A pesticide." The rabbi shook his head in disgust. "Oddly, it seemed fitting because that's what they thought of us Jews. We were vermin that needed extermination."

"Pulling bodies out of the showers is how you survived?"

The rabbi lifted his shoulders, his palms outstretched. "If that's what you call it." He leaned in. "But in 1943, we formed a resistance group. We stole weapons and grenades out of a storeroom with a key we made, and set fire to the building where the Germans and Ukrainians lived. When the buildings caught fire, some of the inmates panicked and forgot our plan."

Now I leaned in, hanging on his every word.

"The Nazis shot at us from their watch towers. I managed to throw a grenade. With one taken out, we climbed over the barbed fortifications surrounding the camp. A lot of us perished on the barbed wire until someone finally lobbed a grenade in the other tower. Too many of us died. If things had gone as planned almost all of us would have survived."

He continued to describe the scene, so intensely, so vividly. I could see the gruesome camp, barbed wire fence, him scrambling over it.

The rabbi narrowed his eyes and studied my face. "You're very curious about this. Why?"

I briefly told him about my patients, Jacob Masinsky, and Mr. C.

Rabbi Dickerstein let out a bitter laugh. "And you think you can make sense of all this? Even the greatest scholars of our time can't do that. Forget about it and move on. If my generation has anything to say about how this world is run, your generation will not know hatred of this nature again."

I didn't know how to tell this man I had learned too much, had become steeped too deeply into his dark world. If I tried to forget the Holocaust, I'd have to forget my patients. I'd have to forget Arik, too. All of them, Arik and my patients, had somehow become lumped together, separate yet whole, deeply ingrained in me.

Dr. Lau agreed when I told him what the rabbi said. "It was a different world back then. Things have changed now."

I disagreed with that analysis of the world's attitude towards racism and antisemitism but didn't want to argue. "Did your country ever experience anything like the Holocaust?"

"Yes. They called it the Rape of Nanking. Done by the Japanese. The number of victims wasn't as many as the Holocaust, but still horrible."

He looked up at me from writing in a chart. "Pamela, sometimes we can't do anything for survivors of atrocities. They have to follow their own path to heal and most won't be able to do that. Forget about it and move on."

Forget about it and move on.

No. I couldn't forget. Every stupid war this world had endured needed to be remembered. Every child needed to study them in order to understand how the hatred and greed of horrid leaders left a huge black void on this planet that could never be refilled.

I wanted the world to know and understand the Yom Kippur war and how antisemitism and apathy nearly destroyed Israel—and me. I wanted to scream at the world to wake up and stop hating and killing each other. But—it wouldn't do any good.

With Dr. Lau's mention of the Rape of Nanking, I went to the library after work to look up the book with the same title.

In 1937, the Japanese forced Nanking's surrender. I threw the book across the table. *Thousands were shot—rape was rampant.* The book had a picture of a young girl not more than ten being raped. The schmuck on top of her hadn't noticed she had already died from his violent invasion. What kind of depravity was that?

I spotted another Holocaust book on the nearby shelves called *Treblinka* and hesitated before picking it up. Why did I torture myself with this? The world had degenerated so much, even from the time of the war, it was beyond repair.

I picked it up. I still had to know.

After reading several chapters, I entered the library bathroom and splashed my face with cold water. A toilet had overflowed and it reeked. The janitor had not emptied the garbage cans in days.

"Why are public bathrooms always so disgustingly dirty?" I asked the walls.

Well, I could not solve any of the world's problems, but I could certainly fix this. I brought out the overflowing garbage to the janitor and confronted him about the filthy stalls and overflowing toilet.

"We start with the little things first, Kilborn," I growled as I left the building. "Little things." I thought of Dr. Luborsky. "Baby steps."

I stopped walking when I suddenly remembered part of my conversation with Rabbi Dickerstein.

"Is that how you survived?"

"If that's what you call it."

My heart sank to the bottom of my being. He wasn't living. He wanted to die. And at that point in time, so did I.

I introduced Rabbi Dickerstein to Rochelle the day after his admission to the unit. She remained slightly confused, but she could definitely manage decent conversations. *Amein* to that.

Rochelle loved discussing scripture and the rabbi certainly knew scripture. She told him that she had been reading Psalms for strength and healing.

"Yes, the *Tehilim*. Those will serve you well," he said. "During our services in synagogue we also sing a prayer for the sick called the *mishabeirakh*. May the source of strength, Who blessed the ones before us, help us find the courage to make our lives a blessing."

The beauty of the tune captured Rochelle's heart and she easily joined in. Learning each other's songs became a daily happening after that. I loved hearing the rabbi turn gospel songs into cantorial masterpieces and Rochelle converting cantorial works into gospel music that begged one to sing and clap and dance.

After a few days, the rabbi held up a sheaf of music. "I have a surprise for you, Rochelle. I've been working on this all week."

He sang "The Lord's Prayer." The man could have been an opera singer, reminiscent of Jan Peerce, a Jewish tenor at the Metropolitan Opera House. Dickerstein's voice had a thick, resonating richness to it, exactly like Jan's. It boomed with emotional power.

Rochelle had never looked so radiant as when she was with Dickerstein. She adored the rabbi and he adored her. I found myself needing to walk away from them several times. I could not understand their love of religion and God, especially after what they had been through.

In my weird mind I had concluded a person could only love God if he was in His favor. No, that's wrong. I believed something worse. God took Arik away because I didn't deserve him. Was that my reality to face? I couldn't bear it if that were true. How could I ever love someone again, if it was?

8

*The Acceptance of Death gives you more of a stake in life,
in living life happily as it should be lived.*
(Sting)

After reading so many books, I came to the conclusion that reality has many definitions. According to Webster's dictionary, reality is the world or the state of things as they actually exist, as opposed to an idealistic or notional idea of them. In my world, reality was the terrible things that happened in hospital—surgeries, coronaries, death, smelly bandages and giving people enemas. Reality for me was also Israeli fighter pilots being gunned down in the Yom Kippur War and never coming back. Reality was learning how to cope with being alone, and nursing a broken heart.

Another totally unexpected harsh reality I faced—getting stuck on Twelfth Street in Detroit, in the middle of a rainstorm, on my way home from my uncle's one night. He lived in Novi, Michigan. The Windsor/Detroit border was friendly and people from both sides of the border crossed freely every day, so being in Detroit was not exceptional. However, there was a detour on the expressway forcing me into unknown territory that night, right in the heart of the city, where the 1967 riots had taken place. For most people, detours aren't a big deal. Not so, for me. I can't get out of a cardboard box without a detailed map, a flashlight, and someone calling my name and telling me to follow their voice, let alone understanding detour directions. To make the situation worse, my old Charger stalled every time I stopped during rain. So, when I came to the stoplights on Twelfth Street and braked, my dear old car stalled.

A gentleman from a corner store ran out and helped me move my junk heap to the curb. "Oh honey, you ain't safe here. You have got to get this car going now."

Too late. A large gang of African American men my age surrounded me. The man ran back into his store mumbling his worries and saying prayers all the way.

"What do you think you're doing here?" said the leader. "A white girl isn't safe in this neighborhood." His friends laughed and moved in closer to the car.

One thing about nursing—it taught you how to handle emergency situations—and sometimes ones like this. My brain went into super focus and I noticed every minute detail of the gang surrounding me. The leader's peers respected him and he didn't use slang. He wore an expensive cologne—Gucci. Both his leather vest and shirt were left open to expose a gold chain around his neck.

After assessing him, I decided to brazen it out. In truth, I didn't have any other choice. "My car stalls every time it rains. Luck of the Irish I guess."

He did not stop staring into my eyes as he reached in and pulled the lever to unlock my hood, which gave me a little hope that he might help me instead of killing me. When I noticed a wound on his forearm, I stupidly went into a deeper nurse mode and grabbed his wrist to look more closely.

"Whatever is lodged in there is causing an infection." I pointed at a red streak that went from the wound down to his wrist. "It's going into your bloodstream. We have to get it out."

He grabbed my throat. "We? You mind your own business."

I nearly fainted when knives and guns appeared. One of the guns poised inches from my face. "Look," I said and gulped, "I'm a nurse. I can get it out for you if you have forceps."

"Why would we have forceps?" said the leader. At this point, one of the guys held my door wide open, getting ready to haul me out of the car and into the street.

I found the determination not to display my increasing terror. "If you smoke pot or hash, you'd have one or something similar." He still hadn't released his grip on my neck. I pulled my purse in front of me and grabbed alcohol swabs and a tube of Polysporin. "It'll take me a few seconds to fix this."

The leader stared at me for what seemed like a never-ending nightmare. I knew from the look in his eyes, killing me had definitely crossed his mind.

He nodded at the guy next to him, who handed me a pair of forceps. Relief swept over me. "Can you run them through a flame for couple of minutes? It'll sterilize them."

While he did that, I wiped the wound with the alcohol.

"Damn, son of a bitch," cried the leader.

"Sorry," I said while concentrating on the wound. "I forgot to tell you it burns."

I took the forceps and gently probed the wound until I found the target, superficial, barely below the skin. Within seconds I held up the object. A bullet. "Here. The offending foreign object." I instinctively knew not to call it a bullet.

I squeezed on the wound and pus gushed out. "You need an oral antibiotic and a dressing." After applying Polysporin, I gave the leader the tube. "Does it feel better?"

He looked at my handiwork. "Not yet. You got any antibiotics in that purse of yours?"

"Yeah, it's for a sinus infection." I handed him the bottle of pills.

"It's a broad spectrum so it should work. You're welcome to have them."

One of the guys had gone into the store and returned with large band-aids. After covering the wound, I shook my head. It was a bad infection. He'd had it for a while.

"Soak your arm in warm salt water a few times a day."

For the first time since our encounter, I dared to really look at the leader. Oh Lord have mercy, my almost killer was one gorgeous man. How can you be remotely attracted to someone who had held you by the throat while deciding whether or not to kill you? Ludicrous! But there I was, finding myself appreciating his good looks.

"You giving me orders, woman?"

My cheeks turned red. "Sorry, I tend to do that. It's a nurse thing."

He had one of those knowing looks in his eyes that guys get when a girl thinks they're cute. Dang. "Can you get her car working, Moe?"

"Yup, for now. She needs a new alternator."

He looked back at me. "Did you hear that, sugar?"

I'm sugar now? I nodded and started the engine. He banged the top of the car. "Okay, girl, get your ass home."

As soon as I turned the car onto the road to the bridge I burst into tears of relief. Too close for comfort. I didn't even want to think what would have happened if I wasn't a nurse.

The staff of Two East took turns going to workshops and conferences to learn about the latest burn treatments. Not even four weeks after encountering my new "friends" on Twelfth Street, I headed for a workshop regarding the treatment of stomach ulcers developing around the nineteenth day post-burn. I felt safer about this location, a hospital in Greektown, only a few blocks from the Windsor/Detroit tunnel. I knew the directions well. Detroit's famous Greektown had long been one of my favorite haunts because of the food.

Cognizant that hospitals and emergency rooms had become the sites to some of the worst violence the angry gangs of Detroit displayed since the 1967 riots, I quickly climbed the stairs to the hospital classroom, constantly looking over my shoulder, making sure no one followed me.

Partway through this lecture, gunshots sounding like pyrotechnics, bounced off neighboring buildings from outside the ER. We hit the floor and crowded together under desks. I covered my head. Bodies laid tight against mine. That brought to mind the NUCLEAR drills we had in schools when I was younger.

Even with bullets cracking all around me, shattering windows and light fixtures, I felt oddly removed from the situation. I still didn't react, even when I could hear some of the other staff crying.

Within a few minutes, a security guard entered our doorway. "No worries, guys, it's a gang war coming to a fantastic ending. The cops are here now. One of the leaders died. Ain't no place in the big D gonna be safe tonight."

A doctor from Henry Ford Hospital lay hunched up next to me. The guy was built. I could feel every one of his powerful muscles that touched me.

"Well, that was a helluva good morning and how-do-you-do," he said.

I turned my head to see this man with pumped thighs and abs. A charcoal-black curl dangled roguishly over his right eye. His lips curled into an incongruous grin, considering our situation. "I'm sure as hell wide awake now." He winked and held out his hand. "David Herzl, MD."

Solid handshake, powerful arms. I shook his proffered hand. "Pam Kilborn, Reg.N. I, uhm, work in the Isolation and Burn unit in Windsor."

We should have been more alarmed about so much gunfire, but danger had disappeared, no one was hurt. More compartmentalizing in action. Getting safely to the car would be worrisome, but for now, we were safe.

"Pleased to meet you, Pam Kilborn, Reg. N." His laid-back voice instantly calmed any frightened emotions I might have felt. "Want to catch some food after this?"

"Sure." I didn't think much past the fact that my stomach had started grumbling with hunger at eleven. I checked my watch—noon. Clockwork.

"If everyone could please take their seats, we'll finish this up," said the lecturer.

David reached out a hand to help me stand. His bright blue eyes sparkled.

"You have blue eyes," I stammered.

He laughed at my surprise. "Wow, nothing gets past you. My mother says I get them from my great-uncle."

Neither one of us seemed to notice or care that we had calmly made dinner plans in the aftermath of a fatal shootout. Definitely not normal reactions from either one of us.

When the lecture ended, David and I quickly found a table at Hellas restaurant. After downing several lamb chops, Greek salad, and wine, lots of wine, maybe we had more nerves to settle than we realized, I learned that David's family came from Cuba. His grandparents and several others managed to escape Europe before World War II and landed on the island. Yes, he was Jewish, and yes, he was a distant relative of *that* Herzl, on his father's side somehow—the brother of a brother who was a cousin etc. etc.

"I have no idea who you're talking about."

He looked at me with shock. "You're kidding, right?"

"Apparently my education has been extremely lacking in many ways." I wondered why he would think I'd heard of his famous family member. Maybe all people with famous families assumed everyone knew who they were.

"Interesting. You're Jewish, right?"

"Wrong. My grandmother was a staunch Christian and went to church every Sunday."

David took another slug of wine. "Wow, I pegged that one wrong. How did you ever become a nurse? I would have thought your parents would want you to be a secretary so you could meet the boss and marry him."

I gave him a sheepish grin. "Actually, those were my mother's precise hopes. I'm a rebel."

David poured us each another glass of wine. "And she's still talking to you?"

"She's German. Stubborn as a mule and still thinks she can convince me to change my mind."

David grabbed another lamb chop from the platter between us. "My family's Hungarian and Austrian. Although they did spend time in France I'm told. My mom's side brought everyone to Cuba. Eventually, I plan on returning there and opening a women's urgent health unit in Havana. The medical care females receive in Cuba is appalling."

I took a bite of lamb chop and practically swooned from the flavors of lemon, oregano, rosemary, and garlic. The meat melted in my mouth like butter.

The time passed quickly. In spite of my obtuseness, I could tell David wanted to date me. Friendly, funny, handsome. Everything a girl could want. I fiddled with the stem of my goblet, tilting the red wine enough for it to glimmer from the candlelight on our table and shine in David's crystal blue eyes. Chateuneuf de Pape. He had excellent taste.

Even though it had been a year, I still wasn't ready to start any new relationship and David didn't deserve being rejected by me. I needed to say something, give him an explanation. "I'm sorry, David," I finally said as he walked me to my car. "I'm just out of a relationship that ended badly."

Ended badly—I couldn't bring myself to say that Arik had died in the war.

"Don't feel bad, Miss Pamela Kilborn, Reg.N. We'll meet again very soon." He wiggled his eyebrows and kissed my cheek. "I'm a patient man. Besides, I know where you work."

I laughed at his antics and climbed into my car. As I headed for the Windsor/Detroit tunnel, I passed another gang fight. The security guard had been right. No place would be safe in Detroit when the sun set that night.

I ran a red light to get beyond the battle. Maybe to get away from David, too. Random thoughts flashed through my mind: burn treatments, gang fights, dashing young doctors with piercing blue eyes. Arik. I tried to think of anything but the hole Arik's absence still left in my heart.

David Herzl. But—the distant relative of some famous Herzl. I rolled my eyes. Every time I met someone Jewish, I ended up in the library. It had become a habit. After parking my car in the parking lot, I squeezed my eyes shut. Did I really want to know about this famous man? I opened the door of my car and stepped out. Yes, I did. OCD in action.

I should mention that from the time I could officially take books out on my own at the age of seven, the library had become my sanctuary. Many an afternoon I had spent there, blissfully content reading fantasies and thrillers, James Bond being my personal hero when I got older. I cringed at the thought of entering the library this time, because of what new horrors I might discover. I checked my watch. Unfortunately, I had plenty of time to explore.

I waved at the head librarian as I entered the building. "Hi Mrs. Smith, how are you?"

Mrs. Smith had given me my first library card. She looked exactly as I thought a librarian should look, hair in a chignon at the back of her neck, conservative gray flannel suit with a white Peter Pan collared shirt, a touch of pink in the flower attached to her lapel.

"What's the topic today, Pamela?"

I grinned like the Cheshire cat. "A Jewish guy named Herzl."

"Interesting reading for you, my dear. Aisle four, middle row. His full name is Theodore Herzl."

I pulled out several books and began my research.

Theodore Herzl was an Austrian Jewish lawyer who became a journalist and playwright. Best known for his critical role in becoming the founder of Zionism and establishing the modern State of Israel.

Holy cow, and I knew someone distantly related to this guy by a brother's brother's cousin etc. etc.

He is remembered as Israel's founding father, his grave located in Israel's national cemetery in Jerusalem, and his Hebrew birthday is observed as a national holiday.

I plopped my hands on top of my head. "I'm not Jewish. Why would I know this?" The bigger question I should have asked was why would I not know about this? Arik and I were going to live in Israel and I had not learned a single fact about that country, except what I researched about the Six Day War in high school. Arik lived on a kibbutz, and I hadn't even bothered to look up what that meant. How would I have managed there? No wonder Israel rejected me.

I returned to work the next day, eager to discuss Herzl with Rabbi Dickerstein. He had passed away in the night from a massive coronary. I closed my eyes and hung my head when I heard the news. "He really was waiting."

In the four weeks Rabbi Dickerstein had been with us, he had brought a sense of peace to everyone. The other staff shed tears at his passing. I tried crying several times as staff discussed his acts of kindness to them, but I couldn't do it. Maybe something had broken inside of me? Of course, it had. My heart. I still didn't connect my lack of emotion to the shock of Arik's death and me not coping with it. I just knew I felt nothing except a lot of guilt. Could experiencing so much shame and guilt be considered emotion?

Rochelle seemed to lack emotion as well when I stopped by her room with a cup of tea and Peek Frean short breads with the raspberry centers.

Rochelle picked up one of the cookies. "These were his favorites."

"Yes, I know, yours too."

Rochelle gazed out the window. "He and I discussed his coming death a lot. Did you know how quickly he would die?"

"No. He could have lived a long time." I hesitated. "Well . . . I had the feeling he was—"

"Waiting?"

I nodded.

"He missed his wife," said Rochelle. "I often heard him praying to God, asking to be taken."

She wiped a lone tear from her cheek. "I surely will miss him, that's for sure."

She gave me a sad smile. "The rabbi cared about you very much. He suspected someone that you loved had died violently."

I plopped in the chair beside her bed feeling gobsmacked. "How did he know? Did you know too?"

Rochelle took my hands between her own. "Yes. Once you've suffered losing someone suddenly, you get a certain look on your face. Like you've been stunned. Only somebody else who's been through that can understand the look." So much compassion appeared on her face. "My husband died in the Vietnam war eight years ago. He was my only love and even though we only had a short time together, it was enough for me. I also had all those children. But life has been good."

She handed me a cookie. "But you, young girl . . . you need to grieve, child. You also need to open up your heart and feel again. Don't you be feeling guilty about starting over. Rabbi Dickerstein wanted to talk to you about that."

I stood, leaned over Rochelle, and kissed her cheek. "Thank you, Rochelle, but you don't need to worry about me. I'll be fine. It's going to take me a little while, that's all."

"I'm praying for you."

Tears filled my eyes. "Thank you."

When I left the unit that day, I drove out to Lake Erie and parked by the water, my usual retreat when I was upset. The sun sparkled on the astral-blue waves, blinding me, dazzling me with its pulsing light. Cormorants, seagulls, and osprey eagles arched and wheeled, playing games with the wind. I closed my eyes and listened to the deceptive music the lake made.

Lake Erie was famous for its murdering, powerful crosscurrents hidden from the human eye. Erie was never smooth. It was always the master conductor, and made its own music, a swelling symphony, oftentimes filled with rage. I opened my eyes, sensing the malicious soul I always believed Erie owned. No, this was not how I would die. Instead of drowning in the lake, I decided drowning my sorrows in drink would be a lot safer. I quickly headed for home. As if to confirm my decision was correct, a lone hawk flew along the car until I left the park, its rasping cry echoing in my ears long after I left it behind.

As soon as I got home, I showered and poured a glass of wine. I burst into tears. "He's dead." Between huge gasps of pain and despair I said the words I'd been avoiding for a year. "He did die in that war. He's gone and nothing is going to bring him back. I'm alone."

9

The Jewish people gave the Ten Commandments to the world.
The Holocaust demands we strenghten them by three additional
ones: thou shall not be a perpetrator; thou shall not be a victim;
and thou shall never, but never, be a bystander.
(Yehuda Bauer)

My transfer to another unit finally came through in 1974, and I started work on the Chemotherapy floor. It had been over a year since that day with Jacob and his response to the smell on Two East. It had also been over a year since Arik died. I didn't think of him constantly anymore. Maybe a twinge a few times a day, a little shock, or a slight whisper rising up from the bottom of my memory, sounding like his voice—*I love you and you know I do*. Before I closed my eyes at night, my heart retrieved the hurt in me and held onto it. I tried to pretend the pain would be gone before the sun rose again, but it remained there until I pushed it back down with force in order to carry on.

Sometimes, I stayed awake wondering how wonderful it would have been to look into Arik's eyes and share how he'd weather life. I would have settled for merely being his shadow. All that I became with him and all that I wanted to be collided against those bitter nights and left me feeling frozen and useless.

I gladly left the burn unit. For the life of me I could not get my weight over the 103-pound mark. The smell no longer lingered in my nose, so I had no excuse not to eat, but every time I tried, I remembered picnics on mountains in Montreal, or eating fresh bagels with cream cheese at dawn after dancing all night.

I had only one regret about my transfer. I had to leave Dr. Lau. He felt hurt, even though he understood as a doctor that having such a low weight for so long affected my physical state.

Four nurses who had transferred from Two East, worked on the Chemo unit and quickly informed me that there were serious problems. Our old Head Nurse acted like a saint compared to this new one. One girl called her the Wicked Witch of the East. I wondered how long it would take me to piss this one off. Exactly five days. She didn't like nurses with new ideas about patient care such as reading to them and giving them afternoon teas. She'd heard about that from my old Head Nurse.

She especially didn't like that I knew how to make cookies. Who knew that could be such an issue?

Head nurse issues aside, I quickly realized I worked with saints. I had already elevated Drs. Lau and Luborsky to sainthood, so it came as no surprise to find myself putting these cancer doctors in the same venerated state. It turned out I had been surrounded by Mrs. Smith's good people all along. Maybe I lived in the right world after all. If only I could get my act together.

We went to conferences to learn the latest in treating cancer. I traveled to Chicago where I met the Swiss-American psychiatrist, Elizabeth Kübler-Ross, the author of the internationally best-selling book, *On Death and Dying* (1969). She wrote about her theory of the five stages of grief, also known as the "Kübler-Ross Model." Every dying individual underwent a pattern of adjustment: denial, anger, bargaining, depression, and acceptance. Elizabeth had also become a force behind dying patients being treated with dignity, and a concept called "hospice," a contained community for patients to enter and die in peace.

I wondered where I stood in her Model. Anger for sure, depression a definite, and maybe I still carried some denial. I didn't think I'd ever get to acceptance. I had no final goodbyes, no grave to visit for closure to that gaping wound.

When his long-term infections developed into cancer, Jacob Masinsky became one of the regulars on the unit. He clapped his hands together with happiness when he saw me working there. "Tea and cookies?" his question loaded with expectation. "And you look healthy again."

"Up to 105 pounds," I bragged with a laugh. It felt good to see him smiling. He seemed more like his old self again. Apparently, he possessed a lot more spit and fire than me.

"I'm finished at 3:30," I said. "Meet you in the lobby by the windows?"

As our lobby teas became routine again, news spread, and I soon found myself brewing and baking for eight Holocaust survivors.

"Where did all these people come from?" I said to Jacob one day. "Did you tell them?"

Jacob downed another cookie. "Never. They're eating all of my favorite cookies." He blushed. "I told Aaron over there. I didn't know he could be such a *Yenta*, a blabbermouth."

The books I read to my group always ended up being Harlequin Romances. The men enjoyed the fluff books the most. Such romantics.

By the end of the second week of Jacob's treatments, our group grew to ten, and the hospital barber, Schmuel, another Holocaust survivor, joined us. He and I had become good friends. The gang dubbed themselves the Harlequin Romance Club.

During that brief time, I read to them, their fear of dying dissipated. I could see them relax, have a nosh, enjoy *kibbitzing* and sharing a laugh or two. A semblance of normalcy settled upon them.

How did they survive what they went through and what they still suffered? A few minutes of suffering made me angry and distraught. What would years of that do to a person? Even mountains can be worn down with enough rain.

All the Club members agreed to make me their adopted sweetheart. "And you make such good cookies," said one of the patients. "Where did you learn how to make such good *rugelakh*?"

"Uhm, it's my grandmother's recipe. She used a lot of butter."

The Club members exchanged glances and nodded their heads sagely. They all agreed I belonged to the "tribe," especially when I told them my mother's nickname was Dollie, a Yiddish term of endearment.

Bayla joined us in the middle of the first week of the other patients' treatments. She had been diagnosed with brain cancer and was about to start palliative chemotherapy. The doctors explained she would most likely die within a few weeks.

When I walked into Bayla's room to admit her, I immediately noticed how her smooth cheeks set off her perfectly round, violet blue eyes. She whimpered every few minutes from the pain in her head. "Oy, this is so awful."

I checked my watch. "They gave you an injection ten minutes ago. It should start working soon."

While taking her blood pressure, I noticed the glaring tattoo against her white bisque porcelain skin. After seeing so many, I thought I could see those numbers without flinching in reaction, but it still shocked me every time.

"You know what those numbers mean, don't you, sweetheart?"

"Yes. Where were you?"

"Auschwitz, then Mauthausen."

I took her pulse. "Some of my patients were there."

"I know. We're all friends. We meet twice a month for lunch whenever we can. It's difficult sometimes with so many getting cancer treatments. The men call themselves the Romeos—Retired Old Men Eating Out Sometimes. They can be so silly."

Despite her pain, she winked at me. "You're our favorite topic at lunch, Pamela. And we're trying to find you a nice Jewish boy to fall in love with." She laughed when I blushed. "Everyone enjoys your little book gatherings, sweetheart. I've always wanted to join the club, but I never wanted to get cancer."

"Club?"

"Yes, I came up with the name. It seemed like a perfect fit. What kind of cookies did you make today?"

"Shortbreads."

They talked about me? It made me wonder what else they discussed.

As the doctors predicted, it did not take long before Bayla became delirious. Her delirium worsened with each passing day. A week later, I was assigned to be her nurse. That morning a kitchen staff member screamed when she brought the breakfast tray into Bayla's room.

I rushed into the room. "What's wrong?"

Bayla had grabbed the staff girl and held a knife forcefully against her throat. She stood on the armchair by the window, her johnny shirt flapping in the breeze of her movements. "Get away from me, or else I'll kill her," she shrieked.

I frantically went through my options on how to get the knife away from poor Bayla without injuring anyone. Came up blank. Crap. I decided to think of her behavior as something "a bit odd," not deadly at all. "Bayla, why are you holding Mary like that?"

"She's a Nazi. She's poisoning our food."

Back to the Nazis again. I kept my face expressionless. "Bayla, do you know who I am?"

She sniffed indignantly. "Of course, I do. You're Pamela, my nurse."

"And where are we?"

Bayla's terrified eyes scoured the room. "Mauthausen . . ."

I inched closer. "We're in Windsor, at a hospital. You have cancer, remember?"

Bayla's eyes filled with tears and she searched my face for some sign that I told the truth. I smiled reassuringly. "It's all right, Bayla. You're safe here."

I eased closer to Bayla and extricated the knife from her hand. "I promise you I won't let anything happen to you, all right?" Bayla never stopped staring into my eyes. "Let Mary go back to work. I'll stay in here with you."

I entwined my fingers with Bayla's and slowly moved her arm away from Mary's neck. "You can go now, Mary."

Once the girl ran from the room, I put my arms around Bayla and helped her down from the chair. "There now, you're okay, Bayla."

She started to cry. "I'm so sorry, Pamela."

The head nurse and two orderlies arrived, a doctor at their heels. Bayla screeched with fear when she saw them and grabbed me by the throat, effectively cutting off my windpipe. "Get away," she cried.

Her eyes lit upon a bedpan sitting on a nearby bed and she snatched it up. "I'll beat her if you come in here."

The doctor bit his lips together to halt a smile, but the orderlies burst out in howls of laughter.

"This isn't funny," I said while gasping for air. Despite being so ill, Bayla had remarkable strength. "Bayla's frightened."

"You're right," said the doctor. "Bayla, I'm Dr. Smith."

She sniffed indignantly. "I know that."

Dr. Smith edged forward and removed the potentially lethal bedpan. He released me from Bayla's hold, put his arms around the woman, and held her close. I held back a snort—tried that and I ended up being choked. Should I warn him? He knows, right? He saw me in her hold.

She collapsed into him, shaking her head in despair. "What is wrong with me that I would do such a thing?"

"It's that nasty old cancer doing bad things to your brain, honey," said Dr. Smith.

He and I helped her into bed. When the head nurse walked over to help, Bayla whipped around and put the doctor in a headlock.

"Oh, for goodness' sake," muttered the nurse. "Stop this nonsense."

Bayla tightened her grip even more.

"Hey, it looks like a great breakfast," Dr. Smith managed to say, his head squashed between the woman's breasts. I should have warned him not to get so close.

"It's poisoned." She pointed at the Head nurse. "She poisoned it."

"Can you help me out here?" said Dr. Smith. He couldn't breathe properly.

The head nurse motioned for the orderlies to grab Bayla and hold her down. In my mind, it would have been the worst thing to do. I took up a fork before they could move. "The food isn't poisoned, Bayla. Watch." I took a mouthful of everything on the tray. "See? It's fine."

Bayla eyed me suspiciously. "You swallowed it?"

"Mm Hmm." I opened my mouth up wide so she could see.

"Well, I am hungry."

"Good," I said. "Why don't you eat and I'll talk to the doctor for a few minutes?"

Bayla chuckled as if nothing out of the ordinary had happened. "Thank you, Dollie, but come right back." She delved into her breakfast with gusto.

The head nurse's eyes shot daggers at me when Dr. Smith patted my back. "Good job, Pam," he said.

Sarah Masinsky, Jacob's wife, had been bunk mates with Bayla at the camps and she brought tea for the two of them every afternoon. I supplied the cookies-of-the-day; this day happened to be Snickerdoodles. According to Sarah, Bayla's most fervent wish if she survived, was to have tea every afternoon while eating cookies and reading.

Each time Sarah entered the room, she held Bayla's hand. "I brought your tea, Bayla my love, the way you like it, two sugars and a bit of cream." Then she chatted about the weather and what a lovely day to take a walk, something else they had not been allowed to do in the camps. After that, she read to her friend from books by Saul Bellow and Sholom Aleichem. It kept Bayla happy.

Sarah explained how they met at the camp. "Within a few days of arriving at Auschwitz, they sent Bayla to Mauthausen. She had a horrible infection from being raped so many times. When the soldiers tired of me, they transferred me there too, for 'sexual experiments.' We became bunkmates again. Both of us went under Dr. Aribert Heim's knife. Oh Pamela, we were in agony. I wouldn't have survived without Bayla. She was so brave."

Sarah's face crumpled. I put my arms around her and let her weep. At this point in time, life seemed like nothing more than a dreadful storm that constantly washed away whatever happiness had been there minutes before, leaving something unrecognizable and ugly in its wake. Surely, there had to be more to living.

I had to admit I reached my own point of no return. Arik's death destroyed me, but caring for my Holocaust survivors and hearing their experiences made me lose any scale of place or hours or human decency. Even ugly wars could not compare to Dachau, Auschwitz and Mauthausen. Compared to them, war seemed—clean—homogenized.

At last Sarah regained her composure. "When the Nazis heard

the British were on their way to free the camp, they gathered us inmates and tried to march us into the forest. The ones too ill to move were left behind. I grabbed Bayla's hand as the others left the barracks and we hid under the floor where the wood had rotted from all the urine and feces. Then everything happened so fast. The British arrived in the afternoon. We were put on trucks and removed from the camp. Bayla and I became separated from each other."

"How could that happen?"

Sarah blew her nose and took a sip of tea. "Because no orders were in place. None of the allied soldiers expected to find anything in the camp. They were in shock. A lot of them wept or vomited. I didn't realize they planned on taking us to different places when we got on the trucks. I assumed we'd be together."

She took a calming breath. "We'd been looking for each other ever since. I registered at the Red Cross in Europe. It never occurred to me to register here until a few years ago."

"Her family says she never married," I managed to say without crying. It amazed me how I fell apart while Sarah regained her strength and dignity.

"That's true," said Sarah. "Bayla died on the inside in Mauthausen. She got pregnant from one of the rapes which is why she underwent the doctor's knife." She hung her head in shame. "Me too."

Not wanting to hear the response I already knew she would give, but feeling compelled to ask, the words escaped from my mouth. "Where did her baby go?"

I was mistaken about Sarah's strength to withstand the telling of this experience. That had been bravado for my sake. Her lips quivered as she gasped out a pained cry.

"Never mind, don't tell me," I rushed to say, but it was too late. The damage was done.

Sarah needed to tell me all of it now that she had begun. For years she had kept her memories at bay, but seeing Bayla and hearing her incoherent cries of terror made her finally face her own horror from that time. Her soul died in front of me.

"She killed her baby boy so they wouldn't make a wallet out of his skin, a real prize for the Nazis—to have a wallet made out of Jewish babies, especially the boys. I buried the baby for her, outside the barracks where all the others were laid to rest."

Sarah clucked affectionately. She tucked another blanket around her friend like a mother hen. This simple act seemed to allow her to distance herself from the memories and return to the present.

"She lives in the past so much," she said softly. "What a horrible place to spend your final days, back in the camps. Now I'm back there too. I don't want to die remembering this. Dear *Hashem*, let me die in my sleep. No pain, no nothing. Quick and be done. I don't want any tears. If someone wants to remember me, they can go dancing or walk along a beach at sunset. And that's it."

The next day Bayla slipped further into unconsciousness and became incontinent. Dr. Smith ordered a Foley catheter. Normally it's an easy procedure to insert a catheter with no pain, but for Bayla this was torture. She screamed and fought every time we tried to insert one.

"Oh, God," said Dr. Smith. His face paled. "She thinks she's being raped." He turned away when his eyes filled with tears. "Oh, my dear God, this is horrible. Don't try anymore. Put diapers on her. It'll be more humane."

He headed for the door. "And start the morphine drip, two milligrams every hour along with Valium ten and Gravol 50 IV."

He had ordered the cocktail of drugs that ended the ordeal of living. I told myself it was merciful to let her die and I felt relief when Bayla took her last breath. But it tore at my heart knowing the last coherent thought she had was of Auschwitz and Mauthausen. And being raped.

10

One should always be among those who are persecuted,
rather than among those who persecute.

(Bava Kama 93a)

I finally had my talk with Tootsie about Arik dying. Over a year later. She had assumed that was what happened and said she gave me room to grieve. Every one of her sisters was like her—needing to handle grieving on their own. Once a Pilch, always a Pilch she claimed and assumed I would be just like her. She was right.

Ever since my talk with Tootsie, I thought about what she said. "Child, you should tell your mama about this. She's right there with you and can help better than a phone call with me."

I really wanted to do that, but I knew the reason why I didn't confide in my mother. She had never let me be close to her. After growing up not confiding, not trusting, I couldn't let her in.

So, I developed a new obsession—drinking wine after work and reading war books I found at the library. I could practically rattle off every word in books by Leon Uris—*Battle Cry, Exodus, Mila 18, QB VII.* I also watched movies about wars and air forces and cried bitter tears through every one of them—*M*A*S*H, Patton, Twelve O'Clock High*.

This habit abruptly ended when I watched *A Guy Named Joe*.

Based on the legend that pilots never die, but return to guide fledgling airmen, this movie included the pilot returning to his widow as well. Joe, Spencer Tracey, is shot down overseas, leaving his wife devastated. I could definitely relate. Joe becomes another pilot's guardian angel who has fallen in love with his widow. Joe gives his widow permission to love again in the gut-wrenching ending

Perfect for causing a girl grieving over a fighter pilot to shut down completely. I didn't have permission to live, let alone love. That evening I became the girl with no affect, and I feared it would become a permanent state of being if I didn't snap out of it.

Dr. Luborsky joined our Harlequin Romance Club gatherings every chance he got. Most of the members were his patients. Collectively, they worked well in keeping him apprised of all of their conditions.

I liked to think he came for the cookies, tea, and camaraderie. Jacob Masinsky thought Dr. Luborsky came to see how I fared. I could tell by the way Ben observed me that he still waited for me to tell him what happened.

I couldn't get the words out, or at this point, make any kind of cry for help.

On my next day off I returned to the library. Mrs. Smith waved hello. "Why are you looking so glum? This isn't like you."

I told Mrs. Smith about my many discussions with Dr. Luborsky and confessed I had an increasing fascination with Judaism and Israel.

"You're right, the Jewish faith is fascinating and it would behoove you to research it." She ruffled my hair with affection, the way she used to when I was seven. "Aisle ten is where you need to go."

My task seemed overwhelming when I saw the shelves and shelves of information I could choose from. I started with *The Mitzvot* by Abraham somebody or other, published in 1937. I couldn't make out his last name.

I plowed through more titles like a locomotive: *The Way of God. The Tanakh. What is Talmud? Judaism for the Modern Age,* although I have to admit I wondered how modern it could be when the book was written in 1955.

I wrote in my notebook what I thought was important from each text, and quickly found myself drowning in a sea of words, most of which I did not understand.

> *In Judaism there is no explicit concept of rights. There is a system of mitzvot, or duties and responsibilities, based on the Jew's love for God, where Jewish obedience to law and Jewish fulfillment of obligations are considered a form of divine worship.*

"How are you doing?" said Mrs. Smith when she walked by my desk area. "You look confused."

"I am confused. I thought the Jewish religion was based on the bible."

"It is, but it is also based on 613 good deeds, *mitzvot.*"

"You're Jewish?" I said with surprise.

"Born and raised," she said absently as she looked up a certain page. She handed it to me. "Read this. It'll help."

I took the book from her, still amazed she admitted being Jewish. I always thought she was an Episcopalian from England and enjoyed tea and crumpets in the afternoon while reading poetry. The book was titled *613 Mitzvot (circa 1934).*

> *Observing mitzvot—that is, acting on our obligations and responsibilities—means remembering the Exodus from Egypt, respecting the "other," and treating the stranger as we expect to be treated, with*

dignity and rights. It means interpreting Jewish tradition in the framework of an interconnected world where famine, war, disease, and poverty anywhere on the globe affect us all.

I was shocked. Jews had such a profound faith in God, that they followed a man blindly into the wilderness. Their incredibly deep faith gave them the courage to face Nazis and concentration camps of horror where most of them died. Even after what they endured, they continued obeying these codes of conduct in their religion to help their fellow man and rebuild Israel into a great nation.

I didn't think I could ever understand, not with my Baptist/Lutheran/United upbringing. I laid in bed that night going over what I had read. One fact remained true and distressing: notwithstanding all of the righteous writing and proclamations about the horrendous atrocities of World War II, the world had done nothing to compensate the Holocaust survivors for what they lost, what they had endured, and how they still suffered.

My patients told me there could never be any compensation, or payment great enough, or apology big enough that would make up for what had happened to them. Even in the seventies, nearly thirty years postwar, none of the countries involved—particularly Germany, Austria, Poland—none of them had admitted what they had done to the Jews. No one confessed to sending millions of Jews to their deaths except for those Nazis who were charged for war crimes. Nor did anyone confess that they had confiscated Jewish properties and belongings after sending them away, and the vast majority never bothered to return any of it. No admission of guilt. These countries did, however, make token reparations to Israel.

Instead, the survivors learned how to live new lives after the War. They could never go back to what they once had. They could never be who they once were. They remained the "Other" people of the world. Unwanted and still despised.

After the war, Sarah Masinsky had returned to her family manor in Poland, only to discover a neighbor down the street had taken it over, along with all of the furnishings and belongings.

"They spit on me and kicked me down the stairs," she explained, "they called the police on me."

The police not only removed Sarah from the neighborhood, they kicked her out of Poland. She ended up in Cyprus where she reunited with her husband, Jacob. A godsend perhaps, a prayer answered. They had been separated during the war. But the pain of that rejection and hatred right after the war made her feel subhuman.

The couple eventually found a new reason to live—to prove to Hitler and the Nazis they had not succeeded in annihilating the Jews. The Jewish faith in God could never be destroyed. Surviving the war gave Jews the determination to go back to their homeland, Israel, and live in peace. They were going to prove to the world that Jews mattered. A Jewish based Israel would matter. It would be a light unto the nations. The survivors would sacrifice almost anything to make that happen.

I gave up on sleep yet again, a regular occurrence since studying about the Holocaust, and at three a.m., put on my sweats, and went for a jog. Running helped me think things through.

I ran down to the riverbank of the Detroit River and stopped for a break. It looked quiet on the deserted Detroit side. More gang fighting had broken out the night before and police placed a curfew on the city. An eerie mist had risen from the river as if dividing our two cities. *Don't look*, Detroit seemed to say with embarrassment. Detroit, the beautiful city I loved, needed time to heal from the '67 riots and all of the bloodshed and turmoil that had happened since. Nobody had given her that time.

My mother and her family were American. Politics and history became the big discussions during gatherings the year after my grandmother had died in 1959. They discussed, argued, roared, especially Uncle Willie, even though they were all Democrats. I remembered the arguments and discussions that took place in 1967 about civil rights—and the trial of the Algiers hotel murders where no justice was served.

The United States of America, home of the free and brave? "Not if your skin is any color but white," I muttered.

Europe had been like that for the Jews—no civil rights and no justice. History kept repeating itself again and again, only with different players. Being stronger in numbers, I hoped the African Americans would succeed in making the world understand this time—the atrocities supremacists continued to make against people not like themselves needed to stop.

When I returned to work, I discussed my late-night thoughts with my club.

"Oh, Dollie," said Sarah Masinsky, "of course it's the same. But now we know we can *never* be silent or accepting. Even a single drop of silence causes catastrophes. We have to take a stance every time we learn of injustice. We will always be in battles fighting for civil rights. That responsibility is part of the privilege of living in a democracy."

One of the survivors from Detroit looked out at her city where smoke rose from another building set on fire by gangs. "The ultimate burden of being Holocaust survivors is having to become an army of righteous fighters for civil rights."

"We write letters now, as well," said one of the other survivors, Mrs. Schönwald. "All of us Jews write letters to the UN and the White House about Vietnam, Apartheid Africa, Civil Rights for Blacks in the United States, and Refuseniks in Russia. We've been doing this for years."

"Why?" I asked. "What good will it ever do?"

"If I might paraphrase Dr. King," replied Dr. Luborsky. "He said our lives begin to end the day we become silent about things that matter. Silence becomes betrayal. We have to do this in order to live."

He grabbed a cookie, then another one. "Atrocities happening around the world cannot be ignored. We need to acknowledge them. Maybe one letter doesn't do anything, but one hundred? And what if a million people wrote letters? That would be tough to ignore."

"And even if it's a squeak of protest no one will pay attention to," said Sarah, "it's something."

Well. It was something all right. Certainly not enough. Instead of hiding from the world with their horrified memories and pain, my survivors had become super-vigilantes against injustices and continuing horror. Even as they became older, some of them in their seventies, they remained determined to fight. According to Dr. Luborsky, survivors often became fierce warriors.

After reading newspapers and articles, it became apparent the rest of the world showed no reaction to any of these infractions of democracy and injustices. I wondered where the worldwide banding together to save humanity had gone.

11

*Some live in darkness and some in the light, but it is the duty
of the Jewish people to carry light with them, and through
their actions, shed that light upon the world.*
(anonymous)

Sarah Masinsky once said her anger kept her going during the
war. That wasn't going to work for me. Maybe it was because I
had been sheltered that I didn't know how to cope with so much
trauma. Whatever the reason, I never figured out how to respond
correctly to what happened around me. I read voraciously instead.
It felt like the safest thing to do.

I certainly couldn't relate to Sarah losing her home and belongings and food. My parents were dirt poor. We had nothing, and
oftentimes, not even enough food to eat. We lived in what Windsor
called a wartime house—two small bedrooms, one tiny bathroom,
a kitchen the size of a closet, and a living room that could only
hold a small sofa, chair, and a tiny coffee table. No end tables.

I did learn at an early age that things would have been much
better for us if one of my parents knew how to cook and sew.

People talk about getting their first string of pearls at their sweet
sixteen party. The only pearls I ever saw were on Holly Go Lightly
from *Breakfast at Tiffany's*.

Sarah Masinsky wore a tiara at the debutante ball her parents held when she turned sixteen. Her family-owned famous paintings and a Degas sculpture. My sixteenth birthday consisted of me boiling hot dogs for dinner; my parents were at work. I bought my own cheap birthday cake with white icing with roses.

The artwork in my bedroom consisted of a lava lamp and a poster of the Monkees. Other art I knew about resided in the Detroit Institute of the Arts. Tootsie and I went there every time she came to town. When I became old enough to cross the border on my own, I went every week. Consequently, I did know a lot about art, especially my favorites, dear old Vincent, Chagall, Klimt, Rodin, and Monet, the Dutch classics.

Music was another heartfelt draw for me. I practically swooned when I heard Puccini on the radio, and I knew all of his operas. And I had been dancing since I was five. My mom had put me in classes because she thought I was a klutz and dancing might help. That may have been why she registered me, but I didn't care. She had given me a gift. When I danced, my heart opened to the music and I soared above the clouds. Every movement became my poetry, my prayers of joy. It was impossible for me not to dance to express my most vulnerable self; impossible not to get lost in music, impossible because I could use it to feel free and unstoppable.

Sarah didn't like dance or opera. So, what exactly did she and I have in common? Being raped. She and I discussed our experiences at great length and those feelings we shared. There was comfort in that, but what a horrible thing to bond over.

As weeks and months wore on, I continued my readings about the Holocaust. While observing news events happening, I concluded that the world had merely expanded its vitriolic hatred of Jews to include Israel. In fact, the Nazis and World War II seemed to have eradicated all of humanity's mercy and opened the dams that kept man's fiendish impulses in place. World War II had become the force of evil that spread filthy malignity throughout the world.

My Harlequin Romance Club patients discussed world events daily with great concern. For years they had taken a much more constructive stance than I would have considered. Many of them had walked in the Civil Rights marches that took place in Washington.

Several had met Martin Luther King Jr. and Bobby Kennedy, my personal heroes. They had traveled to protest rallies all around North America. They shouted slogans, carried placards. Some of them were in their eighties and yet they had marched. These senior citizens eagerly showed me what needed to be done in order to continue the fight for civil rights and peace.

Even though many were too sick to participate in the newer causes, they still wrote copious amounts of letters protesting atrocities and wrongdoings around the world, and when things got rough, they made phone calls to government officials. There wasn't a single drop of silence among them.

A squeak of protest, wasn't that what Sarah had called it? But the word squeak wasn't strong enough to describe these powerhouses of righteous individuals. They proved that letter writers were a lot louder and effective than anyone thought.

I sent my first letter to the Canadian Prime Minister to protest how the rape laws of this country only protected the rapist and made a villain out of the victim. I wrote to every law society in Canada. I had editorials that were printed in several newspapers. Dr. Luborsky said I made him *kvell*, feel pride.

I quickly became a letter-writing fiend and often joined Sarah and the other survivors every Tuesday to write together, over tea. We wrote ten and twenty a piece at every meeting. Squeaks of protest—all of us—almost a roar. I felt as if I was part of something big. I was making a difference.

Dr. Luborsky came to the unit one day and asked to see me in the doctor's consultation room. I knew something was wrong by the frown on his face and the horrible nightmare I had the previous night. He reached for my hand. Someone had died. I knew it.

His grip tightened. "Sarah passed away last night. Jacob woke up this morning and found her with her head on his shoulder. She died in her sleep, right next to him."

No! Sarah couldn't be dead. Hadn't she and I written letters together the day before? We had laughed while writing. We discussed Israel and how much needed to be done in the Diaspora to help that little country while we sipped tea and ate banana bread. Sarah had talked about Golda Meir.

And now she was gone, just like that.

"It was the way she wanted to go," I said after a moment. No real emotion from me again—concern for Jacob, yes. But where was my emotion? I had just lost a dear friend.

"How is Jacob doing?" I said.

Ben paused before answering. He looked surprised by my reaction. I'm sure he expected tears from me. "He is doing better than I anticipated. I don't know how he'll go on without her." He tilted my face up. "Are you okay?"

"I'm fine, Dr. Luborsky. I'm fine."

No, I wasn't.

I swung by Jacob's home during *Shiva*. Ben had explained shiva was a period of mourning that lasted seven days, starting when the mourners return home from the funeral. During shiva, a mourner traditionally stayed at home or at the home of the deceased or the home of other family mourners. He/she wore torn clothing or a torn black ribbon pinned to one's clothes (a practice known as *kriah*). The *mourner did not* go to work or school. Another tradition was friends bringing food when they came to the shiva house so mourners did not have to be concerned about meals.

I brought a pastrami platter from a local deli. "Hi Mr. Masinsky. I'm so sorry. I adored Sarah."

"Ah, my *Chavele*," he cried and nearly collapsed in my arms. "I'm so glad you came. You're here for me." He pointed at a red candle. "I didn't cry until they lit the *shiva* candle. Now it's real. My Sarah is gone."

I helped him into his chair by the picture window. The giant old, tattered La-Z-Boy molded to fit his form from so much use. Comfortable. Another chair, more diminutive stood next to it, Sarah's. Jacob openly wept when his eyes fell upon it. "Ah, Sarah my love," he cried. "You've gone and left me behind."

I went into the kitchen, made him a platter of food, and placed it on the little table between the two chairs. I also brought him a shot of whiskey from the kitchen table full of bottles.

"You have one with me, yes?" he said. Out of respect, I poured myself a shot as well. He showed me picture albums of when he and Sarah had arrived in Canada, crying at every turn of the page. "She was so beautiful, even after all she'd been through. I was the luckiest man on earth to have her. My Sarah had real strength back then, real gumption. I don't know what she ever saw in me."

He broke down and cried even more. I had no words at all. "Well, I guess she's at peace now, *sheyne Meydl*," Jacob said.

My poor, sweet soul of a man. And what was even more heartbreaking was Jacob tried to comfort me and ease my loss of a friend. We were a fine pair.

I looked around the room at the walls. They were bare. No family photos anywhere. One picture of Jacob and Sarah stood on the table by me. And then it hit me. Of course, there were no other family photos. All of their relatives had been slaughtered in the war. Sarah and Jacob escaped into the woods with only the clothes on their backs. They were the only two who survived.

In that moment I realized the real ramifications of the Holocaust. Jacob and Sarah and their lives were obliterated. Who they were in Europe was no longer a memory for anyone. It didn't matter how much I heard their story, I just had not comprehended the full impact of what they had said. But seeing the empty walls and naked tables where photos of joys and *simchas* would have been, made me understand.

"Thank you for coming, *Chavele*."

I kissed his cheek. "I'll see you in a week at the hospital?"

"Yes. For some reason, Hashem doesn't want me to leave yet."

"Maybe because He knows I love you," I said with a tremulous smile. "I can't lose my two dearest friends at the same time, now, can I?"

"No, that would be a *shanda,* a shame. I'll live a little longer for you."

12

Honor thy father and mother.
(Ten Commandments)

At Tootsie's continuous urging, I tried again to tell Mom about Arik, but every time I found the courage to approach, she was either too tired from work, or she wore her don't-talk-to me, I had a bad day look on her face. Several times I made us both a cup of tea and sat by her, trying to find the right words to begin the conversation.

"Mom," I said one night after work, "I have something to tell you. Aunt Tootsie says —"

"Not now. I'm sure you've already discussed whatever it is with Tootsie, anyway. You always do." She closed her eyes, her signal the conversation had ended. I couldn't understand why Tootsie thought it would do any good to tell my mother anything about Arik.

After a few more feeble attempts to talk to my mother, I gave up.

I've never been able to come up with appropriate words to describe my mother. Was she beautiful? Not really, but she had strawberry blonde hair that shimmered in the sunlight like pink gold. Mom's smile lit up a room when she entered, and she possessed a laugh that made me want to join in, even if I didn't know why she was amused. There was only one problem. She rarely laughed.

Mom always looked frustrated and hardly spoke to my dad except to complain. Her face looked like her mother's—depressed, weary of this world. Her blood pressure never went below 180/110 which was an alarming statement to her well-being.

Mom did have a keen sense of family and called her sisters on a regular basis. She also fought with them on a regular basis, especially Evelyn; blood curdling screeches with "I hate you" being the final words of a phone call. And an hour after that, "I'm sorry, too, I love you." It was easy to see why she didn't trust her siblings when these battles occurred.

Mom had a courageous side that I had only ever seen displayed in 1967, during the Detroit riots. She worked at the Woodward and Waverly bank branch as assistant manager. On the morning of July 24th, when the riots raged on, my mom's boss called her to say he wasn't coming in.

"Laura, it's safer for you to go in and open the bank than me," he rationalized. "It's only a few blocks away from the border. I'd have to find a parking spot and as soon as those rioters would see my car, they'd destroy it. The National Guard will pick you up at the tunnel and take you to the bank. They'll stay there with you and escort you home after you lock up. You'll be safe."

"Are you nuts, Mr. Cairny?" my mother cried, fully understanding his cowardice with dismay.

He loudly replied, "How dare you insult me? If you refuse, you can kiss your job goodbye."

Mom didn't say another word. Dad drove her to the tunnel that morning. As promised, the National Guard greeted her at the tunnel exit on the Detroit side and took her to Woodward and Waverly. In an army tank. I remember feeling completely horrified.

After she left that morning, I walked the half block from our house to the bank of the river and stayed there all day. I read, but mostly worried and bit my nails while watching the smoke rise from the burning buildings. They were only a block or so away from where she worked. "Why are you doing this, Mom?" I cried when she returned home the first day. "I don't know of any other mother who gets driven to work in an army tank. Why you?" "We need the money for food and the mortgage payment. Dad's work is closed. And if I can't be safe with a National Guard escort and an army tank, when can I be safe?"

We need the money for food and the mortgage payment. That was the first time I ever saw any part of Mom resemble my grandmother. Grandma used to say that exact same thing whenever she took in ironing, or sold extra fruits and vegetables at the local market. Mom had gumption, like my grandmother and Tootsie.

I gained a lot of respect for my mother during the riot. She never once complained about the people rioting or expressed any fear she might have had. Every day, until the riots ended on July 27th, Mom went to work and returned to the tunnel in an army tank. Only one other teller, a black woman, showed up during that week. She and Mom did everything needed to keep the bank open.

A week after the riots, the bank transferred Mom to Hamtramck and the teller was fired. It took Mom two hours to get to that bank via the Detroit bus system and if she had to stay overtime, she missed the last bus that went into the downtown area, forcing her to walk through some of Detroit's worst ghettos in order to get to the tunnel. Her blood pressure skyrocketed to 200 over 110.

Apparently, her boss didn't like the way she and the teller "disrespected" him. Obviously, they said something once the riots ended. Mom never talked about it, but six months after that transfer, she took a job at Blue Cross Blue Shield as an assistant manager. One of the first people she hired in her new job was the fired teller.

Mom didn't like Christmas. To be perfectly honest, she didn't like any holiday. She didn't know how to cook, so she despaired every holiday when cookies or turkeys were needed. She hated decorating the house but enjoyed how it looked when it was done. She couldn't stand shopping for Christmas presents and complained about nearly every present she received. They weren't personal enough, they were too practical, they were impractical, and lordy, how she hated trimming Christmas trees.

The only real festive moment my mom enjoyed was making fudge—a recipe she and her friend Arlene had learned during World War II. They'd made batches and batches of the confection and sent them to soldiers fighting overseas. Fudge was the big Christmas tradition Mom absolutely insisted had to be done, but if it didn't turn out right, she'd end up in a fit of tears.

By the time I turned ten, I took over decorating the house and setting out the Christmas cards we received. By twelve, I learned how to make the Christmas turkey from Dad. The stuffing recipe I remembered from watching my grandmother.

I found a farm in the county where we could cut down our own Christmas tree. Dad and I went every year and chopped down the biggest Scotch Pine we could find. When its branches settled and spread out, the tiny living room lost its identity and became known as "Christmas tree." We could barely move around the tree without getting pinned to a wall by its branches. I spent the rest of the day stringing it with lights and judiciously placing each ornament on the tree while listening to Christmas Carols and drinking my homemade eggnog.

Once I turned eighteen, I understood Mom suffered from a serious depression at Christmas and I did anything to keep her from sinking into her annual funk. I had taken over the preparations, even baking the dozens of cookies our family gave away. Mom only had to make the fudge.

No matter what I did, Mom developed a full-blown depression before Christmas Eve. According to Tootsie, Grandma Pilch suffered the same depression at the same time of year.

My dad was the opposite of my mother. He always seemed happy. In fact, he was a closet drinker. His entire family drank. Dad didn't think too deeply, didn't discuss politics, had no religion, didn't even go to movies or watch serious TV. He had been in World War II as an apprentice Navy engineer, and accidentally blew up his assigned ship. Thankfully, according to him, there were only engineers and apprentices on board, so no one was killed. Dad was just a laid-back kind of guy who was quite content to sit at home and watch sports, something my mother rarely allowed. I adored him when I was a kid. My parents were as opposite as any couple could be.

Mom pulled me aside on Christmas Eve, 1974, and showed me a wound on her shoulder. I recognized it immediately—a metastasis from a tumor in her breast. She had gone to our family doctor the summer before when she detected a lump and he dismissed it as a cyst.

What I looked at was no cyst. I didn't need a doctor's diagnosis to tell me my mother had a stage-four breast cancer with lymph node involvement.

Some things don't need to be said between mothers and daughters. We both knew in that moment there would not be very many Christmases left for my mother, even though she was only forty-eight years old.

"I'll make an appointment for you to see our doctor tomorrow," I said.

"It's bad?"

"Well, it's not good." I tried hard not to cry. Of the two parents, I related to my mother the most. Losing her would make me feel like an orphan. I had long taken over being a parent to my dad.

"We should go back to the living room and see how Dad is doing," I said.

"Until we know for sure what it is, we won't tell your father."

"All right."

I didn't sleep that night and I watched the sun slip above the horizon and kiss the sugary snow at dawn. An obscene thing to see after looking at my mother's tumor.

I donned a sweat suit and my running shoes. Within minutes, I found myself jogging through the woodland nestled at the end of our street. Of course, this was the run where I saw absolutely everything that could be beautiful in nature on full display. I ran past deer, bunnies, squirrels, foxes. Snow-laden branches of the tallest trees gracefully bowed low as the sunbathed them with light.

I felt as if my lungs would explode from the frigid morning air, but I still ran. The path took me along the river and the mounds of broken ice on the frozen bank. Willow wands gracefully danced in balletic form with the wind, causing snow crystals to swirl with joy. The world could not be more perfect than at this moment.

I ran past our neighborhood church and stopped. Hundreds of giant icicles, some of them over ten feet in length, hung on the long eaves-troughs under the roof—brilliant bright prisms for the sun. Rainbows danced on the wall behind them. Beauty. God's gift to me.

I dropped to my knees. "All right, God, all right. If You're going to take her, all I ask is that it be swift and without pain."

I fell backwards into the snow and stared upwards. The yolk-colored sun gleamed from the cerulean sky. Not a single cloud could be seen. God dared me to find any imperfection. I couldn't.

A rustling in the giant pine tree next to me captured my attention. Two frisky squirrels played together, hopping from snow laden branch to snow laden branch. One chattered when it saw me below.

Splat. The branch dumped its load of snow on my face.

"Are You kidding me?" I jumped to my feet. "I pray and this is what You do?"

I took in a deep breath and calmed. "Okay. So she won't die right away. I get that. But I've made my prayer. You won't let me down on this. I know it." I returned my gaze to the sky. I could breathe again. "Thank You in advance."

Knowing that everything was in God's hands, I returned home. My mind wandered to my patients. Four of the sickest ones remained stranded at the hospital for Christmas because their families couldn't or wouldn't take them home for the day. I developed a ridiculous and impossible plan, but I was definitely going to try and make it happen.

"Dad," I called out when I walked through the door. "How big is our turkey?"

"Why?"

"Do we have enough for four more people?"

"Sure."

"Good. We're having company."

"Who?"

"Four of my patients. They won't be a bother."

Mom walked into the kitchen. "Why would they want to be here?"

I shrugged. "Because they've got nowhere else to go."

After setting the table and making sure the food was prepared and our house was ready to accommodate four disabled people, I made arrangements to bring those patients home.

Dad pulled up to the hospital doors. "Are you sure about this?"

"None of them are going to live to see another Christmas. We can make this last one memorable for them."

"Well, that doesn't seem like a good enough reason for all this trouble." He turned off the engine when I stared at him. "All right. Let's get them."

It took a few quick trips but Dad and I managed it. We didn't have a ramp so each person had to be carried up the steps of our tiny porch. To say our home was crowded would be an understatement. But all of us, including Mom, had enormous smiles on our faces as we chatted, joked, and regaled each other with stories of past holidays.

For the first time in years, I heard my mother laugh as if she didn't have a care in the world. The gratitude of the patients was exactly what we needed to put her pressing dark future into perspective. We were here and living in the moment and loving each other more than we ever had before.

We ate a lot of turkey and stuffing and pumpkin pie. Just about every Christmas carol known to man was sung and we settled around the tree with hot cocoa and the famous fudge.

"I used to make this fudge for my husband when he was a soldier overseas," said Mrs. M. with a wistful smile on her face. "He hated it. He didn't tell me that until twenty years later, God bless him."

"I think every woman made the same fudge recipe during the war," said my mom with easy charm. This gracious southern belle was a side of Mom I never saw. "I add two more jars of marshmallow cream to mine," she said. "It makes it creamier."

At the end of the evening, Mom made packages of cookies and fudge for our four guests. Dad and I returned them to the hospital.

Three weeks later Mrs. M. died. The others soon followed.

One thing became certain that Christmas. I needed to get off the Chemo unit. Every patient who died from breast cancer caused a pain that felt like a dagger in my heart.

13

A faithful friend is a sturdy shelter;
he who finds one finds a treasure.
A faithful friend is beyond price,
no sum can balance his worth.
(Sirach 6:1-17)

We admitted a brand-new wave of Chemo patients to the unit in January of 1975. Most of the survivors who had been used as guinea pigs in the SS camps had died.

This new group of patients had only one survivor—Mr. F. He was a true gentleman in every way, and he loved his family dearly but, as with so many Holocaust survivors, he couldn't express his feelings. On the night he died, his family gathered around his bedside as they did every night. He told them to go home so he could sleep.

When they got halfway down the hall, he ordered me to get him out of bed and into the hall. "I need for them to see me standing."

"Are you sure?" I said with worry.

"Yes."

I half carried him to the center of the hall. When I called out his wife's name, she turned around and gasped when she saw him.

Mr. F. released his hold on me and stood tall. "Goldie, I love you. I always will."

Mrs. F. burst into tears and began to rush back to him. He held up his hand to stop her. "No Goldie. This way. I want it this way."

As soon as his wife and children were on the elevator Mr. F. collapsed. Once I had him back in bed, he grabbed my hand. "Don't call them until I'm dead."

"But why?" For the life of me I would never understand why someone would want to die alone.

"I have things to settle before I die."

During the last hour of my shift, I could hear Mr. F. talking out loud. Then I heard a Hebrew prayer I had become familiar with . . . *"Shema Yisroel Adonai Elohainu, Adonai Echad . . ."* Hear oh Israel the Lord is our God, the Lord is one. The *Shema* is an affirmation of Judaism and a declaration of faith in one God. For thousands of years in the past, for eternity into the future, it remains the prayer that tens of millions of Jews have recited before dying.

Mr. F. had made his peace with God.

I stayed after my shift ended and sat with him, waiting for his death to arrive. Unrushed. Silent. His face wore an ethereal look in those last few moments. By 0200 hours he was gone. An orderly and I bathed him, changed the sheets. We did our best to make him look as if he were comfortably sleeping. Then I called his family.

I turned to my friend, Dr. Luborsky, when he came to the unit the next evening. "What do you think about death and dying?" I said.

As was typical of Dr. Luborsky, his eyes crinkled at the corners when I asked him a question and a smile crossed his face. "What do I know about that?" He shrugged. I wondered if all Jews shrugged as much as Dr. Luborsky did when he talked to me, or did I just baffle him too much.

"Judaism is very specific in its rules about death and I accept that. You've heard the prayer, the *Shema*. In Judaism, death is not a tragedy, even when it occurs early in life or through unfortunate circumstances. Death is a natural process. Our deaths, like our lives, have meaning and are all part of *Hashem's* great plan."

I didn't like that answer. In fact, I hated it. I saw no natural process in six million Jews massacred. And what great plan? So far, all I saw was chaos.

"If someone were to die in my family," I started, "we would be in a funeral home for three days before the funeral. Do Jewish people do that as well?"

Dr. Luborsky took out his patient's chart before answering. "No, my dear. But we sit *shiva* after the funeral for several days. Everybody brings food to the mourner's home, like you did with Jacob. It's much more civilized than a funeral home. Mourning practices in Judaism are done to show respect for the dead and to comfort the living."

He put his hand on my shoulder. "Visiting Jacob was very kind. He said it gave him the strength to get through those days of mourning. Well done, my dear."

Ben Luborsky was the type of doctor who still made house calls and sat with patients when they were about to die. Because he had several older and dying patients, he spent long hours on the chemo unit. When one of his patients lay dying one night, Ben promised him he would stay until his soul passed on.

"Did you eat supper?" I said. I was working the afternoon shift, 4-12 p.m.

"I had a late lunch."

After my shift ended at midnight, I went to the restaurant across the street and bought us sandwiches. I stayed with Ben and kept him company. Vigils are hard to do alone. During those hushed hours, I finally told him about Arik. No tears from me, no sadness. I talked about Arik and the Yom Kippur war in a matter-of-fact, almost monotone voice, but my body had a fine tremor that became more and more apparent as I continued to speak. I also told Ben I thought Israel had rejected me.

Ben kept his steadying hand on my shoulder the entire time. "You do realize the physical country cannot reject you, not that it would even if it could." Ben rubbed my back in a soothing way when my eyes welled up with tears. "You are a wonderful girl, Pamela. Surely you know that."

"It's hard to believe, especially when the person you love gets killed in a stupid war." I got to my feet. It was dawn. "By the way, your patient in room 423 wants to see you before you leave."

"Yes, she wants to be discharged so she can get her hair and nails done."

"But she's so sick. Are you going to let her go?"

Ben chuckled. "I'd never step between a woman and her hairdresser. But she'll be back. She's putting things in order before she dies."

Putting things in order before she dies? Did my mother have things in order? Oh, God.

"Do you think Arik had time to say the *Shema* before he died?" That came out of the blue, but I needed to be reassured.

Dr. Luborsky seemed to sense that. "I am quite sure he did."

I cleared my throat. "I'm leaving the unit in a month. I'm going to the ER."

"Oh? Any particular reason?"

"There's too much death here. I feel like I'm drowning in it. And after my mom had a mastectomy, I'm finding it really hard to take."

"I'm sorry to hear that. You never mentioned your mother's illness. How bad is it?"

"Stage four with metastases. She's just finished her radiation treatments."

"I think you've made the right choice, Pamela. It must be very difficult to see so many people dying."

"It's hell." I walked away before I burst into tears. Ben was the first person I talked to about my mother's surgery and diagnosis.

Dr. Yoshida, my mom's cancer doctor, arrived on the unit as I headed for break the next day. He pulled me into the conference room on the floor. "We got the results of your mom's last tests. The cancer has metastasized to some of her bones. We started her on chemotherapy today, so she'll be getting sick. We'll see where we stand in three months' time." My mother was forty-nine. "This isn't good news, I know," he continued. "I'm sorry."

I'm not sure how I made it through the rest of my shift. All I could think about was how to tell my mom this news. It didn't occur to me that Sam would have already done so. He would never put something like that on my shoulders.

Mom had told me before going in for her scans the previous week she knew something was wrong, and I believed her. Patients always knew. It seemed to be an instinct.

"Uncle," I cried out while sitting in my car after work. "Did You hear me, God? I'm giving up with this shit. Uncle. Make it stop."

I hung my head. "I'm begging you. Help me."

It was an hour before I could even think about heading for home.

14

When I die, give what's left of me to children
and old men that wait to die.
And if you need to cry, cry for your brother
walking in the street beside you.
When you need me, put your arms around anyone and give them
what you need to give to me.
Look for me in the people I've known or loved,
and if you cannot give me away, at least let me live in your eyes
and not in your mind . . .Love doesn't die, people do.
So when all that's left of me is love, give me away.
(Meditation before Kaddish)

I suspected that Dr. Luborsky talked to the director of Nursing after that night because she transferred me to the Emergency Room within forty-eight hours. He had three patients on the chemo unit, all of them with breast cancer, all of them at death's door.

Our hospital's ER was the biggest in Southwestern Ontario. We saw a lot of patients with massive trauma. Nurses not only dissociated in ER and compartmentalized, they went out after work and drank and ate until they decompressed. I soon weighed 144 pounds and didn't care.

My life at this point could best be described as being on a downward spiral of epic, catastrophic proportions—like a Shakespearean tragedy—no resolution to the pain, just a lot of dead bodies on the stage with one poor soul crying "why?" Me being the poor soul.

I dated pretty much anyone who asked me out, a lot of Lotharios who lacked any kind of intelligence or depth. They only saw the pretty nurse with the vacant eyes. On Valentine's Day, I received seventeen bouquets of flowers with letters of undying love . . . and eleven marriage proposals.

My mother thought it was funny. I didn't, not at all. I had become a callous, disdainful bitch when it came to matters of the heart, not deserving of anyone's respect, and certainly no one's love. And not a person deserving of ever living in Israel. I think it was that thought more than anything that forced me to sink into a deeper depression.

Mac was more tenacious than the other men—good-looking, rich, American—and equally as disdainful and callous to me as I was to him. We were a perfect match. I truly believed I deserved no better.

At his request, I set up his best friend with a fellow nurse. Cheryl and I were to drive to the Pontchartrain Hotel in Detroit to meet the guys for drinks before dinner.

Mac's best friend was David Herzl. "As I live and breathe, Miss Pamela Kilborn, Reg-N. How are you?"

I barely remembered David, much to his dismay, but he sure remembered me. He wasn't happy seeing me with Mac. "If you weren't dating my best friend, I'd be making a huge pass at you," he said at dinner that night.

My smile tasted bitter. "I'm not worthy enough for you to lose your best friend, David. Cheryl's more fun. But I have a question for you. Why would a jackass like Mac be your best friend? You seem so nice."

David looked taken aback by the question. After a moment he shook his head. "Good question. We've been friends since grade one. After so many years, you get used to the antics of your buddy and overlook the bad behavior. It's hard to turn your back on a friendship as old as ours."

We double dated a lot after that night. Cheryl didn't last long but there were always other girls. No matter who he was with, David stayed focused on me and watched my every move. He tried to discuss my relationship with Mac almost every chance he got.

"What is with you? Mac is too full of himself to have a decent relationship with a girl like you. You're better than this, kiddo, I know you are."

My response was always the same. I grabbed a drink and walked away. "You're only allowed to talk to me about medicine." My words hung in the air behind me.

David and I often discussed our patients when we double dated, especially my survivors and their cancers. He also elaborated on his goals for a women's clinic in Cuba. He asked how our ER was set up. Relying on my experience, I helped him plan how the rooms of the clinic should look in order to be practical. We discussed at length what supplies he needed. He had researched the best and cheapest birth control that he could provide instead of abortion accessibility. Would Catholic women consider taking the pill, he wondered. They were distraught about the abortions Castro practically demanded for every pregnant girl. David couldn't understand how pills were worse than the abortions ordered by a tyrant. Neither could I.

All of this talk drove Mac crazy. "There are other people in this fucking room," he said one night, "who are not doctors and nurses and couldn't give two fucks about that shit. Come join the party or go home."

To my surprise, I made no retort. I walked out the door, got in my car, and went home. For the first time, I had stood up to Mac. Could this kernel of gumption mean I actually started coming out of my depression? No. It was just a moment.

To hear David express disappointment in me every time we saw each other humiliated me, but I still couldn't pull myself out of my horrible slump. While Mac got drunk and partied with nearly every female in attendance, I sat in the corner of party rooms in drunken stupors. Every time he saw me doing this, David sat beside me.

"Wanna talk yet?"

"No."

"You know eventually you're going to tell me, Kilborn, because I'm not giving up on you."

"Not tonight," I replied.

Weeks passed and I accepted whatever abuse Mac tossed my way. I didn't even like the guy, but breaking up was more effort than I wanted to exert. I also figured going out with him instead of sitting at home was better than nothing. At least I was functioning. Sort of. David told me I needed to "sharpen up." A lot, and in a hurry. I was scaring him. Him? I was scaring *me*.

At one of our all too frequent drinking parties in Ann Arbor, Michigan, Mac made another disgustingly low brow comment about my lack of brains and sexuality, something about being a lump on a log. When I didn't defend myself, he made another comment, yanked me into a nearby room, dumped me on a bed, and landed on top of me with a thud as he pawed me.

The rape from my past flashed before me. "Get off of me, you asshole!"

I kneed him in the groin while gouging his face. He couldn't move away fast enough from my near hysterical wrath.

Jumping from the bed, I snatched the bedside lamp in my hands, getting ready to kill him. Before I could strike, David charged through the door. He grabbed Mac from the bed and slugged him.

Mac sank to the floor. "What the fuck is wrong with you, Herzl?" He wiped blood from his broken nose.

"What the fuck is wrong with *you*?" David roared. He pulled the potentially lethal lamp away from me and held me tight. I turned my rage onto him and kicked him in the shins while still screaming. David winced from the pain.

He held me a safe arm's length away. "Listen very carefully to me, Mac. You're never doing this to her again." His rage had become quiet. Lethal. "And you're never going to see her again either. You're not good enough for her."

He tossed me over his powerful, muscular shoulder, fireman style, and headed for the door. "You're a bastard, Mac. Enough of this shit."

"Put me down David!" I gritted my teeth while pummeling his back.

"I will. Just not here."

After a lot of struggling and screeches of rage on my part, David put me down beside his car. He held my hands tight while opening the passenger door. "Stop it. I'm not going to hurt you. Let me get you out of here."

His voice barely registered in my ears. I still felt Mac on top of me and sliming my neck with his tongue. "I need a shower," I said and promptly went into a crying jag. My blurred vision overwhelmed me. "Oh, God, I'm going to puke."

David held my hair back as I vomited. Puke flew all over my shoes, David's shoes, and down my front.

"Okay, from so much emotional reaction, pretty sure I can assume you were raped at some point," said David while wiping my clothes off with a towel he had in the back seat.

After shoving me in his car, David jumped in the driver's seat and took off.

"Let me out of here, David. I need to go home." I pounded on him while he drove. He swerved to avoid an eighteen-wheeler. "Let me go," I cried.

David put his arm around me and squashed my arms tight, making sure I faced away from him, just in case.

"Ow! You're hurting me," I shouted.

"Calm down."

I kicked on the ceiling of the car, nearly smashing right through it. David whistled low when the fabric tore. "Aw shit. Good one, Kilborn, and you're getting puke all over the car."

"You think you can just take me as your hostage?" I shouted while still kicking at the ceiling and front window.

"Watch me, little girl."

It was by David's sheer strength and determination alone that we safely drove to Grosse Pointe where he kept his boat, a fifty-four-foot Catalina. Like everything else David owned, it was the best—the Cadillac of racing sailboats, something he did on his days off.

David hauled me out of the car. He tossed me over his shoulder again, climbed the small ladder to the boat, and dumped me on one of the benches. I leaned over the side and hurled. Luckily, I had nothing left in my stomach.

He started the engine before I could focus and make a move to escape. Struggling to my feet and barely able to see him, I charged his back and pummeled him while screeching like a banshee. He pointed his boat to the middle of Lake St. Clair.

When no land could be seen from any side of the boat, David cut the engine and dropped anchor. "Okay, we talk now. There's nowhere you can go, so speak."

There is one thing about David that I failed to remember on that night. He always paid meticulous attention to detail. It's what made him a great doctor. In this instance, he remembered I was terrified of water over my head. David was also a very stubborn man when he wanted to be. And right then he was hell-bent on finding out why I had chosen a path of self-destruction.

I was hell-bent on killing him. Or getting off the boat, which-ever came first. I didn't care which one. A toolkit sat on one of the nearby benches. My fingers fumbled while looking for something

I could use to strike him. I grabbed a small mallet and raised it over my head. "I hate you," I screeched.

David couldn't help but laugh. "A mallet? Really? And you don't hate me, you hate Mac." David pulled the mallet from my hands and tossed it overboard. "And you hate the guy who raped you."

The wrench I picked up met the same fate as the mallet. "I'm over that. You don't know what you're talking about."

Hysterical, drunk, and ready for battle, I threw beer cans at him from a nearby case. He quietly caught each one and tossed them into the galley and sleeping quarters below. "Start talking, Kilborn, because we're not leaving this boat until you tell me what's going on. We both have the next two days off, so you're stuck."

When I ran out of things to throw, I did the unthinkable. I jumped into the water. Me, the girl who didn't know how to swim.

"Damn it, Pam! The water's too cold for you to pull this kind of stunt."

David jumped in after me. We both nearly drowned as I floundered and fought him. "Stop!" shouted David. I grasped for his testicles to twist.

David nearly broke my wrist when I succeeded. Aghast at what I had done, I went under and choked on the ice-cold water. David dragged me back to the surface.

"David," I spluttered while clinging to him, suddenly terrified of the position I was in. "I'm sorry."

"It's okay," he said while still groaning. "Ah fuck, that hurt. Let's get back in the boat."

Once he helped me over the ladder, we collapsed on the floor. He put me in a vice grip with his legs in case I became hysterical again.

"Shit," said David while trying to stop the blood from a cut I had inflicted on him. He was still short of breath. "You have got to be one of the most stubborn girls I have ever met. Now, talk to me. Spill it all out." He held me tighter when I squirmed. I could barely breathe. "If

STILL THE SOUL SURVIVES

it's not the rape, then I'm assuming this has to do with all of those Holocaust survivors dying on you."

I collapsed against him. I'd finally met someone stronger and more determined than me. I spilled, spurting out senseless images . . . my mother, my patients, Jacob, Sarah, and even Ben Luborsky . . . not Arik.

Deep, ugly, wracking sobs and wails poured out of me while snot ran down my face. David's legs became a vice again, making sure I understood there was no escape.

"Okay, let's get something straight, Kilborn." He shook me until I looked into his eyes. "Look at me. Now focus on what I'm saying to you and look at me. You need to understand that the Holocaust and what your patients suffer is not your fault."

"But I'm part German." I cringed when I heard the whine in my voice. "And what if it's genetic? I'm never having kids."

I heard a hint of laughter in his voice. "Honey, a lot of the Jewish population of Europe was German. If what happened is because of genetics, then Jews have those genes too."

He swiped at my tears with the pads of his thumbs. "Pam, it's not genetic. Not like you think anyway. Maybe it all happened because of evil human nature. But it wasn't because of someone's nationality."

A fit of shivers made it impossible for me to stay focused. That lake water was so cold and we had been "swimming" for a while.

"Shit." David abruptly went below deck and returned with a giant duvet blanket and one of his sweatshirts. He had changed into dry clothes. "Here, you're shivering so violently I can barely see your eyes. And your teeth are chattering. Get out of those wet clothes and put this on. Do you need help?"

"No thanks." Wrong. I realized how wrong I was when I lost my balance and nearly fell overboard again. David stripped me down with clinical expertise and had me dressed in his shirt within seconds. He wrapped both of us in the blanket and stretched out on the bench, using cushions for pillows. He held me close while I tried to calm down.

David didn't have a lot of answers to the questions that had driven me into such despair, but he had enough that I finally had hope another Holocaust could be prevented.

"And the Jews have Israel back with their own democratic government. We have our homeland again," he said.

"I keep hearing that," I said with a hiccough and promptly went back to near-hysterics with the mention of Israel. At last, I spluttered about Arik, how I didn't understand why there was a Yom Kippur war. I confessed my guilt for not calling Arik and begging him to return. And for not going to Israel to try and find his grave.

David gently stroked my hair and kissed my forehead in brotherly fashion. "Wow, sweetheart, I am astounded at your brain. Why does your mind go so nuts to make you worry about such awful things? Let's put this into perspective. You may be upset about the war and all of its carnage, and maybe you're upset about not going to Israel and finding his grave, but that's not what's bothering you."

He had my full attention with that statement. "What do you mean?"

"Arik didn't keep his end of the bargain with you. He promised to love you forever and come back to marry you. But you think he chose Israel over you and died. And that's why you're so fucking angry and confused. You don't understand how he could do that."

I pulled away and stared at him. He knew me too well. How had I exposed myself so much, not only my body, but the ugly parts of me—my guilt, my rage? Had I really been so drunk in front of him these past weeks that I'd let my guard down?

I would have tried to leave again but I suddenly felt played out. The quiet rolling of the boat, the serenity of the moment, and the heat emanating from David's body lulled me into a deep state of lethargy.

I sank back into his arms. "Arik had a job to do. It was his duty. I always knew that."

"Well, maybe you knew, but you weren't expecting him to die, were you? Even he didn't know he would never see you again."

119

"If he had stayed with me, he'd be alive."

"Yeah, but he didn't. He had to return home. Arik loved you, kiddo. You were the one he was born to love, that's why he recited *Shir ha shir'im* to you when he first met you."

My brow knit into a frown of confusion.

"It's kind of a Jewish guy thing. You find your true love and you recite that poem."

His voice dropped to a near whisper. "And Arik believed you were his *besheret*, his fate, his soulmate. Never in a million years would he have done anything to hurt you."

I could almost hear Arik reciting the *Shir ha Shir'im*. David's quiet reasoning reopened the wound that hadn't healed. "I . . . I know that. I—"

David kissed the top of my head. "You're gonna have to forgive him, honey. I'm sure he's up in Heaven constantly asking you to do just that—forgive him."

The image seared into my heart. "I do, but I don't want to lose him. . ."

David pulled me tight against his chest. "Aw, sweetie. You'll never lose him because he hasn't left you. He's always going to be there in your heart. Sure as you breathe, he's inside you forever. You're gonna have to find a different way to love him so that you can go on living. He sure as hell wouldn't want to see you like this, trying to destroy yourself."

He handed me a box of tissues from a nearby table.

"I guess you're right," I managed to say while mopping my face clear of tears and snot and mascara and whatever else was on there. I was such an ugly crier.

David sighed with relief. He knew his words had begun to reach me.

"And here's another killer you're dealing with," he said. "Because you're a nurse with that nurturing soul of yours that I love so much, you're desperately trying to fix your patients." He wrapped us tighter in the blanket, making sure my feet were covered. "And I know you're trying to come up with a scheme to fix the world so there's no more wars. But, honey, it would take a miracle to fix this world. And that's what has you even more fucked up."

I nodded hopelessly. He was right. He went back to stroking my hair.

"You can't fix a Goddamned thing, Nurse Pam. You can't fix the hate that Israel faces and you can't fix your Holocaust survivors. All you can do is what you're doing now. Love them and care for them."

If he was trying to encourage me, he failed. The world was hopeless. My patients were hopeless. I was hopeless. I took in a shaky breath. "There has to be something."

"Here's what I've figured out in my added eight years on this earth than what you have. You and I are alive, human, and as all humans do, we have good and bad in each of us. We can only live within the boundaries God has set for us." He pulled me in closer when he felt me shudder at his words. "And in those boundaries, we can despair and curse God, like your Mr. C. did, and not make any changes. And people who do that will more often than not choose evil, and they will make the world ugly."

Hiccoughs started. David handed me a bottle of water.

"There's nothing we can do?" I whispered.

"Well, we can try to make things better in our own way. Not fix but make better. We make a difference."

I rested my head on his shoulder while listening to his words.

"Me, going back to Cuba is my way. You making cookies and tea and being a nurse is your way. And here's the good part in this. You and I have a lot of years left to make changes for the better, to stop evil. It's going to be done with little steps, like a clinic or a cookie made with love, but think about it. We're only two people. Imagine if there were more people like us, like thousands or millions? Imagine what the world would begin to look like."

At that moment, snuggled in the warm blanket with David's protective arms around me, I felt comfortable, safe—worthy of being a human and getting lectured on why I needed to still live.

David tilted my chin up. "You sure you're not Jewish?" he said in a teasing voice. "You're certainly carrying enough guilt around on your shoulders to be a Jew. And this fixing obsession is so like a Jewish mama. My mother can't hold a candle to you."

The lake had misted over while we talked, and stars faded one by one until the only color seen in the sky was lavender. It felt as if the earth had taken a moment to relax when dawn and daybreak met on top of the water. I held my breath when a sliver of sun suddenly appeared and forced the shades of night to begin disappearing. With each passing second the sun became braver and braver until eventually it gained strength to completely chase the night into oblivion. My spirit thrilled when everything around me became illuminated. I felt human again with a heart that could feel and love. Nothing in the future was clear, absolutely nothing at all, but it didn't matter anymore.

David let out a tired sigh. "When my family went camping every year, my sister and I would sneak through the woods to see the sun rise over the lake. She used to say that sunrises were God's way of saying let's start over again."

"Smart girl." I turned and looked up at him. "David, I have to ask. What did you ever see in me to keep chasing me? I mean I'm glad you did, because I'm pretty sure you just saved my life, but what was it?"

David grinned. "You made one helluva good impression at that conference, especially when the bullets flew. In case you didn't notice, you were the only girl not crying. Hell, even some of the guys wept like babies. But not you." He laughed and tweaked my nose. "And you're a dainty eater. Your mouth didn't get all greasy when you ate those lamb chops at Hellas. Let's catch some sleep, now, then get a late breakfast."

David had bombarded me with facts, ideas, and corrections that night on the boat, and he was right about everything. I couldn't repair anything or anyone. Maybe Sarah Masinsky had been right. Maybe all we could do was be a squeak of protest.

Or—maybe there was more. I could certainly do more for the future. I could write more letters of protest and fight for Israel in my own way. I could try to write stories like authors Leon Uris, John le Carré, and Ken Follett did about the wars and the soldiers who fought them, only my heroes would be Holocaust survivors and Israelis. I could fight for Black civil rights in the States and stand in the crowd being counted.

One thing I couldn't do was turn back the clock and change history. Like David said, a very hard fact to face. Maybe that night was the witness of the rebirth of me with a new capability of putting things into perspective. David, with his quiet, laid-back voice and heart as big as the world, really had saved me.

After he dropped me off at my car, I gazed into the sky. "God, I apologize for anything derogatory I may have said. Maybe You are looking out for me."

A great blue heron landed beside me.

"But let's get something straight. I'm not strong enough to let go of Arik. I really loved him. I may need a lot of help from You, all right?"

The heron flapped a wing in disapproval and moved in closer. I decided it was a male because it promptly regurgitated a dead fish on my foot and flew away.

I glared at the sky. "This fish does not serve as an adequate replacement for Your help. Just letting You know that. And maybe I can do anything, but only if You're by my side."

As if in response to my tirade, a single strip of a rainbow appeared before me. I laughed. "Okay, that's better. Thank you."

I shook my finger at the sky. "You really had me going there with the dead fish."

15

You can't force anyone to love you.

(Jewish Proverb)

My relationship with David deepened after that night. We spent hours on his boat during our days off and he talked about his family history and Theodore Herzl. He mesmerized me with his thoughts on Israel and its future. He loved the country.

"And you don't want to move there?" I said with surprise.

"No. As much as my mother would love me to make *Aliyah*, my heart is in Cuba. It's where I was raised."

David and I dated for over a month. He was my hero, my guardian angel. He eased me into allowing my frail heart to feel again. He loved me, why he did I would never know, but he did. And I adored him. Unfortunately, I didn't love him the way he wanted me to, but I tried. Desperately. I couldn't.

We went back to Hella's several times. It became "our place." The owner got to know us and enjoyed watching what he thought was a young couple falling in love.

"We Greeks are the best lovers in the world." He winked. "You let me know if he needs pointers, eh?"

One night David announced he was leaving for Cuba in a week to assess the area where he could build his Women's Urgent Care unit. "Come with me," he pleaded. "I love you, Pam. I want you to help me find the right place. I want you to meet some of my relatives who still live there. It'll be fun. What do you say?"

His face was so hopeful. I thought he had understood how I felt about a relationship with him. Obviously, I was wrong, but I sure wasn't ready to have yet another serious talk with him. God, it was so hard to say no. "I can't, David. You are my dearest friend, the most noble and kind human being I have ever met. You deserve better than me."

David groaned. "Dammit girl. You're wounding my pride here. Why don't you let me decide what I deserve?" He let out a sigh of frustration. "How about I go to Cuba and when I return in three months, we discuss this further. I can't imagine life without you."

I reluctantly agreed.

I finally decided I needed privacy, a place to gather my thoughts, and deal with my mother's declining health, my work, and all of the other crap. I looked for my own apartment. My mother thought it was a selfish move and in all probability it was. But for me, it seemed necessary.

Instead of facing my problems and finding that apartment, I took up tennis. My tennis pro was a guy named William. He was what my mother called scary-smart.

William—a great tennis player and I believed he was one of Ontario's top pros —he had a body of sinew and muscle. My girlfriend called him a major stud muffin. I found myself constantly staring at his knees and *tuchas*.

William found humor in everything. While I learned about tennis and the man who played it, I found myself laughing and smiling more and more. I had not felt so carefree in a very long time.

"Want to play a couple of games of tennis tomorrow and then go to Wendy's after?" he said after one class. That was the first time he asked me out.

He had me at Wendy's, my favorite takeout. "I'd love to," I replied.

That innocuous little date led to another and another. Before I knew it, Will and I were seeing each other nearly every day. He made me laugh almost constantly and called me after work every night.

I counted the minutes until I'd see him again. My tennis game got really good.

Three months later, the night I had dreaded, happened. David and I went out for dinner after his return from Cuba. He told me he found a place to start the clinic and intended to move there within six weeks when renovations were completed. "Have you thought about coming with me? I really need a good nurse. I also really need a girl."

I hung my head, feeling so guilty. "No, David," I said, "I can't."

David took my hand in his. "I get it. I mean, I don't want to get it, but I do. I had hoped that my absence would make your heart grow fonder but it hasn't, has it? I think this is the last time I'm going to see you."

"But why?" Of course, I knew why. Was I really so selfish that I wanted him to still be my friend? I had to let him go.

"Because you're never going to feel for me the way I want you to." David took a huge gulp of wine. "And you've fallen in love with someone while I was away. Who? The tennis pro?"

"No," I cried. "I want to be in love with you. I do love you."

David brushed my hair over my shoulder. "Yeah, you are in love with this guy. You just don't want to admit it. Falling in love again scares the crap out of you." He looked at me with such longing. "God, you don't know how much I love you."

He gave me a soft, sweet kiss. "But your life is going to be with this guy sitting here between us as big as hell. My life is going to be in Cuba, running a clinic for women, fighting Fidel Castro. He's actually forcing abortions on women now. Looking for that perfect race kind of thing, and we both know how it turns out when a leader starts talking about pure races."

My heart started doing flip-flops. Was he going to be in danger like Arik had been? Oh, dear heaven, I never thought about that. "You never talk about what you're going to face in Cuba. You're not going to be in any danger, are you? Should I be worried for you? Please, David, tell me you're not going to be in harm's way there."

David shrugged his shoulders. He looked a lot like Dr. Luborsky when he did that. "I guess you really do care. That's comforting to know. There's not much to say about my pal Fidel. Cuba is one of those communist countries where even aspirin is hard to come by. A patient gets better care if they bring a bar of soap with them so the doctor can clean his hands properly before touching them. Cuba desperately needs to be brought into the twentieth century." He hesitated. "Well, they won't have to bring soap to my clinic. I'll have plenty."

He abruptly got to his feet. His stunning blue eyes glistened and shimmered with tears under the antique crystal chandelier on the ceiling of the restaurant. He must have known how this night was going to go because he had chosen a different place to meet.

Damn, I had hurt him so much.

"Keep fighting the fight, Kilborn. And remember that in Cuba there is a guy who will always know how wonderful you are, and if life ever changes your mind about us, you come and find me. I hope this tennis guy realizes what a treasure he has in you and how much love is in that heart of yours. I love you."

I never saw David after that. It was as if he never existed. I had the weird thought he might have been one of the thirty-six Righteous

Souls. Months later I heard Castro arrested every doctor who disagreed with his policies on women's rights and abortions. He shut down their clinics. I feared the worst. David would have been all over those policies, fighting with everything he had. I prayed his father had managed to somehow find a legal means to get David out, but those chances, his friends told me, were slim to none.

Running and tennis weren't enough tension releasers to handle my fears and worry anymore. I decided to learn how to swim. It seemed like something that would come in handy if I was ever on a boat again.

16

Trust yourself. Create the kind of self that you
will be happy to live with all your life.
Make the most of yourself by fanning the tiny,
inner sparks of possibility into flames of achievement.
(Talmud Commentary)

Another month passed before I called Tootsie and told her what was really happening with Mom. Now that I experienced emotions again, my eyes became floodgates and I cried at a moment's notice. Tootsie cried right along with me.

"Are you holding up all right, sweetheart? You hadn't even gotten over your young Arik dying, and now this."

"I'm actually doing a lot better." I explained about David, dating William, and transferring to ER. "And I'm looking for an apartment I can afford. I need to move out and be on my own."

"Emergency Room?" she exclaimed. "Kind of like moving from the frying pan into the fire, isn't it?"

"Yeah, but I can't watch so many people dying of cancer anymore. Especially my Holocaust survivors."

"You do what you need to do, sweetheart, to take care of you. I was worried for a while there. Keep me posted on your mama."

Within a few weeks, I found an apartment on the west side of town, as far away from my parents as possible. I wasn't elated about this move, not at all. Making dramatic changes traumatized me every time. I was what people called a creature of habits. Mom telling people I ran away from home did not help. She refused to visit my new place. It was moments like that when I could see she was exactly like Grandma in many ways. Grandma had sat in mourning for a month when Tootsie moved out.

William liked the place. "It's huge." He walked out onto my main floor balcony and placed a pot of pansies out there. "And this is a great view of Ambassador Bridge and the river."

I joined him. "And I'll be able to watch the July first fireworks from here."

I loved the view. I could sit on my balcony and watch polluted sunsets painting the water blood orange and gold. There was one big negative—it was the most polluted section of the city, a scuzzy neighborhood with rats running around the building. I didn't care. It was mine.

"Let's get these rooms painted, so you can set things up," said Will.

Once I decorated my apartment, I was quite content to leave it exactly the same way. No moving furniture around, no redecorating of any kind. My idea of excitement was buying a new plant.

My mother, on the other hand, loved to change everything in her living room every two years, like clockwork. I guess it was a tradition for her. I didn't want to think about what all that new furniture really symbolized.

Moving out wasn't the only major change in my life. My transfer to the ER was still very new. Emergency Room nursing was an altogether different game from anything else I had ever done. A nurse had to use all of her training—Pediatrics, OB-GYN, surgical, psychiatry, and even Chemo. As my experiences grew, I became Jack-of-all-Trades-Master-of-None.

Nurses who worked in ER were tough, fast-moving, no-nonsense, get to work and do your job kind of people. They had no time to deal with emotions and reactions. Don't get involved with the patients and their problems, treat them. I had to admit, I liked that attitude.

On an even brighter note, I dated William and played tennis with him nearly every day. Thanks to David's intervention on the boat and Will's continued presence in my life, I stopped the self-destruct mode. I ran three miles every day, played tennis, and had taken up dance again. I did give up on the swimming, though.

Unfortunately, my body decided to handle my compartmentaliz-ing by developing irritable bowel syndrome. All that pent-up anger and emotion had to come out somehow. My body chose the squirts. I wasn't going to be allowed any dignity in my dysfunction. "Thanks, God," I muttered after every bathroom visit, "for reminding me of my lack of coping skills. Good one." I swore I heard Him laugh.

Quite a few ER nurses had IBS as well. In fact, the line-up to the bathroom was huge after any particularly distressing case. We seemed to be members of our very own special club of dysfunctional women. This bizarre camaraderie made me feel good in a way. I teased the others and suggested we make badges. Member of the ER-IBS club since 19___ and then we put in the date of our diagnosis.

"You're so strange, Kilborn," said our Head Nurse as she charged for the nearest bathroom. "There is nothing remotely funny about this." Well, I thought it was funny.

A huge benefit to working in the ER was getting to meet some of Windsor's more fascinating doctors. One of my favorites, Dr. Jova-novich, a part-time ER doctor from Serbia, was an extraordinarily large man. He reminded me of a giant bear.

When we first met, he roared with happiness. "Hallo, my darling!"

He paused a moment. "German, a little Austrian, and Czechoslo-vakian." He grinned. "Right?"

"You forgot Dutch and Irish."

"Ah, that explains the twinkle in your eyes. And a little bit Jewish, no?"

"No sir."

Jovanovich had a deep, booming, jovial voice, a head full of con-stantly ruffled snow-white hair, and merry eyes that actually did twinkle, and he wasn't even Irish. He loved little children. Surprisingly enough, they weren't afraid of the giant man. Most of them thought he was Santa Claus. To see him treating them, I almost believed he was.

One night, he brought me out to his huge, dilapidated car and opened the trunk to show ten bushels of vegetables from patients. They had given them for payment of his services. "See what my patients gave me today."

I was stunned at how many bushels sat in the trunk. "Why did they give you all of this?"

He filled a plastic bag with various vegetables and handed it to me. "They don't understand that seeing a doctor in Canada is free, so they insist on paying me with whatever they grow. I'd hurt their feelings if I said no."

He tossed me a rutabaga.

"My grandparents used to grow these in their garden," I said. "What do you do with them?"

"They are good for soup." He watched my reactions with eyes wizened from facing years of people's pain. He was a good man. "I bet your grandma was a good cook."

"She was. She made an incredible chicken soup with dumplings."

Jovanovich's laughter made the windows shudder. "Not dumplings, my dear girl, matzah balls."

I nicknamed Dr. Jovanovich the Gentle Giant. That's how I thought of him.

Nurses switched shifts every two weeks and we had to do all three shifts. The afternoon shift was always the busiest. During one afternoon shift, police brought in an auto worker with a beatific smile on his face. They caught him smashing windows of houses while he shouted threats to the "whores" who lived there.

As I filled out admission papers at the staff desk, Joe talked amiably to the air in our Psychiatric room across from me. He chortled. "That's a good one."

"Who's he talking to?" I said to the cop who stood guard outside the door of the room.

"Jesus. They're best buddies." He tilted his head toward the man. "Careful. His co-workers said he suddenly went berserk."

I knocked on the door of the room. "Hi, Joe," I said. "May I come in?"

"Sure, hon. We're shootin' the shit."

Joe looked lovingly at the space next to him. "Sure, sure," he said to the air. "You go on ahead while I talk to the nurse."

He grinned. "You're wondering what happened, tonight."

"Yes, I am." I craned my neck trying to see who he looked at with so much fondness.

"It was the most amazing thing. My wife had left me and took our kids. I crashed my car and the roof on the house caved in. So, I'm working on the fender line at work, feeling mighty sorry for myself, when all of a sudden Jesus came walking down the line. He was as magnificent as I always dreamed he'd be. And then he stopped right in front of me. He said, 'Joe, it's time for you to stop working here. I need you to do the Lord's work. You have to clear out all of the whores in this town. I'll show you where they live.'"

He suddenly nodded his head and laughed. "Yeah, okay, man. I'll tell her." He grinned. "Jesus wants you to know we was both hungry, so we stopped at Burger King before getting started." He was so sincere. I almost believed someone was there. Only the nurses laughing at me made me stop from looking where Joe had his eyes fixed.

Joe laughed even more. "Yeah, me too."

"What did he say?" I grimaced for asking. We weren't supposed to acknowledge hallucinations.

"He says he always gets the squirts after eating at the BK."

Joe frowned. "No, just because she's got big boobs don't mean she's a whore. She's a nurse, very innocent looking." He looked at me. "He thinks you're a whore because of your boobs. Women didn't have boobs like that in His day."

The roar of laughter from the nurses' station made me blush.

"It's the way I'm built."

"I don't know, man. Ask her yourself."

"What?" I cringed. I really had to stop asking him what they were discussing.

"Jesus wants to know what you're doing after work. He and I are going to the bar across the street for a few brewskies."

I cleared my throat. "I'm busy." I winced when I saw the ambulance staff had joined the nurses at the station—all of them listening to the conversation and nearly crying from laughter—re-enforcing for me I was handling this situation all wrong.

Joe continued to tell me about the night, stopping every few minutes to laugh at something his "pal" said.

"Joe, I don't see Jesus. He's here?"

"That's a real shame, sweetheart, because He is beautiful." He leaned forward. "And He's a helluva good joke teller. Raunchy, though."

"So, he's in this room?"

"Oh, yeah, yeah, for sure." He pointed towards the bathroom. "He's on the toilet, taking a dump."

The other staff howled even more when I looked in the bathroom. Dr. Jovanovich took the chart from me when I returned to the nurse's desk. "You handled that perfect, little one. You gained his trust. We must always remember to respect the people coming in here and gain their trust. Unless they are no-good human beings."

"And how do you know the difference?" I said, feeling better. The staff had stopped laughing when they heard his words.

"Believe me, you know. They can never hide who they are for very long."

We admitted Joe to the psychiatric unit.

Several days later I saw Joe in the coffee shop of the hospital. His delusions had cleared up within a few days of medication being administered. Because of that, his psychiatrist gave him dining room privileges.

In spite of recovering so well, Joe looked dejected, disconsolate—lonely. He looked like he needed a friend.

"May I join you, Joe?"

Joe nodded.

"How are you doing?"

"He disappeared."

"You mean Jesus?"

"The Doc says I was delusional. But He seemed so real. I felt so happy with Him around, like I had the strength to do anything. Now he's gone." He held up a Bible. "Doc gave me this. He says Jesus only exists in here." His shoulders sagged when he studied my face. "I guess you don't understand."

"I understand. It's really hard to lose your best friend. I know. I've lost three of them."

I took the Bible and thumbed through it. "You ever read the Bible, Joe?"

"No."

I read several Psalms to him, the joyful ones. The ones my grand-mother used to read to me on a regular basis. "What do you think?"

"They're beautiful. Who wrote them?"

"King David. He loved God. And his life was no bed of roses, believe me."

Joe took the Bible from me. "I gotta go. Thanks."

And with that Joe was gone, running back towards the Psychiatric unit, grinning from ear to ear.

17

"Two dogs were bad friends.
One day the wolf attacked one of them.
Quoth the other: 'If I do not help him today,
the wolf will destroy him and tomorrow attack me.'
So they joined forces and killed the wolf."
(Talmud, Sanhedrin)

Code Five coming in," shouted the charge nurse. "ETA three minutes."

Code Five in layman's terms meant the patient had no vital signs. He'd stopped breathing and one of the ambulance attendants pounded on his chest trying to get the heart to start pumping again. It also meant all hell was going to break loose the moment that patient arrived.

Within seconds of the charge nurse's warning, the huge glass doors burst open and a patient gurney rammed through, two ambulance attendants racing with it to the resuscitation room, and a third attendant on top of the patient pumping his chest. The staff charged after them.

I put the leads on the patient's chest so we could read the EKG on a large screen and see what his heart was doing. Another nurse pushed the ordered meds through the IV tubing. This man's heart raced a mile a minute, skipping beats along the way, and getting absolutely nowhere. His oxygen level was low, seventy-four percent. After another bolus of lidocaine, his heart slowed down to normal— eighty. He was stable. Our next job was to stabilize him even more and get him to the OR for placement of a pacemaker.

When the patient came to and saw Dr. Jovanovich's face, he practically jumped off the table with joy. "Moishe! This is a miracle. How have you been my dear, dear friend?"

Dr. J. held the man down, flat on the table, with one hand. "I am very good, thank you Michael, but you must stay still until we put a pacemaker in you."

"Okay, I understand." He beamed at all of us. "You people are so lucky to work with this hero. He saved all of us during the war. He kept us alive in the woods for years. And he is the toughest, wildest fighter around. You should see him fight. Powerful."

He turned back to Dr. Jovanovich. "It's wonderful to see you again. Ruthie will be thrilled."

"It will be good to see her too." He nodded at us. "Take him to the OR stat."

Three hours later, Dr. Jovanovich walked into the staff lounge with a huge vat of soup he'd made. When I entered the room, he offered me a bowl. "Here, little one. Cabbage, potato, and rutabaga soup. It puts hair on any man's chest."

It was awful.

Dr. Jovanovich chuckled when I made a face. "Eat up, eat up, Pamela." I loved the way he said my name. It was the same way my grandfather had pronounced it, with the accent all wrong, all endearing. "It keeps you warm, especially on a cold winter's night."

He held up an enormous loaf of Black Russian Rye bread, pulled off a huge chunk, and tossed it my way. "Tell me what you think. I made it myself."

"On top of being a doctor, you make bread?"

"Yes, I made bread every day for three years when we were in the woods." Wagging his finger at me, he continued. "And you know what? I think you would have been a really good partisan."

He tossed me another piece of bread. I looked at it with longing. I hadn't had bread in three months while being on my latest diet. I grabbed that hunk of heaven and stuffed it in my mouth. "This is really good."

Dr. J. chortled with delight. "You need to fatten up a little bit, Pamela. Can't make babies when you're this tiny."

And this was the toughest, wildest fighter?

During my visit with Jacob Masinsky on the Chemo unit the next day, he asked me to check in on his friend Michael. They had been partisans together in the woods.

"Oh, you must know Dr. Jovanovich then," I said. "I work with him sometimes in the ER."

"Yes, I do. We are good friends. I was worried that you should be in such a terrible place to work, but if you are with Moishe, then there is no need."

"Why do you call him Moishe? That isn't his name and he's not Jewish."

"Because he was our Moishe. Just like Moses led the Jewish slaves out of Egypt, he led us into the woods and taught us how to fight back. He saved a lot of Jews in the war. Hundreds of us. Unfortunately, Sarah and I didn't stay with him. She wanted to go south to her aunt's home."

"But if he's Serbian and you were in Poland, how did you meet?"

"Germany had taken over part of the northern section of his country and those Nazis traveled through the area recruiting every young man they could find. It didn't matter if they wanted to be in the army or not, they were recruited. Moishe and his brother escaped and tried to reach Poland through the woods and mountains. There was safe passage from Poland to Russia.

"We all met in the woods on the Hungarian border by accident. Our group of Jews would have all died if we hadn't met Moishe and his brother. Moishe taught us how to fight."

"That's incredible. I can't imagine him fighting."

"But me, you can see me as a partisan fighter? *Oy vez!* You're some funny girl."

I giggled and kissed Jacob goodnight. "Don't put yourself down, Jacob. You're a real fighter. I'd trust you to protect me any day."

"*Oyyyy.* I couldn't protect Sarah. How can I protect you? Goodnight my Chavela."

18

Never say this is the end of the road.
Wherever a drop of our blood falls, our courage will grow anew.
Our triumph will come and our resounding footsteps will proclaim:
We are here!
We'll have the morning sun to set our days aglow . . .
But if time is long before the sun appears,
let this song go like a signal through the years.
This song was written with our blood and not with lead.
It's not a song that summer birds sing overhead.
It was a people amidst burning barricades that
sang the song of ours . . . with pistols and grenades.
(A Partisan Song by Hirsh Glik)

After leaving Jacob's room, I headed for the ER to work the afternoon shift. I thought about how unmanned Jacob felt. I couldn't help him with that.

It was Saturday night. Not only was it a Saturday night, it was a full moon, the worst. Working in an emergency room during a full moon pretty much guaranteed that something bizarre would happen. Older and wiser nurses accepted that. Whatever the reason, ER had gone crazy that night and no one dared leave the unit until reinforcements appeared. Even though my shift in the ER had ended at eleven pm, I stayed on after midnight to help ease some of the chaos.

At this stage in my career, I had worked enough shifts with full moons that I was a firm believer about the moon's capabilities of disturbing the force and making people stark raving mad. To prove me right, police cars arrived with two members of the Satan's Choice biker gang. Almost like in the movie West Side Story, two gangs had met under a bridge and fought it out—only without the singing and dancing. Satan's Choice guys needed stitches. If these brutes looked this bad, I wondered what the other gang looked like. Satan's Choice members were frightening guys. Big, huge muscles, tough.

Windsor had two predominant biker gangs. I had gone to high school with the other gang, the Lobos. There was an unwritten rule with them—if a girl was from their high school or the neighborhood, leave her alone and keep her safe.

Satan's Choice had the reputation of being meaner back then, more menacing, and as far as I could tell, did not have any kind of moral code when it came to girls.

The cops brought them to ER because these guys had knife wounds that needed stitches before going to jail. One had a gash down the cheek. The other guy had been slashed across his forearm.

I led the two bikers down the long hall to the suture room. Chains hung from their belts and rattled as they moved. They looked me up and down as if I were a slab of fresh meat. I just knew this wasn't going to go well.

Dr. Jovanovich needed to see three kiddies with croup before he could sew up their wounds. He looked worried when he saw me heading down the hall. The cops who brought these guys in were nowhere to be seen.

I asked the men to lie on the stretchers while I set up the suture kits. They refused. One of them checked out our supply of surgical instruments that hung on the back wall. He fingered Kelly clamps and forceps, hot items for drug addicts. They used them to hold joints and hash. As I suspected, the guy started shoving our supply into his pockets.

"Come on, put those back," I ordered, using my sternest voice. At that point I still thought I was fairly safe. Someone would be here soon. Right?

"Or what?" said the guy. He had a lascivious grin plastered on his face and stalked towards me. "Whatcha gonna do, bitch, hurt me?"

He undid his belt. I nearly gagged. He reeked of old semen. Somewhere out there in the city, some poor girl had been raped.

His partner shut the door and began to undo his belt as well.

I backed up against the wall. We were nose to nose. From the looks and smell, he had not brushed his teeth in days. The prevailing odor was regurgitated beer and pizza.

I fumbled at the wall behind me in search of the call bell for the Nurses Desk. Missed that but managed to get the intercom on.

"I'm gonna have a good time with you, little girl."

I heard a thunderous stomping of feet tearing down the hall and what sounded like the roar of a massively large bear. Before anyone could move, the door banged open and Dr. Jovanovich filled the doorway. "Get away from her!"

He roared again and slugged one guy, sending him flying through the air. The biker crashed into the wall of instruments and became impaled there.

Dr. Jovanovich picked up the guy in front of me, and threw him out of the room, into the hallway wall. Plaster cracked and crumbled all around the unconscious bastard.

More footsteps. The police showed up, their guns drawn. They looked around at the damage and then at me. I stood there in shock. I had never seen anyone so big and powerful move so fast.

"Get these bastards out of here," bellowed Dr. Jovanovich. "You never should have left them alone with her."

He turned his face creased with worry lines when he saw me still up against the wall. "Are you okay?"

"They didn't touch me."

"Good." He stormed out of the room. "Get these pieces of garbage out of my Emergency Room," he thundered at the cops. "You never leave your charges alone with one of my nurses." He dragged one biker behind him. The guy looked like a dead rat.

I sagged against the wall. That sure was no Santy Claus. I never expected Dr. J. could be so violent.

When things settled down, Dr. Jovanovich served staff more homemade rutabaga soup to calm us. None of us needed or wanted to discuss what happened earlier. Events like that happened nearly every time we worked. I've heard people say ER nurses were a hardened group with no feelings. Now that I was one of them, I knew differently. We just never showed any emotion to the public.

I scooted my chair next to Dr. Jovanovich in the lounge. "Mr. Masinsky said you saved hundreds of Jewish lives."

Dr. J. slurped the contents of his bowl into his mouth all at once. "I didn't save them. I showed them how to be defiant and fight. There is a difference." He chewed on a piece of bread. "We weren't able to do much as a single unit, but around Europe there were over 50,000 Partisans, doing the same as us. We targeted railroad infrastructures near Warsaw to stop the cattle cars of Jews from getting to Auschwitz. But when that happened, the Nazis just pulled everyone off the cars and shot them. So, we went after the bridges. That's where Jacob came in handy. He very nimble and could climb the bridge trellises to place dynamite up at the top. We took out some other railways and supply depots, too. But it was not enough to stop the Nazis."

He practically spoon-fed me when I stopped eating. "We missed all of the signs in the thirties of what was about to happen with those Nazis," he said. "When I look back there were three years, 1931 to 1933 when we could have done something if we had known. It took Hitler less than six months to destroy Germany's democracy and turn it into a dictatorship filled with hate. Europe didn't hear Hitler's words as threats back then either, like we would have today.

By the time we figured it out, all that was left to do was run into the woods and fight back if we ran into any Nazis."

"How did you know where to go, where to hide?"

"My brother and I used to go hiking in those hills and woods when we were kids. We knew the area like the backs of our hands." He held up both of his hands. "His hand knew Serbia and part of the woods, and my hand was bigger so it had the rest of the map." He laughed at his own joke while he poured himself a cup of coffee.

"I watch you, you know," he said. "You're different from most of the nurses. You don't take anything for granted. That's why when tyrants of today speak, it grates on your ears. Mine too."

He gave me a giant piece of homemade strudel. "You know what else you do? You look every person you meet right in the eyes and you talk to them. You're trying to make them act normal. It's why that young man who thought he had Jesus with him, trusted you. He knew you were trying to help him. No bad guys will get past you and he understood that. He felt safe with you."

Dr. Jovanovich picked up a sheaf of charts and a pen. "But you need to learn how to fight."

"Where did you learn to fight like that?" An errant memory of me twisting David's testicles flashed before me.

"My papa. He made sure all of his sons could fight and shoot a gun. He knew something evil was going to happen."

I was asked to work a double shift that night. Full moon, devil moon, didn't matter what a person called it, the moon never disappointed and it didn't this time either. Now that the biker gang was gone, Dr. Jovanovich was his usual jovial self, tending to every person coming through the door with the same care and respect.

Definitely one of those good people, I thought. *You were right, Mrs. Smith. They're around.*

19

Whoever does not see God everywhere does not see Him anywhere.
(Kotzker Rebbe)

After my double shift in ER, Will met me at my apartment with breakfast in hand. "Happy anniversary." He handed me a McDonald's bag.

"Anniversary?" I said with a yawn, grateful to see food. My stomach had gurgled all the way home.

"Yes, it's been six months since I first asked you out."

"I didn't realize you were romantic in any way."

Will pulled out the food from the bag. "I'm not. But you are. So, happy anniversary."

Arik and David had made me a hopeless romantic, craving all the love songs, bouquets, poetry, and love letters. I wanted to be swept off my feet and carried off into the sunset. William wasn't into any of that. His lack of romanticism was a major problem for me and he knew it.

When we first dated, William reminded me of Woody Allen for thought processes and John McEnroe, the tennis player, for looks. However, the more I dated him, the more I realized he was so much more than Woody—more like a JFK, or John Quincy Adams mixed with Mort Sahl and George Carlin. He was even smarter than Ben Luborsky.

Will was the kind of guy who disarmed me with a smile. He was also exasperating, and irreverent. He claimed to be bored with politics, even though he knew way more about politics than any other man I'd ever met. He hated dancing and musicals (I loved them), and barely tolerated movies. But if the movie was *avant-garde* or weird, he was on top of it. He could make quotes from *Casablanca*, *The Manchurian Candidate*, and he knew the final speech by heart from Charlie Chaplin's *The Dictator*.

He read every book he could lay his hands on and he brought them over for me to read so we could discuss it. He wasn't a die-hard left-wing voter, nor did he like the right wingers. Will called himself a Centrist.

He renounced religion. He claimed he didn't believe in God. That made me think our relationship through several times. "But Will, I do believe in God."

"Good for you. Believe what you want. I won't hold it against you. Let's talk about something more important. Why do you read Harlequin Romances?"

"They're fluff. Mind numbing. And my patients like them."

"I have never in my life met anyone who reads Harlequin Romance novels outside of my sister Ruth," he announced. "And I won't date someone if that's all she reads."

"I read a lot more than romances."

"All right, what's your favorite book?"

"The Great Gatsby."

William did a double take. "You liked that book?"

"I loved it. I also love John Steinbeck, Ian Fleming, Leon Uris, William Shakespeare, and—"

"All right, you made your point."

William and I were complete opposites and I had no idea why

I felt so attracted to him, but I did. I knew manners, decorum, and ballroom dancing from the Pilch clan. My mother had forced me to walk around the house with a book on my head for hours—torture for a tomboy. I had learned etiquette for high tea before I was six, and how to dress impeccably on a dime. Mom insisted on dignity.

"A person doesn't need money to behave like royalty," Mom often said. "But money helps."

William had none of those skills. He never held a door open for me and most times he walked five paces ahead. So, what was the draw? After a lot of speculation, I realized he painted my ugly world in a whole new way, filled with nature and music and laughter. He pointed out cloud formations, rainbows, murmurations of starlings, wildflowers. I liked his world a whole lot better than mine.

Will handed me a lovely white peony one night, after we had yet another argument. He called it a peace offering. "Did you ever notice how we argue about the same thing?" he said. "It's always about my beliefs. You seem to think I'm shallow and without feeling, that I only have a bunch of acerbic opinions."

"That's the only side of you that I ever get to see. What am I supposed to think?"

Will thought about that a moment. "Okay, want to see what really matters to me?"

I immediately became skeptical, wondering if he was being serious. It was hard to tell most of the time. "Sure, I'm game."

"I'll pick you up early tomorrow morning, before four. Wear a jacket and hiking boots. It'll be cold."

"But what are we going to do at dawn?"

"Bird watching."

Will picked me up at exactly 0400 hours. Before dawn. Way before dawn. "Come on, we're late." He handed me a Thermos of hot tea with a warm buttered bagel. Will might not have opened doors, but he attended to my comforts. He even placed a blanket over my legs.

We drove to Point Pelee National Park, forty-five minutes from where I lived. Even after we parked the car, the sun had not bothered to rise yet. I could hear birds chirping and squawking as if they had been up for hours.

"I've never been here before dawn," I said in a hushed voice.

"This is the best time to show up." William pulled out two sets of binoculars and handed one to me. "Do you know about this land?" He handed me a giant garbage bag as well.

"What do you mean, do I know about the land? It's swamp and beach."

"And a Carolinian forest. There are over twenty kilometers of trails. We're going to walk five of the trails." When he saw the confusion on my face, he put his arm around me. "The park is a sand-spit formation, that's why it's surrounded by beaches and water. Migrating birds land here to rest before flying over the next lake. It's the largest bird migration path in the world."

He held up the bag. "For garbage. We'll start with the Woodland trail; it's about six kilometers."

The Woodland gracefully wound around the lush, green swaying trees that stood like ever watchful guardians over the groves. When we passed through the musky swamp woody incense engulfed us. We were being beckoned into the woodland's pulsing heart and I eagerly followed its path. Coils of mist sensuously enshrouded the tops of the trees and writhed around my feet. I gasped with delight when I realized the rustling sound of leaves on the forest floor came from birds, squirrels, and foxes just rising from their slumber. With each rustling leaf a tiny face appeared, shyly peeking out.

I rediscovered music in the gentle lapping of waves against narrow beaches, and the sweet songs of hundreds upon hundreds of migrating birds. Will suddenly held me back and pointed at a doe and her baby where they still slept. The giant fronds of the forest ferns cloaked them from predators—us.

As we continued to walk, I could see Will ahead of me through the mist that soothingly drenched us with droplets of water. He pointed at a coffee cup and wrapper he had missed. I dutifully put them in my bag. Muskrats played in the swampy pond to our left. Giant lacy cobwebs taller and wider than me dripped with dew. They glistened in the slowly rising sun. This was Heaven, an ephemeral moment in time.

Deer startled as we passed by their beds of zebra grass drifting near the ponds. One doe stood five feet away. "Hello beauty," I murmured.

Each trail we walked displayed new wildlife—turtles climbing onto logs to await the sun, fish swimming in ponds. Will pointed out raccoons in the hollow of a tree above the swamp area. On the fourth trail, scarlet tanagers foraged for food.

The fifth trail took less than twenty minutes to walk, but we passed hummingbirds feeding on a nearby patch of pale pink blossoms. The sun had fully risen by the time we finished our trek. It was mid-morning, 1000 hours.

"Time to go," said Will. "Too many people are on the trails now." He placed the full garbage bags by a disposal area.

"Do you do that every time?" I said, pointing to the bags.

"Yes. People are idiots. Wildlife confuse garbage for food." He pointed at a nearby muskrat home in a small pond. "Look what he used in his roof, electrical wiring."

We walked to one of the many beach areas and had a picnic while gazing out over the lake. "I used to come to this place with my parents on Sundays," I said, "and we'd barbecue hot dogs. But we never saw any of the trails or birds the way you showed me today." I turned to Will. "This was incredible. Thank you."

"You're welcome." He picked up a stone and made it skim over the water, touching down several times before sinking. "You're right about me, I guess. I'm weird in a lot of ways. I'm not the romantic guy with flowers and chocolates and poems about undying love. I don't do public displays of affection. And I'd rather crack a joke than express my feelings." He turned to me. "I've never understood the need for that. But I am loyal. I never betray someone I love. And I will always be there for you, no matter what."

He turned back to the still lake and skimmed another stone. "I have passions and they are deep. They're just not what other people hold dear. I don't need a church or synagogue to know there is a greater being. I come here and this is all the proof I need. Beautiful music seeps into my soul and almost makes me weep. Not the crap on the radio, but stuff like Meditation from Thais, and Jazz."

I stood next to him.

"Can that be enough for you, Pam?"

"Is there love involved?"

The intensity of his stare made me weak. "Yes. You would never doubt that you are loved. Not even for a day."

I slid my arm through his. "Yes then. It can be enough."

In that first May together, during the great bird migration, we saw nearly 280 species of birds and collected over forty bags of garbage. Point Pelee became the place where we could always connect and decompress. It brought romance to us in a different way. William's way. His thoughts seemed more ethereal and on a whole different scale of intelligence than any man I had ever met. He loved nature and jazz and classical music and exploring the meaning of life through philosophy.

He was beautiful.

20

"He who is full of joy is full of love."
(Baal Shem Tov)

My dad was an anti-Semite, although not intentionally. He didn't understand how hurtful his comments were. He often made cracks about the cheapness of Jews. One of his favorite lines was "I jewed somebody down." His Jewish boss had not given anyone a raise in over three years. Dad made five dollars an hour only because he was a senior employee. I could understand his bias, didn't like it, but I understood.

The entire Kilborn clan hated Jews and people they didn't understand, except for my great grandfather. He loved everybody. His being continuously sloshed had kept him mellow.

My mother was the opposite of my dad. She didn't have a prejudiced bone in her body.

One day she pulled me aside while watching Will chat with my dad. "I like him. It'll be interesting to hear what Uncle Willard has to say about him. You're in for a rough ride."

Rough ride?

On our drive to my place that night, Will asked me about my mother's diagnosis. My heart rose in my throat. I never discussed my mother's condition with anyone. The end of her life was drawing closer and I knew it, just didn't want to say that out loud yet. That would make it real.

"I need to know what we're in for, Pam. She doesn't look good."

I debated in my mind if what he said was true. Did he need to know? I glanced over at his worried face. It wasn't fair to him as a boyfriend for me not to tell him what was going to happen. I randomly wondered if I had become a better human and passed God's worthiness test to be able to have love again. I certainly trusted Will, like I had trusted Arik. Was that a sign?

"She's on her third bout of chemo," I said, "and it's been really hard on her. She vomits for a week after every injection."

"I can tell you two are close."

"We never used to be, but we've certainly become closer since she's gotten so ill. I'm taking her to Florida next January for at least a month. She can't handle the cold."

Will held my hand and squeezed it. "Sounds like a solid plan. I'll be here when you return."

21

"L'fum tzara agra, according to the effort is the reward."
(Ben Hei Hei, Ethics of the Fathers, 5:26)

I continued to devour the books Will brought over and we had heated discussions about every one of them. Growing up as a staunch socialist caused major problems for me with Will's more conservative-Centrist attitude. He was almost business-like about topics. I was all over the place with my arguments—loud, passionate, and using my hands for emphasis.

One evening we argued about some political issue and, after screeching like a banshee, I kicked him out. He arrived at my door at two in the morning with a bouquet of dead chrysanthemums in hand. I could tell he was upset about our fight and this was his weird way of demonstrating that distress—dead chrysanthemums.

"For you." he said. "They bring out the color in your cheeks."

"Not funny, William." His humor didn't work on me this time. "Where did you get these?"

"From some person's yard. They didn't seem to have any use for them."

I stepped back to let him in, trying to ignore his smirk. "Do you finally see things my way, now?" he said.

"Careful, Goldstein, I have a wicked temper and I bite."

"Well, let's kiss and make up and I'll explain again why you're wrong."

Will and I fought a lot. He called them heated debates. I called them major battles and worried we might not be as compatible as I had thought on the beach that day in May. After nearly a year of dating, I thought of us as a couple which made me feel vulnerable around Will. He knew so much about me and my family. Did I want someone to be that close again?

I began to make lists of pros and cons of our relationship. Will was smart and philosophical. I was practical, down to earth. I was a nurse for crying out loud. I had to be that way. Our saving grace was I loved to read and discuss philosophy. In that way we were perfect for each other.

And there was the romance thing. As much as I hated to admit my shallowness on this, I realized I needed something more from him. Other couples had "their song." Beautiful songs with beautiful lyrics. *Oh, my love, my darling, I've hungered for your touch . . .*

I mentioned this to William one day while we ate our Wendy's hamburgers. He looked at me with an annoying grin. "So, you're expecting a romantic song?"

My eyes squinted with suspicion. "Yeah, that would be nice."

"I've got a perfect one," he said. "It's one of my favorites."

And then he proceeded to sing:

> *Spring is here, a-suh-puh-ring is here.*
> *Life is skittles and life is beer . . .*
> *All the world seems in tune*
> *On a spring afternoon,*
> *When we're poisoning pigeons in the park . . .*

"How's that for romance?" he said expecting me to laugh.

Most girls would have slugged him and run away, but I seemed to be stuck in a mire of horrid fascination. I finally stopped spluttering. "And who exactly wrote that?"

"Tom Lehrer. I can play it on the trumpet, too."

"You play trumpet?"

"Yes. I taught myself. I guess I'm pretty good because the Windsor Symphony asked me to join them when I was seventeen."

I had no words for that bit of information.

Not only was Will a tennis pro in those earlier days of our relationship, and trumpet player extraordinaire, he had taken on the job of being a mailman. He ran his route for exercise. And because he couldn't figure out what to take at university, he thought it might be fun to get a business degree.

And I had fallen in love with him. Damn. Why? He completely confounded me. He cracked a million jokes. Nine times out of ten I didn't get the punchline.

After I complained to Dr. Luborsky about William, he laughed. "You're in love."

I groaned. "No, I'm not. We argue all the time."

Dr. Luborsky put his arm around me. "You've met your true Romeo, my dear. In Hebrew, we say he is your *besheret*."

Besheret again. Again?

Ohhhhh crap.

I took a long run that night, along the river, and thought about all that had happened to me in such a very short time. Not even five years had passed since Arik's death.

Jacob and Sarah had sent my world into a vortex of fear, confusion, and anguish. Ben Luborsky became my rock, encyclopedia, and confidant. He still was. And there had been David. Sweet David who saved my life and put me straight. The more I thought of it, the more I believed he had been one of the thirty-six Righteous souls of Judaism.

Then along came Will.

It seemed as if God had strategically placed these people in my life like chess pieces in a game, trying to thwart disasters from my bad choices, and preventing opposing forces from declaring checkmate and destroying me.

My thoughts turned to Will. My mind did not match his brilliant one, and his theories on life had so much more depth than mine. I loved traditions. He certainly did not.

I looked up at the cloudy night sky. "What am I going to do, God?"

No heavenly answer. I got the impression He thought I needed to try making wiser decisions—alone.

Will and I did have one important thing in common. He knew a lot of my Holocaust survivors.

"You're Jewish?" I said when he mentioned it.

"Well, yeah."

"Why didn't you tell me?"

"With a last name like Goldstein, I didn't think I'd have to. You didn't figure it out?"

In truth, I had never given his surname a second thought. I still compartmentalized. I saw him as separate from my Holocaust survivors. Separate from Arik. Separate from Ben and Israel. Will was the guy I dated. I had labeled him as Will, the tennis pro.

Dr. Luborsky laughed uproariously when I told him William was Jewish. "So, he's not a Romeo. He's your Moses." On a more serious note, he said. "Are you going to convert when he asks you to marry him?"

"Marry?"

Dr. Luborsky chuckled. "Yes, marry. It is inevitable."

Well, spit.

During the following weeks, Will and I continued to discuss, debate, and argue. According to Will, he had core beliefs only. They were all he wanted to discuss, not the differences between Christianity and Judaism. He became annoyed when I pointed out his basic tenets remarkably resembled Judaism's basic "tenets."

"Don't be cute. They don't. I don't believe in God."

"So, you've mentioned a few times. You're an Atheist."

"No. I don't believe in God."

"But isn't Atheism someone who doesn't think God exists?"

"Atheism is not a disbelief in gods or a denial of gods; it is a lack of belief in gods," snapped William. This conversation made him feel uncomfortable. My mind whirled. What was I missing?

He stuck his palm up when I started to speak. "End of discussion."

I harrumphed. "Why do you get to end discussions and I don't?"

"Because I brought Chinese food for dinner. Let's eat."

My eyes narrowed into slits. "Sly. Sly and conniving. You'd be an amazing lawyer. I can see you in court, even. Every argument we have, I feel as if I'm on the Defense stand and you win. You're rationalizing to match what you believe."

He had set the table and put out the food. "Come and eat."

"Don't think you're off the hook with serving me food. It's just I'm hungry. We're gonna talk about this a lot more because I do believe in God."

Will nodded. "As you wish. But then I get the last piece of cake."

22

*They will fight against you, but will not overcome you for I am
with you and will rescue you," declares the Lord.*
(Jeremiah 1:19)

After the Last Name Revelation, as I liked to call it, Will suddenly
became more Jewish. I can't even explain how he did that, but
he did. Yiddish words crept into the conversation, more of his jokes
had Jewish themes.

He took me to some of the more popular Jewish delicatessens in
the Windsor/Detroit area. One day, we went to a place where the
owner barely spoke English.

After William ordered pastrami sandwiches, the owner looked
at me questioningly, "moostapikapeppa?"

"Excuse me?"

He sighed. "Moostapikapeppa?"

After the fourth attempt at asking me the same question, he
threw his hands in the air and called for his wife. "Rutie! *Da Goyishe
nicht vershtayen.*"

At that point William laughed so hard tears ran down his cheeks.
My embarrassment was at an acute high.

When Rutie saw Will, a big smile broke out on her face. "*Velvel!
Nu?* How is your mama?"

"She's fine, Mrs. N."

Rutie frowned when she saw me but quickly nodded. "My husband is asking if you want mustard on your sandwich and a pickle on the side, or some fresh peppers."

Moostepikapeppa—Mustard, pickle, pepper. I glared at Will. "You could have told me."

"This lady makes the best cinnamon buns in the world." William completely sidestepped my outrage. He took our sandwiches and drinks to the only table in the room. "No raisins."

Rutie blushed at Will's compliment. "I made a fresh batch this morning. I'll pack some up so you can bring them home to your mama."

Rutie studied my face for several minutes, then beamed another smile. "Now I know where I've seen you. You're the nurse that ordered a platter of food for Jacob Masinsky when his wife Sarah died."

"Yes, I did. It was a beautiful platter. Thank you."

"Sarah and I were good friends. We were partisans in the war. Enoch and I came from Vilna though." She shuddered. "Such awful memories." With that, Rutie returned to the kitchen.

"What's Vilna?" I whispered to Will.

"One of the largest Jewish towns in Europe, before the war." He took my hand. "You don't need to know about that."

Yes, I did. Will still didn't understand my OCD about research. Vilna. Back to the library I went.

"Oh, you look distressed," said Mrs. Smith. "What are you looking up this time?"

After I mentioned Vilna, she walked around from her desk. "Ah, you've been to Mr. and Mrs. N's deli then. They're lovely people." She pointed to her left, "Aisle Nine. Middle shelf."

According to the Britannica, Vilna was known as the "Jerusalem of Lithuania," and had been home to more than 60,000 Jews. That

Jewish hub was destroyed during World War II and most of the Jews killed. Some escaped into the woods and formed a group called the Partisans of Vilna. Using guerilla warfare and taking it to new levels of violence, they became known as some of the bravest and ruthless fighters against the Third Reich.

Rutie and Enoch certainly did not fit the bill of being ruthless. But then again, I thought Dr. Jovanovich was a gentle giant. Obviously, I had a lot to learn about human nature when it was tested.

Several weeks later, I returned to the delicatessen without Will. I had become addicted to their pastrami sandwiches.

Rutie was at the counter. "Pamela! Nice to see you. Pastrami with mustard?"

"Yes please." I had immediately developed a soft spot for Rutie after we met. She pronounced my name the way my grandfather did.

"Dollie, what's wrong?"

I wiped my eyes. "You say my name like my grandfather did. He died a few years ago."

Rutie sat beside me. "Which old country did he come from?"

"We're not sure. Austria, Poland, Czechoslovakia. He could never remember."

Rutie laughed. "I think I know the border. Nobody living there ever knew what the name of the country was from week to week. At least we didn't have that problem from where I come from."

I wiped some mustard from my mouth with a napkin. "Do you mind if I ask a question?"

"Ask."

"Will said you and your husband were Partisans of Vilna during the war and you were very brave. What happened?"

Rutie hung her head when her lips began to tremble. "Nothing that was any good. The Nazis never made anything good. Hitler was Satan. Just like in the rest of Europe, the Nazis came in and made ghettos for the Jews outside of town so the other people couldn't see what they did to us. They put all of the sick and old people in Ghetto Two and killed them instantly. Then they started on Ghetto One, sending most of them to Ponari to be slaughtered like sheep. Young people like Enoch and me, couldn't bear that idea, so we fought them when they arrived to take the rest of us. After killing most of those Nazis, we escaped into the woods. We stole food and supplies from the people in the city, even sticking guns in their faces, demanding food. Then the boys found out where the Nazis had camped and we kept stealing ammunition and explosives."

Rutie went to the counter with my empty plate. I thought she had finished, but she returned with a plate of cinnamon buns. I bit into one and groaned with a sugar addict's delight. "What did you do with the explosives?"

I shouldn't have asked, but I had never heard of partisans or Jews fighting back against the Nazis until I met Dr. Jovanovich. My reading at the library claimed more than 30,000 Jews were partisans. Dr. J. said it was more than 50,000.

"Just like Sarah and Jacob's group, we blew up roads and railway tracks." Her voice softened with shame. "We blew up hundreds and hundreds of Nazis marching into battle as well. I have so much blood on my hands."

"Surely it was necessary," I said with conviction.

She watched her husband catching a housefly and turning it outside. "No. Such a terrible thing to have done as a Jew. Everything we did went against the Torah. One Nazi boy I shot wasn't even as old as me. He had pink cheeks."

She took a deep breath and patted flour off of her apron. "Enoch was studying to be a rabbi before the war. After what we did . . . he hasn't been able to set foot in a synagogue since then."

"Where did you marry?"

A nostalgic smile appeared on her face. At least that was a fond memory for her. "In the woods, under the stars, by one of the rabbis who fled with us. The rabbi tried to assure all of us we were doing the right thing, that Jews have had to fight many times to save themselves." She folded her arms in front of her. "But I will never forget that boy's face. He haunts me every night."

As I was about to leave the deli that day, I noticed a plaque on the wall. A man named Abba Kovner had written a tribute to his fellow partisans who had fallen in their battles. I just knew Enoch and Rutie had been part of this man's troupe of fighters.

Each one of us, we the last ones, let us remember our dead that fell in battle and sanctified their names and the honor of their people. On its altar they gave the prime of their lives. Let the movement remember.

Its loyal members, heroes of the destruction that in the hour of catastrophe and death rose up the banner of battle and of revenge for the catastrophe, and even with the last of their might, carried it to the very end! Let the homeland remember.

The memory of its zealots—the last that fell on foreign soil, soaked in the blood of millions of our brethren, and the cry of revenge was on their lips."

These two elderly souls, where the man escorted houseflies outside to fly free, and the woman with skin as white as flour, baked wonderful confections daily and gave them all away, were Partisans of Vilna. They fought and killed Nazis. They stole food and clothes from the people of Vilna. And they felt shame at their heroics instead of pride.

For me, the real marvel was that they came to Canada and made a new life together. A miracle. Except—Enoch had been a pious and righteous man who wanted to be a rabbi before the war. Because of what he did to save himself and other Jews, to avenge the deaths of millions of Jewish souls, he could no longer face entering a synagogue and praying. And according to Rutie, he had never uttered a single word of Kaddish ever again.

When I mentioned this to Will, he put his finger over my mouth. "You don't understand. After the war, he just wants to lead a normal, quiet life."

"No, Will. It's way more than that. And what about Mrs. N.?" I said. "She's obsessed about baking."

"My mother says she bakes every day so she can feel sane. She'd panic if she couldn't bake. And that is all she wants to do."

I disagreed with Will's assessment. The way I saw it, she thought surviving Auschwitz was better for Jews, more pious, than fighting back. And in my mind, that was just wrong.

23

"Sometimes love is stronger than a man's convictions."
(Isaac Bashevis Singer)

January finally arrived and couldn't have come too soon. My mother suffered horribly in the cold of December. The cancer was in her bones, and getting cold made her cry out in agony. After months of saving holidays, days off, and money, I booked the two of us at the Palm Beach Hyatt Regency in Florida for the entire month. Dad stayed behind and went to work.

The night before my trip, Will brought over a stack of numbered envelopes, a rubber band around them, with my name on each one.

I fanned through them. "What are these?" Letters like this were a first for him.

Will actually blushed. "I've written you a letter for every day that you're gone. Open them in chronological order."

"But why?"

He pulled me close and gave me an incredibly passionate and wild kiss. "Because I want to make sure you won't forget me while you're gone. I'm not going to be there to keep the other guys away from you. I love you, you know."

"Oh," I whispered. I was in a state of shock. Will loved me. "Why?"

Will laughed at the dumbstruck look on my face. "Because you always surprise me. I never know what you're going to do next."

While flying to Florida, my thoughts lingered on Will and his declaration of love for me. For the first time, I actually wondered what life would be like being married to him. I eagerly read each letter in chronological order while basking on the beach with my mother. They mostly discussed school, what he planned to do after this degree, where he'd like to buy a house in Windsor. The letters were filled with inane and stupid jokes, famous quotes he liked, and the occasional newspaper article he had found interesting. His charms made me homesick for him.

The last letter began differently. The tone of the words was different, more serious.

I have started every letter with salutations like Dear Pam, Hey Good Looking, Hiya, Hi, etc. But I have never started a letter the way I've wanted to, with words from my heart. I wasn't sure if you'd believe them. So here goes. My Beloved,

I woke up this morning and smiled with relief. This is the last day I have to spend without you. You're coming home to me tomorrow and my solitary loneliness will end. The sun might even come out again, once you get here. It's a funny thing about being alone for a month, after spending the better part of a year with you—I realize how much I depend on hearing the sound of your voice to make me happy, and watching the sparkle and shine in your eyes when you see me come through your door makes me melt. I love how I can make you laugh at my silly jokes. And I love how you tilt your head and smile shyly when I embarrass you.

I miss having your arms around me. I miss kissing you. I miss taunting you and getting to watch you become riled—it's like watching fireworks go off. I miss everything about you.

I'll see you tomorrow, my sweet love.

Will.

I read and re-read the letter several times. Was I that obtuse that I didn't see how Will really felt about me? There was that moment on the beach last May, but we never really discussed love again.

Will loved me. He actually put it in writing.

I refolded the letter and held it to my chest. "Such beautiful words, just like Shakespeare's sonnets." A giggle escaped. "That dufus."

When I returned from Florida in February, things changed between William and me. A lot. Every time we were together the conversation became so serious. We discussed the differences between Judaism and Christianity. He asked me thoughtful questions. Could I ever live without Christmas? Could I ever convert to Judaism? Could I ever marry a Jew?

And then Valentine's Day arrived. A yellow rose was delivered to my apartment. Will had written "I love you" on the card.

A single yellow rose without thorns means our love is pure and true and will last forever. It means I am very happy with us.

My lips turned up at the corners into a smile of delight. I couldn't help but think Arik had just moved aside so I could love someone as much as I had loved him. And as ridiculous as it sounded, I finally felt as if Arik had given me permission to live, just like Spencer Tracey had given Irene Dunne permission in *A Guy Named Joe*. That movie had torn me apart five years earlier. Now, the thought of it made my heart soar into the atmosphere.

I loved Will!

Will came over to my place for dinner that night. I laughed with glee when I saw the Wendy's bags. My favorite.

"I want the whole nine yards," Will said later. "I want you to convert to Judaism. I want us to be legitimate. I love you."

I couldn't stop smiling. "I love you, too. I've got an idea."

"What's that?"

I sat on his lap. "Let's get married."

Will nearly dropped me on the floor. "Geez, I've been trying to say that all this time. Okay. Let me check my schedule. I'll have my people contact your people—"

I kissed him solidly on the mouth. "You talk too much, Goldstein. Do you know of any good rabbis?"

After Will left for his house, I called Ben Luborsky. I told him about Will and me planning on getting married. And me converting to Judaism.

"Well, it took him long enough. *Mazel tov.*" He chuckled at how breathless I sounded. "It's good you're going to convert. Our survivors already think you're a Jew. You should visit the local reform rabbi and discuss it with him. Steer clear of the orthodox man."

When Will and I met with the rabbi, his first words were, "*Oy vez,* have you got a problem. This will kill your mother." William's mother was famous in the community for being emotional. And that was putting it mildly.

I wasn't impressed with the rabbi. He was nice enough, but his brain and knowledge didn't hold a candle to my William.

My William.

"Well, you certainly have your answer," I said as I looked in the mirror hanging on the wall of my bedroom. "You're in love again. Only this time, Kilborn, don't screw up and let him die. You have to take better care of him."

I finally understood why I was so attracted to Will. He made me feel whole again, significant, eager to explore life. And clean. William made me feel clean again.

24

Who is wise? He who learns from every person.
(Pirkei Avot 4:1)

Thanks to William and Mrs. Smith, I had read well over one hundred books about religion, Judaism, World War II, and the history of the Jews of Europe. When the rabbi gave me a layout of what we would cover in his conversion classes, I groaned. Will had spoiled me. I was used to debates and loud discussions about all topics Jewish. In this class I'd have to be polite. *Yes sir, no sir, how high would you like me to jump, sir.* The man wanted regurgitation. This was going to be torture.

To keep my sanity during these classes, I decided to take matters of actually learning into my own hands. Detroit was home to several large and fabulous bookstores and one of them was famous for its Jewish content. I set my eyes on that one.

Later that week, I returned to my library and told Mrs. Smith about the Jewish bookstore I intended to visit. I also told her about Will asking me to marry him.

She looked at me over the rims of her glasses. "So, you're going to convert?"

"He's asked me to, but I was thinking of doing that anyway. From what I've read so far, Judaism sounds so beautiful."

Mrs. Smith was not pleased. She brushed a wisp of her gray hair back and tucked it into her chignon. "I'm surprised William has asked you to convert. It's such a selfish thing to do on his part."

My eyebrows rose in shock. "Selfish? Why selfish?"

"Pamela, you of all people have seen first-hand what the results of being Jewish are. If you love someone, why would you put them through that?"

I didn't know how to respond, but I knew I didn't like her criticizing William. He loved me. Of course, he would want me to convert to his religion. That's what women did in the seventies. They converted to their husband's faith. That's what all the women in my family had done.

"We're a very small community," said Mrs. Smith. "I've known William since he was born." She gently placed her hand under my chin and pushed my mouth closed. "Oh, do keep your mouth closed, you look like a carp with it open. The Goldsteins are not exactly the in-laws I would have chosen for you. But William is a sweet guy and very handsome. I can understand your attraction to him." She glanced upwards when she realized what she had just said. "And no, we will not be discussing Esther and Maurice and the children in any great length. Better you discover them on your own."

I took a deep breath. "I haven't met them yet. But answer this. Why is it selfish to ask me to convert?"

Mrs. Smith stepped away from her desk to stand directly across from me. "Have you not comprehended what you've been reading all this time? The Holocaust is not a one-time persecution of us Jews, Pamela. It happens every seventy years or so. What will you do when another Hitler comes along? Have you thought about that? You will have to be fiercely strong and brave, and ready to fight. Will you be able to do that?"

"Will you?"

From the look on her face, I had, in turn, shocked Mrs. Smith with my question. "You know what, Pam? I honestly don't know. What I do know is I'm moving to Israel when I retire next year. It's safer there for Jews. And friendlier."

The silence painfully lingered between us. "You're leaving me?" I said with a pained, horrified voice. My eyes welled with tears. I couldn't help it. Mrs. Smith had been part of my life since I joined the library at the age of seven. She understood my love for books, my research fascination. We had discussed deep topics for years, read books together, and talked for hours about life, especially now that I was an adult. I considered her my perfect mother.

"I'm not leaving you, dear girl. I'm going home, where I belong."

My throat had become thick and closed up. She was leaving me. Truly leaving. She was the one who had always been there, always been my one constant friend.

She cleared the emotion from her throat. "You'll need to do a lot more research if you're going to decide whether or not to convert. You're right to go exploring in Detroit. There is a lovely deli down the road from the bookstore you mentioned. Make sure you eat before going to read. Tell them Gertie Smith sent you."

William wanted nothing to do with conversion classes, so I assumed he would feel the same way about going to Detroit. On my first adventure into the store, I practically squealed with delight when I saw the endless rows of books. So many wonderful books, thousands of them. I spent the first hour touching covers with awed delight. Eventually, I decided to break down this precious time in the store into sections—traditions, prayers, Torah, history, Israel, theories and philosophy.

I grabbed a few books about Judaic philosophy and quietly sat in a corner in the back, where no one would notice me. After creating a little nest with my coat, I extricated my notebook and pen and began reading. After several hours passed, I returned all of the books back to their shelves, save one.

"I'll take this, please," I said to the owner, a Chasidic, middle-aged man with black-rimmed glasses, and beard.

"*Nu?* It took you six hours to pick out one lousy book?" His *payes,* ringlets, jiggled as he spoke.

I nervously licked my lips. "I'm sorry, I'd love to take them all, but I can only afford one on a nurse's tight budget."

"I see. Do you plan on coming here often to do this then?"

"I'm hoping to, for a little while at least. If you let me, please?"

After a long stare and a gruff clearing of his throat, he nodded. "So long as you buy one book." He wagged his finger at me. "Each time."

Relief passed through me. "Thank you."

"*Zaye Gezunt.* When is next time?"

"Next week."

Every day off work, I went to the back of the bookstore with a pile of books, plopped on the floor, and read, taking down notes whenever I didn't understand something, or wanted to discuss an issue with Will. At the end of my day, I would select a book I felt I needed to read more closely. A nurse's pay didn't cover much. It certainly didn't cover the cost of new Jewish books every week.

My fourth visit in, the owner looked at the title of the book I wanted to purchase. "*The Holocaust Chronicles.* Why this book?"

"I take care of a lot of survivors and I'm trying to put all of their stories into perspective."

"Ah, it's too bad Rabbi Dickerstein died. He could have helped you with that."

My eyes widened with surprise. "I knew him. I took care of him."

We chatted for several minutes about my patient. It felt good to hear about him from someone who knew him well.

The following week, I placed my latest book choice on the counter. The owner gave me a cookie. "For your journey home." He blushed a little and wiped cookie crumbs off his beard. "You can call me Isaac."

"Thanks Isaac. I'm Pam. See you next time."

Going to the bookstore on days off became a tradition of sorts. The library lost its allure, perhaps because it pained me to see Mrs. Smith, now that I knew she was moving. The other draw for me was so many different types of books at my fingertips. Isaac's store contained volumes about the greatness of Judaism. The religion, traditions, and history were interwoven into a magnificent tapestry that lovingly wrapped me in a shelter where I could read and study for hours. I enjoyed exploring this fascinating religion and culture that I had grown to love. The more I read, the more I didn't understand how William could reject Judaism.

Isaac was always polite and very curious until one day he shouted, "You're driving me *meshuginah*! What are you doing reading all these books like a Talmudic scholar?"

Maybe I owed him an explanation, so I told him about my Holocaust survivors and William and my plans to convert. He plopped in his chair by the till. "So, are you going to really convert or do that Reform thing?"

"I don't know, Isaac. I love William, but he's Reform. And I adore the traditions, especially Shabbos." We spent nearly an hour talking. Isaac enthusiastically described the joy of dancing on Simchat Torah and eating meals in a Sukkah to celebrate the harvest. I listened with an almost unbridled joy to this man's love and devotion of his faith.

"It sounds so wonderful, Isaac, the way you describe it," I said with longing. "I can hardly wait to be Jewish. I don't relish the idea of classes with this Reform Rabbi though."

"Being converted by an Orthodox rabbi is the best way. After all of this studying you've been doing, you need to follow your heart. Then you have no problems down the road when you have kids."

His eyes scanned me from head to toe. "You're too skinny," he declared, "you should eat more. Take half my sandwich."

I agreeably devoured half his pastrami sandwich and a pickle, (Will was right, Mr. N.'s in Windsor *was* better).

"*Nu?* When will you be coming back?" said Isaac.

"I'll be here Tuesday."

On my next day off, I arrived at my usual time, waved hello to Isaac, and took the sandwich he had placed on the counter for me. "This is wonderful," I mumbled as I took a second bite. "What is it?"

"Beef tongue. It's a Jewish delicacy, my mother's specialty." He pointed at a pile of books on the counter. "You're missing this whole section of Judaism that you should know about before converting."

"Thanks." I grabbed the books while trying to figure out how not to gag. Beef tongue! Ew.

I went to my usual corner where a small table flanked by two chairs had been placed. "Thank you, Isaac," I said. "And thanks for the food."

"Don't mention it," he replied. "You need at least another twenty pounds on you. I consider it my *mitzvah* to fatten you up before you get married."

An elderly gentleman arrived shortly after and asked if he might use the chair next to me. I assured him that would be fine and returned to my reading. After several minutes passed, he leaned over to see what book I held. "Ah, Hillel. Are you enjoying it?"

"I'm reading his seven rules and not really understanding them. The only one I do get is *What is hateful to you, do not do to your neighbor, that is the whole Torah. Everything else is commentary.* That one is straight forward."

We spent the afternoon together discussing Hillel, traditions, and the history of the Jewish people, and my favorite, *Shabbat.* We shared the beef tongue sandwich and I told him about my Holocaust survivors.

He chuckled. "So, you own them, do you?" When I looked confused, he explained. "You call them your survivors. It's an endearing thing to do. You care a great deal about them."

When I felt my cheeks burn with embarrassment, I looked down at my hands. "I love them," I said with feeling. I hadn't realized I called them that.

We talked for another hour about his life as a rabbi, my survivors, and their need to forgive. At last, the man rose to his feet. "I must leave. It's almost time for afternoon prayers."

"Thank you for spending time with me. I wish you held conversion classes. It would be so exciting to learn from you."

His eyes shone like stars when he turned back to look at me. "If you were in my conversion class, I would be signing your conversion papers and welcoming you into the Jewish faith right now. I hope you continue your studies."

He handed me a book, *To Be a Jew* by Hayim Halevy Donin. "You might find this helpful. You can use it as a how to book when you forget a rule."

"Like a Cole's notes?"

He laughed. "Yes, exactly." He waved his hand. "Cole's notes. I'll have to remember that." He shook hands with Isaac. "Shalom, Isaac. *Gezunt zolstu zein.*"

I asked Isaac the name of my new friend. He pointed at the book. "Rabbi Donin. He's a great man. It was a very sad day for this community when he moved to Israel."

Rabbi Donin had been the rabbi of the B'nai David congregation in Southfield, Michigan, where he remained a rabbi until he made aliyah in 1973. The rabbi was also the co-founder, and the first president of Yeshivat Akiva, the first modern and Orthodox Hebrew day school located in Detroit. He happened to be in town, visiting family and did Isaac a favor when he came to meet me.

Isaac leaned over the counter a little. "He wants you to have that book for free, so you can pick out another one now. Two for the price of one."

Meeting Rabbi Donin changed how I looked at life and Judaism.

Anything was possible he had said. He was the epitome of what I thought a rabbi should be. Donin convinced me to convert the way William wanted for now. "When you have children and are running your own home, then you have an orthodox conversion, then you become kosher and *Shomer Shabbos*. The woman decides how to run her house." He nodded his head in a sage manner. "You will do well as a Jewess. This is your *besheret*, your fate."

Besheret had another meaning?

Swallowing my misgivings, I signed up for conversion classes at the Reform temple in Windsor the next day. I would continue coming to the bookstore to prevent a rush of boredom hysteria.

I giggled at the sky. "You're still watching out for me, aren't You?"

Yeah, not so much. For these classes, I found myself still on my own. If I wanted to be Jewish, I needed to really fight for it. My first stumbling block came when the rabbi insisted William had to come with me to classes. I refused. "It's my conversion, not his. I don't want him here."

"But you are marrying William. If you weren't doing that, you would never consider converting."

And that's when it hit me. That wasn't true. I thought back to when I had first explored Judaism and it had nothing to do with Will. In fact, I didn't even know Will then. Jacob and Sarah and Ben, with their deep faith and contentment with being Jewish was what motivated me to study the religion.

"If you don't do this my way, you'll have the longest Reform conversion in history, young lady. This is my temple and I make the rules."

An ultimatum? Why so hostile?

I could feel my temper rising. *Steady Kilborn, steady.* "Then I guess I'll have the longest Reform conversion in history. It's my conversion, not his, and I don't want him present."

After great deliberation, I discussed with William the idea of me converting to Orthodox Judaism. He nearly freaked out. "I only want you to do this for my mother's sake. Being Orthodox would be a nightmare for me."

I didn't ask why. I should have.

It ended up that I really did have the longest Reform conversion in history—two years. The rabbi had met his match in me. I did not want Will in my class and that was that. I argued with the rabbi every chance I got about why his approach to converts getting married was wrong. Boy, did I argue. My point was the temple *should* have classes about the wedding and marriage before the ceremony. The congregation *should* welcome the couple into the synagogue with open arms. And, most important, the rabbi *should* make converting something that a person would want to do because of Judaism's beauty. Not a punishment for falling in love with someone who was Jewish. All three *shoulds* were ignored.

I wondered during my very long and boring classes if I might be a tad stubborn. I asked that question when Will came over after class one night.

Will drew me close. "Ohhhh, whatever gave you that idea? It's part of your charm."

"Can't I go to Detroit and have an orthodox conversion? It would be done in a month."

William growled. "No. I don't believe in any of this crap. As I've said before, it's only important for you to convert so my mother will accept you."

I pulled away from him. "So, you think we're not going to practise Judaism in our home?"

"Wasn't planning on it."

"Oh no you don't, Goldstein," I said. "I'm converting because I love all this stuff. And the first thing I'm buying when my conversion ends is a pair of candlesticks. So, get used to that idea."

Will pulled me close again. "I think I created a *Golem*, a Yiddishe monster."

25

*Sometimes you will never know the true value
of a moment until it becomes a memory.*
(Talmudic thought)

C ode Five coming in." shouted the ER supervisor. "ETA four minutes."

As happened so many times, the patient gurney crashed through the open ER doors, two attendants rushing the cart into our resuscitation room, one attendant on top of the patient, pumping his chest.

All we could see at first was the frailty of this person. The attendant had cracked the man's ribs from pumping so long. A shiver ran down my spine when I heard ribs grinding together with every pump on the chest. The same reaction as nails on a chalkboard.

I placed the leads of the EKG on the patient's chest. The lines were erratic, a dying heart. Still, we tried to save him, hope against hope a miracle would happen.

Every time we resuscitated him, he'd raise his arms up to make sure his kippah was still in place. And every time he did that, he'd go back into Defib. I placed the kippah back in place and held his hands.

"Oh my God," I whispered when I saw his face. "It's Jacob Masinsky. He's Dr. Luborsky's patient."

The doctor glanced at the charge nurse. "Get Luborsky in here. Maybe there are DNR orders on this old guy. You know his diagnosis, Kilborn?"

"Metastatic ca."

When Jacob came to, he tried again to make sure his *kippah* was in place.

"For Christ's sake, someone strap this idiot down," shouted the doctor. I grabbed a small roll of gauze and wrapped it around Jacob's head so the *kippah* stayed in place.

"What the hell are you doing Kilborn?"

"Keeping it in place," I replied while holding onto Jacob's hands.

I held tight when Jacob came to again and kissed his cheek. "It's all right, Jacob, it won't fall off again."

Jacob looked into my eyes. "Oh, it's my Chavela. I'm not alone."

I whispered so the doctor and staff couldn't hear me and held his hands tighter. "Your Chavela is here."

"Say the *Shema* with me."

I understood what was about to happen and I nearly burst into tears. In my heart I knew it was time for him to let go. I just wished it didn't hurt so much.

"*Shema Yisroel, adonai elohainu* . . . Hear O Israel, the Lord is our God, the Lord is one . . ."

The doctor looked at me as if I'd gone nuts. "That's melodramatic, Kilborn," he sneered.

"No, not at all," said Ben Luborsky from the doorway. "He's about to die." He moved to my side and joined me in the prayer.

A look of serenity lit Jacob's face. Within seconds his heart stopped beating.

Ben held his arm over Jacob's chest, preventing another attempt at saving his life. "Let him be," he said. "He's had enough."

When the ER doctor was about to protest, Ben held up his hand. "I'll take responsibility. He's my patient."

The rest of the evening flew by in a blur. I had become so attached to Jacob. My heart ached. The ER doctor entered the staff lounge while I was on break. "So, you knew that old guy?"

"He was a patient on the chemo unit."

"Maybe the heart problem was a side effect from the chemo. It makes ya' wonder what made him die."

"I think the more important question is what made him continue to live after all he had gone through. He was an incredible man."

The doctor shrugged after pouring himself a cup of coffee. "Doesn't really matter, does it? None of us make a difference."

Will met me at my place after work and tried to console me, but it was to no avail. I needed a break from the ER and disdainful doctors. I transferred to the OR and *that* was like going from the frying pan into the fire.

26

There may be times when we are powerless to prevent injustice,
but there must never be a time when we fail to protest.
(Elie Wiesel)

The OR area was set up like a ladder—two long aisles where various Operating rooms stood with their scrub rooms, materials rooms, rooms with surgical instruments and dirty utility rooms down each long aisle. Cross aisles every now and then joined the two sides. I felt as if I had entered an industrial zone with very little humanity.

I spent the first six months in the OR training to be a scrub nurse, meaning I assisted in passing surgical instruments to surgeons. I preferred being a circulating nurse where I made sure everyone in the OR was happy—anaesthetists, surgeons and their assistants, scrub nurses, head nurse, supervising nurse, and the patients and cleaning staff. Least of all the patients. Even though they shouldn't have been, patients were low man on the totem pole.

Being a circulating nurse meant I could fix situations whenever they went wrong. And every time I did that, I thought of David Herzl. I still tried to fix things and I doubted I could ever change that habit no matter what David had said.

My supervisor and head nurse were both tough as nails and ran a really tight ship filled with so many characters with wild personalities. They were fascinating to watch in action—both of them staunch feminists—a near impossible feat during the 1970's. I used to joke with William and say I wanted to be just like them when I grew up.

As for the doctors—it seemed the more talented the surgeon, the quirkier the personality. One Jewish surgeon, Dr. Asher, whistled while he performed surgery. If he whistled Jingle Bells or some other frivolous song, all was well. Classical music meant the surgery had become difficult but things were under control. Opera—things were becoming dicey; call for the supervisor. And Wagner meant all hell was about to break loose, which was my cue to hit the Code Red button to call in all staff, run for the Emergency crash cart, and start up the defibrillator. Good times.

After nearly a year of working there, things became routine. I had favorite doctors and Dr. Strathman, an anaesthetist, was one of them. She stood less than five feet tall and if she weighed a hundred pounds that would have been a miracle. She had a round face, a gentle soul, and put patients at ease with a single smile before putting them to sleep. More amazing to me? We had the same color of hair—burnt auburn. Dr. Luborsky had been wrong. People with that color hair weren't just from Holstein County in Germany. But she *was* from Germany.

The most senior anaesthetist, Dr. Dornanalty, thought he had the power of God and a nurse or a female anaesthetist did not want to be on his bad side. He ignored Dr. Strathman, and when she tried to discuss something important with him, he sloughed her off like an annoying fly. She was a woman in a man's position. Strathman in her quiet way, fought his asinine attitude every chance she got, and surprisingly enough, won nearly every battle. I became her number one fan. She demonstrated to us women the power of quiet tenacity and upholding moral principles.

My fascination with warped and sick minds had me observing Dornanalty every chance I got. The man hated anybody who was not a WASP (White Anglo-Saxon Protestant). I liked to think he hated himself as well because he wasn't Protestant—he practiced Catholicism. I saw him as the Pillsbury Dough Boy. Same doughy face, beady eyes, and thin lips. His appearance mocked his revered position.

When I circulated in his OR, I knew by the end of the day I'd feel shattered because of his derisive remarks and rudeness. I thought of my survivors and how they'd react to him, or more to the point, what they thought they should have done when facing someone like him. And just like Strathman, they would have maintained that quiet tenacity, their moral principles, and above all else, dignity. That was going to be really hard for me. I had a temper.

Other doctors complained to the supervisor about Dornanalty nearly every day. "That obnoxious bastard called me a fucking wop!" "He called my patient a Nazi throughout the surgery!" "If he mentions I'm an Arab again, I'll sue you and this entire hospital!" "He called me a Negro bastard."

My supervisor would mutter, "They don't pay me enough to put up with this shit."

When Dr. Dornanalty heard I dated a Jew, his nickname for me became "the little kike-lover." I had not heard kike before, but I didn't need to consult Ben or Will about its meaning. I knew it was profoundly derogatory.

Not knowing what to do about him yet, I took notes and observed. Working women in the seventies were safer if seen and not heard. Because of Dornanalty's stature, staying quiet seemed the best course of action.

And then he made his first mistake.

I circulated in Dr. Asher's OR one day where Dr. Dornanalty was the anaesthetist. He entered the room prior to the surgery and placed his very unsterile newspaper and coffee on his anaesthetist's table standing at the patient's head. Stupid ass.

It took all of ten minutes before he started with his "kike-lover" routine.

The surgeon stopped whistling. His assistant looked from Dornanalty to me not knowing what to say or do. He was Jewish. If Dr. Dornanalty had been an observant man, he would have noticed all of this. Instead, he asked derogatory questions, including wanting to know what it was I found so special about my kike. I didn't answer. His attacks happened every day, and unless he threatened me, I felt the only course of action was to stay silent.

After the surgery ended, Dr. Dornanalty and the surgeon transferred the patient to Recovery Room while I helped Cleaning Staff prepare the room for the next surgery. Same surgeon. Same anaesthetist. The next assistant was Dr. Luborsky.

I was happy that I still got to see Ben, who was a regular in the OR. By Canadian law, surgeons needed assistant doctors and Ben was a favorite. No matter what happened, he remained calm.

I felt especially glad to see him on this day. The tension between the surgeon and Dr. Dornanalty had reached a frightening high. I could hear Dr. Asher complaining bitterly to someone in the hallway about Dr. Dornanalty in-between surgeries.

Dr. Luborsky walked into the room after that and nodded at me. "Hello my dear. You and I haven't had a chat in a long while, have we?"

My brow frowned in puzzlement. I could tell by his stance and demeanor something was horribly wrong and I was part of it. "No, sir," I replied. "It's nice to see you again."

The surgery was fairly simple as surgeries go—a cholecystectomy, gall bladder, but the ice-cold tension crackled through the air. I felt the iciness between the doctors in my veins.

Dr. Dornanalty called me kike-lover four times and he yelled at me once for not refreshing his coffee. He whined when he saw his daily newspaper had been removed during cleanup.

"The other patient's blood was on it," I said in a matter-of-fact voice but I braced myself for a major battle. "It had to go to the dirty utility room."

He left the room and returned with his filthy newspaper. I grabbed a plastic bag, snatched the paper from his hands, and put the contaminated newspaper inside. The room suddenly felt hot to me. Was that rage sizzling through the atmosphere? I think I preferred the ice. My instinct was to call the supervisor, but I had no idea how to explain what was happening.

"You can't bring that in here, sir," I said quietly. *Be like Strathman* had long ago become my mantra. Be like Strathman. Quiet. Determined. Dignified.

Dr. Dornanalty bellowed something about noble kike-lovers not being welcome in his OR. I ignored him and began final count of sponges and instruments before the surgeon began closing up the "wound.

When the surgery ended, I remained behind with the cleaning staff. We joked about Dr. Dornanalty "He needs a couple of high colonic enemas," I said, "to clear out the crap that keeps coming out of his mouth."

The staff all laughed until they saw Dr. Dornanalty filling the doorway.

"Is this what you do in your spare time, make fun of your bosses?"

"No, sir," I said with a smile. "Just making a polite suggestion. You upset the doctors today."

"I did no such thing," he roared.

"Dr. Dornanalty I need a word with you," said Dr. Asher. "In the head nurse's office."

"Whoaaaa, that was close," said one of the cleaning staff when he left.

I checked the list of surgeries, trying to hide my nervousness. Maybe the doctors thought I had caused a scene with the newspaper and I was going to lose my job.

"Hey guys," I said to the cleaning staff, "we're done for the day. See you tomorrow."

I did the end-of-day routine—checked the drugs on the anaesthetist's stand and replaced the ones he used, and replenished the other supplies in the room.

When I returned to the Scrub room to check on scrub brushes and masks, several doctors stood there, as if lying in wait for me. What the hell?

I knew Ben Luborsky, the opera whistling surgeon, Dr. Asher, three Jewish surgeons, an Arab surgeon, and a Japanese anaesthetist thoroughly despised by Dornanalty because of the war. This guy, barely in his thirties, had been born and raised in Canada.

One lone OB-GYN surgeon stood at the doorway with a haunted look in his eyes. He was Jewish as well.

Ben got straight to the point. "How long has he called you kike-lover?"

When I told him, he groaned. "*Oy gevalt!* Why didn't you come to me? This is antisemitism. We can do something about this."

Was he criticizing me? "Am I supposed to know this is different from the other stuff he says?"

Dr. Asher showed his concern with a frown. "I didn't realize he was mean to the staff."

The supervisor of the OR had entered the room. "He's awful to them," she replied. "My girls eventually develop a tough skin and ignore him. But my best nurses end up leaving, like I fear Pam will in a few more months."

"Well, it's not acceptable, not at all," said Dr. Asher. "What can this young lady do to stop it?"

Me? What could I do about getting rid of some bully doctor? That was Asher's job. I really didn't think this could ever be listed in my job description.

Asher didn't know my name which is why he called me young

lady. As concerned as Asher was about the situation, he'd never really bothered much about getting to know the nurses before. And that was the problem. Because he was a thoracic and cardiac surgeon, he was the one doctor who worked closest with Dornanalty. He saw the anaesthetist in action the most, but he never noticed the abuse towards the staff. Or his blatant racism.

"This can't fall on Pam's shoulders," said my supervisor. "We may be able to do something as nurses, but it's up to you doctors to report him to the CMA. Pam, talk to me before you leave."

Well, at least she understood. After she left the room again, the doctors discussed the many racist comments this man had made in their presence during surgeries. What really alarmed me was that none of them had ever uttered a complaint about him.

They all agreed that unless something terrible happened, or that he put a patient's life at risk because of his racism, nothing could be done by the doctors. It would be up to the nurses to figure out what to do.

And they all looked at me again.

Well, wasn't that just the good ol' boys club in action? I lost a lot of respect for every one of those doctors in that moment, even Dr. Luborsky. And that cut me to the core. They were all talk and no action when it came to antisemitism. A devastating thought slithered across my mind. A drop of silence—this was exactly how the Holocaust began—no action. No words of reprimand for the antisemite.

When the room cleared, Dr. Luborsky remained behind. He was reluctant to make eye contact. "Now that you're practically engaged to young William, you are considered one of the tribe, Pamela. You should have come to me with this."

Really? He expected me to have come to him. And for what? So he and his fellow doctors could tell me to handle this ass of a man on my own? I couldn't go there. Ben had to have seen my look of shock and disdain.

"Excuse me, sir, but what tribe?" I said while observing him.

Ben crossed his arms. My inane thought—at least he hadn't used his typical shrug this time. However, when I looked more closely, I could see my condemnation might have been unfounded. This was a different Dr. Luborsky trying to talk to me, not the gentle soul I usually saw. He was angry and ready for a battle, but what fight was he planning on?

"I forget how much Gentiles don't understand," said Ben. "The tribe is the Jewish people. We've been persecuted and hated for so long that we've learned to stick together. Especially in situations like this. How are you supposed to take on the Goliath of racism by yourself? You need to come to someone like me or Dr. Asher, or any of the other Jewish doctors and we will help."

No kidding! "But all of you just told me to handle this alone."

"Yes," he said with infinite patience, "but we said that for show."

"I'm not understanding," I said.

"What do you think Dr. Asher and I were discussing in the hall before this surgery? He was appalled when he heard how Dornanalty treated you. Asher notified the CMA and while he did that, I notified B'nai B'rith and other Jewish organizations that deal with antisemitism."

I almost burst into tears. My lack of trust had really jeopardized my friendship with Ben this time. I felt so ashamed.

"There are a lot of people who still hate Jews and think we are the cause of all the troubles in the world, Pamela. We've never really been allowed to fit into society. There is a veneer of politeness and propriety that makes one think we do, and we at least get invited every now and then to parties, but that's pretense as well. If you scratch all that away, we still do not fit in. It's where the term The Other People comes from. Jews have always been The Other People, the ones nobody wants for neighbors."

He turned on the faucet and scrubbed his hands. "It's why Israel is so important for us. We have someplace to return to, someplace to call home, especially if and when another Hitler comes along."

I felt as nervous as a cat in a room full of dogs when I remembered what Mrs. Smith had said to me. *You will have to be fiercely strong and brave, and ready to fight. Will you be able to do that?* "So, have you been to Israel?" I said, hoping to change the subject because I was totally unprepared to find an answer to Mrs. Smith's question.

"Yes, many times. I feel as if I've come home when I go there, the emotional pull is that strong. The first time I went, I actually wept when I set foot on Jewish ancestral soil. You will especially fall in love with Israel because of your tie to Arik."

Ben gave me one of his measured stares. "Come, Miss Kilborn, why so quiet? I'm used to receiving a bombardment of questions by now."

"I don't know what to say. I've never really seen antisemitism or racism in action. This is frightening."

"You weren't here in 1967 to see the riots in Detroit? What did you think that was about if it wasn't fighting the Big White powers that seem to rule every corner of this planet and put down the African American race?"

"It didn't occur to me to label it as racism. Civil rights issues, yes."

"The riots were fights for civil rights and more. They were a reaction to white institutionalism keeping people in an impossible situation—slums, no education, no jobs worth having."

Ben walked over to me and gently kissed my forehead as if he tried to repent for what had taken place earlier. "And now that you're going to be part of the most hated, singled out tribe of people on the planet, you need to learn how to connect dots a lot better. The world isn't different from before World War II. Racism and antisemitism are still fueled by ignorance and fear. We'll talk more about this later."

"Thank you, sir." It was then that I noticed Dr. F., the OB-GYN doctor, sitting in the OR room, staring straight ahead. He had moved from the doorway of the scrub room to sit in the quiet. Ben and I rushed in the room.

"Dr. F. what's wrong?" I said while taking his pulse.

"It's happening again," he said. His voice had a tremor to it. He looked up at Ben. "We can't stop it this time either."

When Ben tried to respond, Dr. F. held up his hand. "No Benjamin. We never can. Until I saw this poor girl being attacked, I hadn't faced how bad antisemitism has become again. I can't stand this anymore. I can't—bear it. Why is there another generation of young Jews being persecuted? Didn't we put up enough defenses to protect our young ones?"

I frowned when Ben didn't say anything. He just put his hand on Dr. F.'s shoulder. What was wrong?

I got on my knees in front of Dr. F. "I'm okay, Dr. F. I've got this covered. We're going to stop Dr. Dornanalty."

Dr. F. patted my cheek with a profound sadness. "It won't be enough, my girl. It's never enough." He rose to his feet and walked away.

I turned to Ben. "What was that about?"

Ben could barely speak. "Dr. F. was the first Jewish doctor in the British army to enter a concentration camp—Dachau. He went stark raving mad from what he saw and he's never gotten over it." He shook his head. "Damn. Of all the doctors to be involved with this today. I'll see you later."

I stopped by my supervisor's office before I left for home. "You wanted to see me?"

"Shut the door." She pointed at the chair for me to sit and handed me a sheaf of papers—incident reports. "I've been making one out every time I've heard him call you kike-lover. Can you think of other times?"

"Every time we work together."

She sighed with exasperation, slid the papers in a file folder, and handed it to me. "Okay, take these home and fill one out for every time something like today happened. I've put in a few that I've filed so you see how it's done."

"But will this do anything?"

"If we get enough of them. It covers our asses at the very least. And one day something awful will happen and we'll be glad we have the documentation. With these filled out and filed with administration, we'll be free of repercussions."

She leaned back in her seat. "There's not much we nurses can do, except maybe make a squeak of protest. But sometimes that squeak can be made at the right time and it turns into a roar and brings the monster down."

My head shot up from the file folder. I remembered the last time I'd heard someone say "squeak of protest."

"Like letters of protest," I said.

"Exactly."

"Is there any part of Dornanalty that's good?" I said. "I mean, doesn't he do charity work or something?"

"Yes, but because you're a doctor and do fifty wonderful things, does not give you the right to be abusive to other people. When we ignore bad behavior like his, staff morale is damaged and everyone is on edge, and that causes mistakes to be made. Patients become at risk. We have to try and stop him. It's the ethical thing to do."

Later that evening, while eating dinner with Will, I talked it over with him. He didn't joke or make his usual wise cracks, which scared me even more. He looked as serious as I'd ever seen him.

"There is a story from World War II," he said while eating, "about an SS officer who ran one of the camps. He was a devoted husband and father and he showered his children with open displays of love and affection. Because of his kindness to his own, the Nazis put him in charge of keeping Jewish kids calm—before he put them in those Death showers and killed them."

Will put his arm around me when he saw my distressed face. "By society's standards, he was a good man—except for that one thing, one evil thing—he did wrong. Would you have a problem reporting him in order for him to be stopped?"

"But it's not the same thing. Dr. Dornanalty hasn't killed anyone."

"Not yet." He continued. "Okay, let me put this another way. How do you think it makes me feel that because my girl is dating me, a Jew, she gets called kike-lover and is harassed at work?"

He lifted my hand and looked at my fingers. "So much so that she nervously bites her nails. I'll tell you how I feel. Frustrated as hell. Useless as a man. I'm not only angry, I'm worried something is going to happen to you because of this guy. He could get you fired or destroy your reputation as a nurse. I've always known how to handle antisemitism when it's directed at me. I grew up with this crap. You didn't. You don't know how to defend yourself."

He picked up the folder and leafed through the papers inside. "Your supervisor is telling you this is important to do. And give Ben credit, he'll back you up on these. Reporting this guy to B'nai B'rith and the Anti-Defamation League is just the start of what he's going to do. So, fill out the forms. You want to be a Jew? Then this is your part in this fight. I can help you if you like."

My lips trembled and tears rolled down my cheeks. "I'm scared, Will. If he finds out I'm doing this, my life will be hell."

"Your supervisor is showing you how to protect your ass. Documentation of the truth always becomes the iron-clad protection that Jews need."

I went over the day's events while lying in bed that night. Will often quoted phrases of famous people to me. This time he had recited something by John Donne:

Send not to know
For whom the bell tolls,
It tolls for thee.

I pulled the blankets over my head. "I sure hope it's not ringing for me this time." I promptly fell asleep.

Life in the OR kept rolling along, and Dr. Dornanalty with his racist slurs, helped me add more fuel to the folder every day.

The following week the oral surgeons took over OR Six for their routine full day. The head surgeon, Gary Parent, made sure to bring pizza and doughnuts for the staff.

Dr. Strathman needed to give anaesthesia to one of Gary's high-risk, physically unstable patients. Under normal circumstances, because of this man's health profile, no surgery would have taken place, but he had an ulcerated gum that had become infected. It spread to his sinuses, heading for the brain.

Dr. Strathman asked me to get the new cardiac monitor from OR One, Dr. Dornanalty's room. He didn't have any surgery for three hours and we would be finished long before then. This more sophisticated machine detected even the slightest of arrhythmias.

Halfway through the surgery, the patient coded. For a wild hour, the surgeon tried to finish the surgery while the rest of us pumped on the patient's chest and brought him back to the living. We collectively sighed with relief when the patient stabilized. Ten more minutes to go. The surgery would be done and we'd be out of the woods.

At this moment of quiet stress and worry, Dr. Dornanalty thundered into the room. "How dare you take my equipment, Kilborn. It's mine and stays in my room."

"I requested she get it, Daniel," said Dr. Strathman without looking up from the monitor. "This is a difficult case and we needed the newer monitor. He's just come out of an arrest."

"Never touch this again, Kilborn," he mewled like a moose as he grabbed the monitor. "I don't care what state your patient is in." He tore the leads off the patient. "It stays in my room."

I pressed the Code Red Alarm button and scrambled to place the old leads on the man. Time elapsed was thirty seconds.

"Daniel, you son of a bitch," shouted Dr. Parent, still frantically working to finish the surgery. He had only four more stitches to put into the wound to keep it closed. "Put that back on my patient. Now."

Dr. Dornanalty ignored him and prissied his way back to his room, taking the monitor with him.

When the supervisor arrived, the surgeon glared at her. "I want that fucking bastard gone. He took the fucking monitor off, right after my patient coded. Who the fuck does he think he is?"

"God," I said in a quiet voice. "He thinks he's God."

I could tell by the look on my supervisor's face that she wanted to strangle me for that unprofessional commentary.

"I'll make sure you never get him again as the anaesthetist, Gary."

"Not good enough. I didn't have him as the fucking anaesthetist today and look what he did. He is a danger to patients. Either he goes or my entire office of surgeons leaves for Hotel Dieu's OR rooms, your competition. It's up to you."

"We'll take this up later," said my supervisor, "in my office." She leaned into me. "I'll help you document this incident."

Dr. Strathman and I exchanged glances when the surgery ended and we collectively sighed with relief. We made it. The patient survived.

A week later, Dr. Parent and his associates took their practice to the competition. Dr. Dornanalty had won again.

February brought another, far more sinister incident with Dr. Dornanalty.

An OB-GYN doctor of Chinese descent needed to perform a Caesarean section on a woman whose baby was in distress. Dr. Dornanalty was on call. He refused to be the anaesthetist unless another OB-GYN agreed with the decision for surgery.

An Egyptian OB had arrived at the unit for one of his patients. I immediately grabbed him and explained the situation. "That Dr. Dornanalty again," he growled and went to examine the patient. He agreed the woman desperately needed a C-Section.

Still Dornanalty refused to cooperate. "You've got an Arab and a Chinaman saying she needs surgery. Get a white man."

Forty minutes later Dr. Dornanalty felt satisfied with the "white" doctor's assessment and would give the anaesthesia—but only if the white doctor scrubbed in. Rushing madly to save mother and child, the white doctor broke the baby's arm while trying to get it out of the womb. Both doctors worried that the babe had been anoxic too long and might have brain damage. Because of the delay caused by Dr. Dornanalty, the original APGAR (a scoring system doctors and nurses use to assess newborns one minute and five minutes after they're born) was a five. It should have been ten.

"You have to report this," said the primary OB man. "This is racism. It shouldn't happen in a hospital like this."

I held out the form I had already begun. "I know, sir. Will you stay and sign it once I've finished filling it out? It will be more powerful if I have witnesses."

He read the document. "You've been making these out after such incidents?"

I nodded. "For a while now. It makes them more concrete if the doctors sign them as well. No room for doubt."

The doctor understood. "Finish it up and I'll sign it when I return." He left to look after his patient.

After my third draft, I groaned and ran my hands through my hair. No matter how I wrote it, the words ended up being a scathing account of blatant racism by Dr. Dornanalty.

I ended up asking all three OB men to sign it. The Caucasian OB refused. "This is my friend you're condemning here. I can't be part of this."

I felt my eyes fill with tears. Why did this fall on my shoulders? "I'm asking you, sir, to agree that my account is true and accurate." My voice quaked. "That's all."

William had insisted I ask the involved doctors to sign the nursing incident reports. It was way out of line, but if I did not have the signatures from witnesses who saw his bad behavior, it would merely be my word against his. Just like when the cops told me to forget making a report after being raped when I was a teenager. Nothing had changed when it came to the he said/she said routine. If this doctor, who was his friend, didn't sign the report, it would be thrown out and I would become the scapegoat.

I looked at the Egyptian, silently begging him to understand and step in.

He nodded and took Dornanalty's friend aside. They argued for twenty minutes before the doctor finally threw his hands in the air. "All right, you've convinced me." He grabbed the papers and signed them.

I handed in the report to my supervisor the next morning.

Her face paled as she read the grim documentation. "Shit. This is bad. I'll take it to the executive director today so he and the lawyers can decide what to do. Dr. Dornanalty is going to lose his license."

She was right. Dr. Dornanalty lost his job and would not be able to practise for five years. My supervisor brought me to her office to tell me the news. "We did it."

"But at what cost to me?"

"I know, me too. You and I are in this shit storm together, kiddo. The good ol' boys will give us a lot of hell. Dornanalty's got friends. He's not done, not by a long shot."

Doctors and nurses were going to take sides, many of them defending Dornanalty out of fear of what he could still do to them. In my mind, I knew I had done the right thing, but the consequences of my actions were going to bite me in the ass, big time, unless Ben and the other surgeons backed me up. Fighting antisemitism and racism was a lot more frightening and difficult to do in real time. It was definitely more frightening than writing letters of protest.

27

When history looks back, people will know the Nazis weren't
able to kill millions of people and get away with it.
So long as people don't forget.
(Elie Wiesel)

On one of my midnight shifts, Dr. Strathman came in to give anaesthesia for an emergency surgery—an appendectomy. She still sat in the staff lounge after I finished cleaning up post-op, reading one of the conversion books I had left on the coffee table.

"You're not going home yet?" I said.

"I'm awake for the day now. I've been reading your book about the Jewish faith. How much longer until you convert?"

"At least another six months. The rabbi is being difficult because I don't want my boyfriend present during my conversion lessons. It's my conversion, not his."

"Yes, I can see why he'd be upset. It has nothing to do with you, Pamela. It has to do with your young man and why he wouldn't have fallen in love with a Jewish girl."

I made myself a cup of tea and sat down. "William keeps alluding to that. Why is it such a big deal?"

"Because of what happened during the war."

The war again. It seemed all the recent stresses in my life had everything to do with unresolved issues from World War II. In fact, if I looked more closely, almost all the world's tensions stemmed from WWII. Nazis still existed. Ku Klux Klan members marched in the US. The Cold War. After all of my reading and experiences, I knew one thing to be true. Fear and ignorance begat hatred, hatred begat violence, violence begat wars.

I opened my sandwich from home and offered her half—liverwurst, lettuce, cucumbers and mayonnaise, a very German sandwich. She eagerly took it.

"The evil that the Germans perpetrated in that war and how they spread it throughout Europe and beyond can never be forgiven," Strathman said between bites. "I'm surprised the Jewish people have anything to do with the rest of the world after that. And now the UN regrets giving them back their country."

I didn't want to discuss Israel, even though I could have learned a lot about it from her point of view. "Did your family get involved with the Nazis?"

"No. My father and his associates took a stand against them. Even before the war, in 1933, they were terrified of the Nazis and they tried to fight against the degenerating morality in the medical profession. If the Nazis were able to convince doctors to follow their depraved protocols and morality, convincing the rest of Germany would be easy."

She wearily rubbed her eyes. The more she talked about this, the heavier her German accent became. "Ironic isn't it, that the United States, the home of the free, will be remembered as the country that started this 'pure race' thinking before the turn of the century. They were the first to perform vasectomies on the criminally insane prisoners, 'racial hygiene' they called it, preventing the rest of the nation from 'national degeneration.'"

After finishing my half of the sandwich, I offered Dr. Strathman one of my cookies.

"The United States," she went on, "also had laws prohibiting people of different races to marry, nor could people with epilepsy and mental retardation and diabetes. Germany based its 'pure Ayrian race' on those US policies."

Strathman stared into her teacup. "The Nazis told everyone that the *Volkstod*, the German people as a whole, were in grave danger of being destroyed by these 'lives unworthy of life'."

"But your father disagreed with this." I marveled at how she became more and more technical while talking, almost like a textbook. Maybe she coped with what she said by doing that.

"Yes. He and several of his colleagues knew where this would go. Especially when phrases like 'cultivator of the genes,' 'physician to the *volk*,' and 'biological soldier' began being used to describe doctors. The key aspect of the transition from sterilization to direct medical killing or nazification of the medical profession was achieved by a combination of very ideological enthusiasm and systematic terrorism."

The hairs on the back of my neck rose. "That's diabolical."

"Yes." Strathman's lower lip trembled. "My father and his friends were some of the first people to be put in a political prisoner camp in the thirties. Dachau. For years." She wiped her eyes and blew her nose. "None of them were ever heard from again. A rumor said they were beheaded before the attack on Poland."

Strathman very neatly folded her tissue and placed it beside her cup of tea. I knew it was her way of keeping order in a disorderly world. Her eyes still swam with tears.

"One of my father's friends, a professor of philosophy, helped some students put a movement together. They called it The White Rose movement. Their slogan defined the minority's purpose—'We will not be silent. We are Germany's Conscience.'"

She wiped her eyes again. "We Germans should have been destroyed because deep down that Nazi evil is in our genes. I've always thought I should return to Germany and live out my life there. I don't deserve a country like this."

"I think you're a wonderful human being," I said in a rush of emotion. How could she think so little of herself? She was one of the gentlest humans I knew.

"I'm not, you know," said Strathman. "I'm just good at hiding what I think. It's why I never married. But I'm ready to go back and face my Germany and whatever Hell it is now."

She tried to get her emotions under control. "My biggest fear is that nothing has changed. That people are still the same disgusting animals they were back then. And I couldn't bear to see that. I'd kill myself if that were true."

She looked at her watch and got to her feet. "It's after three and I am due back at seven. I'll see you soon."

I felt unnerved by Stathman's conversation. She had voiced what I always feared—that somehow people with German ancestry were demented and twisted with an evil nature.

I considered her a dear friend—a true *mensche* of a soul. *Please God*, I prayed, *let her be wrong about the Germans.*

On my next day off, I returned to my favorite bookstore.

"Pamela," said Isaac with a wave of his hand. "How are you doing?"

I liked how he considered me part of his "tribe" now. One of the tribe. "I'm okay, Isaac. I need to look up the White Rose group from World War II."

"I haven't heard about that in years." He headed over to a small German section and returned with a book no more than forty pages long, in German and English. Isaac had confessed one day how

much he enjoyed the way I studied because I always chose interesting topics to research. "There isn't a lot known about them. You
met someone who does?"

"One of the doctors I work with. Her father's friend led them."

He handed me the book. "Let me know what you find out."

I went to my little cubbyhole of a corner, pulled out pen and paper,
and opened the book, *Gedenkstatte,Deutscher Widerstand.*

> In the summer of 1942, a group of students from the University
> of Munich and their philosophy professor formed a non-violent
> resistance group in Nazi Germany. They became known for a leaf-
> let campaign that called for active opposition to the Nazi regime.

That fit with what Dr. Strathman had said. I began to chew my
fingernail and squirmed in my seat. I wasn't sure I'd be brave enough
to do something like that. Letter writing is one thing post-war. Doing
something like this at the height of the Nazi regime was another.

They co-authored six anti-Nazi Third Reich political resistance leaflets. Calling themselves the White Rose, they instructed
Germans to passively resist the Nazis. They had been horrified
by the behavior of the Germans on the Eastern Front where
they had witnessed a group of naked Jews being shot in a pit.
Okay, I thought. Pamphlets. Perspective. I needed to put this into
perspective. Was that really such a big deal?

> Producing and distributing such leaflets sounds simple from
> today's perspective, but, in reality, it was dangerous. Paper was
> scarce, as were envelopes. And if one bought them in large quan-
> tities, or for that matter, more than just a few postage stamps (in
> any larger numbers), one would (have) become instantly suspect.

I closed the book and shut my eyes. "Well, thanks for answering
that question," I muttered.

When I returned home, I called Tootsie. I got straight to the point. "Do you think Germans are evil and demented?"

Tootsie didn't laugh at the question. It seemed as if she knew my research would bring me to this. She took her time answering because she claimed she had wondered the exact same thing. "I thought they were after the war ended, especially when word got out about the concentration camps. But in 1962 your Uncle Joe and I were stationed there. After living with the Germans, it became clear there were two camps; the older people who still believed everything the Third Reich did was correct and justified, but—"

"But what?" I asked with impatience.

"The greater majority of children and grandchildren of that generation were horrified when they learned of those Nazi evil deeds and tried to make reparations. They vowed that this would never happen in Germany again and taught their children the evils of the Reich in schools."

I mulled that over before asking my next question. "How can that be true? I see Nazis marching all over the U.S. and Germany."

"Yes, but what you don't see are the huge numbers of people pushing back against them. It may not look like it, my girl, but the people of the world are still reeling from the war. We are fighting hard today to put things in place so it can never happen again. In fact, I'm on my way now to a meeting of women doing exactly that."

I didn't know what to say.

Aunt Tootsie let out a gentle laugh. "I guess it will take you a while to absorb that your aunt is out there fighting for rights like you, won't it?"

"You're a political activist? What are you protesting?"

"How the Armed Forces of the United States treats its women."

"I love you Aunt Tootsie."

"I love you too, dear girl. You have my heart."

28

*Freedom: Independence is not a gift or an entitlement. It needs to be
fought for and encouraged every day.*
(John F. Kennedy)

A big surprise for me came when no real repercussions arose from getting Dr. Dornanalty fired in 1977. No tolling bell either. Just a lot of nurses avoiding me and talking behind my back. Typical. Most women in the seventies were still ardently passive aggressive.

My mother called me at work one day, nervous as all get out. "I did something without your father knowing," she said breathlessly.

"Okay, I'll bite. What did you do?"

"Ohhh, don't you yell at me. I was having lunch with Ann and we happened to be by the Ford dealership and there sat the cutest little car, all orange and white. They called it a hatchback, I think. Well one thing led to another and before I knew it, I bought it. I used up all of our savings. Your father is going to kill me."

"You what?" I practically shouted. After taking a calming breath, I held the phone back up to my ear. "Well, if you think you made a mistake, you can always cancel the purchase."

"No. I want you to teach me how to drive this thing so I don't have to wait around for you to take me places. You're older now and more independent, and I decided I wanted to be independent too."

You could have knocked me over with a feather with this revelation. My mother had depended on Dad and me to drive her around her entire married life. I always thought she wanted it that way.

"Way to go, Mom. I'm off tomorrow. I'll take you for your beginner's license, then."

So, at the ripe old age of fifty-three, my mother studied hard and received her beginner's license. Three months later, she became a full-fledged driver, an absolutely terrible full-fledged driver.

In addition to teaching Mom how to parallel park, turn left and right, and switch lanes, I taught her how to 'flip the bird' at obnoxious drivers. She was thrilled.

One afternoon, Mom picked me up and we went in search of violets.

"What?" I said when she called. "You used to call violets Grandma's one folly. What happened?" When I was young, Grandma had rows of violets on her windowsill, all of them with names. The deep purple she had named Bobby; he was the youngest son who was killed in the Korean war. The pink, Victoria, after her mother. White stood for the angel, Gabriel, the only violet not named after a deceased person. Gabriel represented strength, courage. There were eleven violets in all. Each one with the name of a dead member of the family.

"Because I think she might have been on to something about them representing Death and the resurrection of that soul," said Mom. "I'm praying they have the power to shun away evil spirits from all of us. I need the souls of my family around me right now, to help me get through this cancer."

"Like Guardian angels?"

"Exactly. These violets are my Guardian angels. Besides, I want you to see what a good driver I am now."

Mom drove slowly. Very slowly. Very, very slowly. One guy rode her tail for a mile and then pulled alongside her. "Bitch," he bellowed.

My mother boldly held out her index finger. Then she stuck her tongue out at him.

"Uhmmmmm, what was that, Mom?"

"I gave him the finger like you taught me."

I giggled. "Mom, you used the wrong finger. The index finger means you're one with God. It's the middle finger you need to use."

"Oh, no! I've been doing it wrong all this time?"

"Well, not if you're a good Christian, you haven't been."

She let out a dainty harrumph. "I can't even do that right. I never wanted to be a good Christian woman like my mama. It never did her any good and it hasn't helped me much either."

She pouted all the way to the flower nursery. I felt bad for having corrected her.

Mom picked out several kinds of violets: pink, violet, deep purple—every single color the nursery had. Twelve pots ended up in the back of her car.

"What are you going to do with all these flowers?"

Mom slammed the hood of the trunk down. "I don't know. I thought of my mother and her violets and then I realized I'm tired of always scrimping and not getting anything I want. So today I want violets. If there is one thing you learn from your mother's life, Pamela Jean, it's to do things and take care of yourself. Buy nice clothes. Travel like Aunt Tootsie. Explore the world. The only trips I've ever been on were the ones you planned for me. And that isn't right. Let's go home now."

"It's about time you started thinking about you for a change," I said. "I'm proud of you."

She burst into tears. "Don't be. I am fifty-three years old and I have not done a single thing to have made my life matter. And I am sick of it. All anybody can ever do is matter and make a difference in this world, and shame on me for not doing a damn thing. How did I ever get to be this old and not have a single thing to show for it?"

She got into the driver's seat. "Get in. We're going out for Chinese food."

I tried telling her being a supervisor at Michigan's Blue Cross Blue Shield health care organization was a major achievement, but she didn't listen. "I don't even read books," she shouted.

Mom never talked about that day again. She put the violets on the living room windowsill, but forgot to water them. They were dead within the month.

Maybe the violets were an omen of things to come.

29

When you look into your mother's eyes, you know that
is the purest love you can find on this earth.
(Mitch Albom)

March rolled in like a lion. Mom developed every awful chemo side-effect, including constant vomiting and shingles. They stopped the treatments two weeks later and began a regimen of palliative care, which meant the end of the road.

At this point, I didn't know what was more stressful, visiting my mother or going to work, but I patted myself on the back, thinking I managed both fairly well. I deceived myself. William told me that whenever he saw me. "You're white as a ghost. And look how much weight you've lost. You're skinny again. Let me help you."

My back stiffened. "I'm fine. I don't need your help."

Will's eyes narrowed. "But you'll let me know when you do."

I leaned my head on his shoulder. Who was I kidding? I desperately needed William. "I'm sorry. I'm trying to get through one day at a time. It hasn't even registered with my dad how sick she is."

"Then tell him so you don't have him falling apart. Maybe he'd even give you some support."

I let him put his arm around me. "It's just going to be so hard, though," I choked out.

One wintry day I found my mother's clothes flung throughout the house. She sat in the kitchen with all of her medications, plus large bottles of Dilaudid and Tylenol with codeine on the table in front of her. From the mound of tissues by the medications, she'd been crying a long time.

I walked over to the table and quietly collected all of the meds, counted each bottle of pills to make sure she hadn't taken an overdose.

"They're all there," said my mom.

"I see that. What's going on? Cleaning out your closet?"

"Nothing fits without my breast and—and this huge ugly scar. How am I supposed to go anywhere when nothing fits?" She threw her wig across the room. "Look at me, I'm a monster with no hair."

My mother had finally reached the saturation point for horrible diseases and debilitating side-effects. It had taken five years. Her misshapen body owned a huge scar where her left breast once sat. It had turned into Keloid tissue and protruded through whatever clothes she wore. She could not wear the lousy mastectomy bras with cups using birdseed to fill out the shape. They didn't sit right over the raised Keloid scar.

"I have nothing to wear," said Mom. "I need clothes that hide my chest."

"Well, let's go shopping."

"No. I don't want anyone to see me."

Not for the first time, I wondered how I would react if I were in my mother's position. I suspected not half as well. "Tell you what," I said. "I'll get us some Chinese take-out and be right back." I had a plan . . . sort of.

I ordered at the restaurant then walked across the street to Women's Fashions, my mother's favorite dress shop, and explained my mother's situation. As a breast cancer survivor, the owner understood exactly how she felt. She selected a dozen outfits. "Return what she doesn't want, sweetie."

It ended up, my mother loved them all, but I returned five. I couldn't afford so many. In fact, I couldn't afford any of them—that venture cost me three months' wages. It was worth it to see her smile when she looked in the mirror.

Mom dropped a bomb on me after she put her new clothes in the closet. "Listen, there is only one thing I need you to do for me so I can die in peace. I need you to make friends with William's mom. It's obvious you're going to marry him."

I made an inward gasp. I wasn't ready for any conversations about her death. "Mom, cut it out. You'll be here for my wedding no matter who I marry."

"No, I won't. And I'm not going to die in peace unless I know she loves you like a daughter. Promise me, you'll talk to her. I'm not sure why she refuses to meet you, but you have to try at least."

I nervously rubbed my forehead. "All right." I didn't know how I could pull this miracle off. "I'll try but don't get your hopes up. She's upset because I'm not Jewish."

"When she meets you, she'll love you."

Right. I'd been doing everything by the book, which isn't like me, taking care of my mom and doing the conversion classes. Will's mom still refused to acknowledge my existence.

I guess it's true what they say: no good deed goes unpunished. And boy did I feel punished. I should have been a bitch about everything from the get-go. If I had any courage, I would have run away from all of it, including my mother.

When William came over that night, I explained what my mother wanted me to do. "What do you think?"

"Let's go talk to my dad."

Maurice shook his head when he heard my mother's request. "I can see why my son has fallen in love with you, but Esther will never accept you. There's not a chance in hell she would ever meet with you, let alone become friends."

Even though I had never met this woman and she had no logical or acceptable reason to behave in this manner, I felt crushed by her rejection.

Weeks passed and Mom continued demanding I meet with Esther. It became an obsession with her. She even brought it up to Will. "Make her see how wonderful my daughter is."

"I'll talk to my dad again," said Will. We went back to Maurice.

He thoughtfully ran his hand over his bald head. "She'll get hysterical, but I suppose it's inevitable. Come by on Thursday and I'll have her prepared for you. It will probably be better if you see her on your own."

What? He didn't want Will to go with me?

"Okay, fine, I'll be there alone," I said, feeling defenseless and thoroughly annoyed. Prepared for me! I had worked hard as a nurse, and patients loved me, including Jews, Holocaust Survivors, and other patients. I was converting, I was giving up Christian holidays. And if my mother's not so subtle comments were correct, I'd be giving up my own family.

And Maurice needed to prepare her for me. I could not recall a time when I felt so angry and frustrated by someone. He had to *prepare* this woman to meet me? This just gnawed at my soul.

Thursday came around and I arrived at the agreed time. When Esther opened the door and saw me standing there, she blanched.

"Hello, Mrs. Goldstein, I'm—"

"I know who you are. Come in."

She led the way into her living room and sat in a wing-backed chair that almost looked like a throne. Her face remained white. She didn't look at me once, didn't even acknowledge me. After a long silence I decided to get to the point.

"Mrs. Goldstein, I'm not sure if Will has you told you, but my mother is ill. And because Will and I are getting married, her dying wish is that you and I become friends. It's all she wants."

Esther's knuckles turned white as she clutched the arms of her hard backed chair. "His name is William, not Will. I call him Velvel. It is unfortunate for your mother that her dying wish will not be granted. I can never be friends with you. Ever. Now leave."

Ever? Ever! I clutched my car keys in my lap. "But I love your son very much and I've almost finished conversion classes—"

"You're not Jewish. You'll never be Jewish." She crossed over to the door and held it open. "You'll never be good enough for my son."

"But . . . but it's her dying wish."

Esther lifted her chin with stubborn pride and said nothing. She still wouldn't look at me.

That was that. "Thank you for your time." I fled to my car, determined Esther would not see my vulnerable tears.

My mother put her arm around me when I told her what Esther said. "If I could attend your wedding, I'd ask my friends to throw their wine glasses at her when they shout mazel tov."

A sad smile played at the corners of my mouth. Together we looked out the window at the cold heavy rain. It seemed as dark and depressing out there, as it was in the house.

"Well, you tried," said Mom. "Maybe you and Will should reconsider. This marriage will only give you both a lot of grief. His family has already rejected you and God knows how my side will be."

"So you keep saying. You really think Uncle Willie will be upset?"

"Yes. He says the right stuff when it comes to religion and racism and he believes it, but only if it doesn't affect his family."

Later that evening, Will and I discussed the situation. "I'm sorry Will. I don't think we should get married. If you saw the look on your mother's face . . . she wants me dead. I have no big need to marry. Just come and live with me."

Will was as stubborn as his mother. "No. She doesn't win this time. I'm going to marry you. As soon as you've converted, we're planning a wedding. I'm thinking June."

For once in my life, I decided to keep my mouth shut and not argue.

30

Families are a gift from G-d to be treasured and cared for.
(Anonymous)

April should have been a better month. It really should have. Spring came early and flowers already peeked out from their beds of slumber.

Although Mom felt marginally better and her tests came back clear, my nurse's instinct told me something wasn't right about her. And she had become resigned to dying in the summer.

The Pilchs always held an annual Easter event and this year I invited Will to meet my extended family at Uncle Willard's house. He and Willard had a lot in common, including their nickname—Willie. They spent the entire afternoon with Uncle Joe, sprawled in front of the TV, watching sports with ongoing snarky commentaries and challenging each other with exchanges of ridiculous jokes. Will became a huge hit with everyone.

Uncle Willie announced at one point, "you're all right there, Willie. You're all right."

Willard brought up only one concern, the "Jewish thing," especially when I told him about Will's mother. "For twenty-five years, I taught at a high school full of Jews, kid. They never get involved with Gentiles and they always do as their mothers say. Your Willie there, is a great guy, Pam, but he doesn't strike me as someone strong enough to stand up to his mother. You better think about this long and hard because you're going to be rejected your entire life and you're not strong enough for that. You're just not a strong person. They'll never accept you."

Again with the not strong! What had I ever done in my life that made my family think I was some frail, idiotic weakling? I really wished I had brought that list of questions I had written all those years ago. I would have definitely asked them then.

Willard's comments aside, Tootsie and Evelyn loved the idea of me taking conversion classes. "You know that rumor went around for years," said Evelyn. "Some of our Texas family members thought your great-grandmother came from Jewish stock. Something about a long line of Jews from the German county of Holstein—rabbis even."

Tootsie let out a boisterous laugh that could be heard in every room. "And we were supposedly related to royalty, too, which is why the Jewish identity had been hidden. What a turn of events that would have made on world history."

A wistful look slipped across her face as she stroked my hair. "Although, I do remember Mama used to light candles on Friday night. She never said anything, but she did light candles."

"I remember she had that Al Jolson record," I piped in, "that had all those Jewish songs on them."

"What songs?" said Tootsie.

"*Belz, Kol Nidre, Cantor on the Sabbath*, and a lot of others I can't remember."

The two women exchanged looks. "I never knew," said Evelyn.

Nobody in the family sensed I felt closest to Tootsie. It was almost as if Tootsie and I were in a secret sisterhood together. I thought she was so seriously cool. Brilliant. The only one in the family with black hair and blue eyes, Tootsie stood regally tall and loved to read.

Her insights and intelligence were off the charts, and she made it so easy for me to confide in her.

When we found time alone, I told her Uncle Willard's opinion about William.

"Shame on Willie for saying that to you. You're a grown up now. You have a real career and it's a hard one. You're not a glorified secretary until you marry, and you'll never have a dull life, no matter what, because you're interested in the world like I am. What your parents and any of this family think should have no influence on what you do, Pamela. That goes for your William too. If he loves you, it shouldn't matter what his family thinks. Love with the right man is absolutely worth everything. Enjoy the relationship."

I told her about the books we read together and Will's plans for the future. Tootsie delighted in Will's intelligence. "Judaism is one of the most beautiful religions I know. If I had not met Joe, I, too, would have converted."

She cut us both a piece of German chocolate cake. "Personally, I think those rumors Evelyn mentioned were true. I think your grandfather is Jewish too. And being Jewish would explain so much about your grandmother's Baade family in Texas."

After downing our cake, she brushed my hair while we sat together, something she did every time we saw each other. "Jews have incredible morals and traditions. They are a fantastic people. It would be an honor to be considered one of them."

Tootsie looked out the window at the swimming pool where her kids splashed and played with Uncle Joe. "I'm glad you're taking care of Holocaust victims, sweetheart. What a fulfilling experience for you to be able to care for the ones wronged in the war. I wish I had your strength to do that."

"I didn't have much say in the matter." I glowed on the inside. Tootsie always acknowledged my strengths and skills and took pride in me as a niece. I felt so pleased she cared about what

I did. "I've learned so much about life from them. They are extraordinary."

"Yes, only brave souls survive such heinous history." Tootsie glanced at her watch. "Okay my sweet, almost-to-be-Jewess. It's time for me to pack for the journey home tomorrow." She moved toward the stairwell of Uncle Willie's house in one smooth, regal movement, the epitome of grace.

"Finish your conversion. Call me when it's over and tell me how you feel the moment they say you are Jewish."

31

Join the company of lions rather than assume the lead among foxes
(The Talmud)

Dr. Strathman again announced her intention to return to Germany. "To welcome spring, I'm moving back to my hometown. If you hear I've committed suicide, it's because nothing has changed." She looked at me with a sad smile on her face. "Remember what we discussed that night." Without another word, she just disappeared, leaving me feeling bereft. Strathman had been one of the bigger reasons why I enjoyed working in the OR.

Spring came and went without any major calamities, much to my relief. I graduated from Conversion class and went for my mikvah, a type of bath. William did not go with me. I wanted to do this alone.

The theory is a convert has this mikvah and "purifies" oneself to show the convert is leaving the old life and religion. While in the bath, there has to be three rabbis behind a curtain listening to the *naked* convert reciting prayers. Easy. NOT.

When I arrived at the mikvah house in Detroit, freshly showered and bathed, the receptionist assigned me to a private room and attendant (a complete stranger!) whose job was to assist and witness me rewash first in a bathtub, and then a shower. I also had to re-clip my already clipped nails and brush my teeth. My hands shook and I dropped the clippers several times, to the point the attendant laughed.

After my attendant inspected me from head to toe, really inspected me, she offered me a large towel. "The rabbis are in position to hear you."

She led me to the main ritual bath area, a beige room with mosaic tiles in beiges and browns, no windows, and a small deep pool about the length of an over-sized bathtub. If people suffered from claustrophobia, they needed to avoid this area, especially the tub.

Another horror for me—they didn't change the water in between each mikvah. I found this so unbelievably revolting, considering why orthodox women use that thing.

The attendant took my towel and motioned for me to enter the pool. "Submerge yourself," she whispered. "I'll make sure your head is covered over with water."

I cringed. Just get it over with, just get it over with. *"Baruch ata Adonai Elohenu melekh ha'olam asher kideshanu b'mitzvotav v'tzivanu al ha'tevillah,"* I said, loud and clear, so the rabbis heard. I desperately needed another shower to clean myself after this. "Blessed are You, Oh Lord, our God, King of the universe, who has sanctified us with Your commandments and commanded us concerning the immersion."

I submerged myself three times. "Did I do it right?"

At her nod, I stepped out of the water with relief. The attendant recited her own congratulatory prayer over me. "Mazel tov."

The rabbi and cantor of Will's congregation met me outside the change room after I finished trying to sterilize myself with diluted Dettol disinfectant and dressed in my own clothes. I reeked of the disinfectant and I had gargled so many times, I used an entire bottle of mouthwash. I was going to be soaking in my own CLEAN bathtub for hours when I got home. Maybe after that I wouldn't feel so-so-so *traif,* dirty.

"Mazel tov," said the rabbi. "Now we figure out a Hebrew name for you, to make it official."

"Oh, it can't be anything but Shoshana," said the elderly cantor. "It means a beautiful rose. Look at the blush on her cheeks. She is such a beauty."

"Thank you, Cantor." I didn't have the heart to tell him the blush came from me scrubbing my face raw with that Dettol.

I felt incredible relief when the rabbi announced the entire ceremony had officially ended. When I thought about it, roses were one of my favorite flowers and had great significance in my life. It was a perfect name. Shoshana.

The rabbi filled in my official Jewish name on a certificate with a beautiful script. In Hebrew! He handed it to me. "Your document, proving you're a Jew."

As soon as I got home, I showered in the hottest water my body could stand. After that, I sat soaking in a scalding hot bubble bath with a glass of wine in my hand, and I called Tootsie. I could barely tamp down my exuberance. "*Shalom*! I'm a Jew. My Hebrew name is Shoshana."

"Mazel tov. I am so happy for you, darling."

We spent an hour discussing whether or not I felt any different. And I did. For the first time in my life, I felt whole, complete with a soul and conscience, ready to face the world.

When I lit my first Sabbath candles that Friday, I felt a solid connection to the Jewish world. Shortly after, I headed for the temple to attend services. William refused to go, just as I anticipated. I didn't care. I had wings lifting me higher and higher. I was a Jew.

Esther also attended the Temple that night. She never missed.

When I entered the sanctuary, I saw her immediately, as big as life. She refused to acknowledge me. I had secretly hoped that if

Esther saw me there, we might bridge a gap of sorts and become friendly to one another, but I knew as soon as I saw her face that would never happen.

As soon as Esther noticed me talking to someone, she'd rush over and grab them by the arm and tug them away from me. She tearfully spoke to them and I observed them frowning in horror at whatever she said. They glared at me and refused to talk to me again.

One of her friends had the temerity to suggest I worship someplace else. "This is Esther's temple." she said. "She and her husband founded it. You need to find another house of worship." Even the rabbi who converted me had changed his friendly demeanor and spoke in clipped and iced tones.

"Kilborn, what the hell are you doing here without William?" I whispered. I decided to escape to a dessert table at that first evening service. The tradition of desserts after Friday night service was called an *oneg*. With each step I took to the table, people scurried out of the way. I nodded and smiled, "Shabbat shalom." Their movement reminded me of Moses parting the Red Sea. I never knew I had such power. Maybe I still smelled like Dettol. It had only been a few days since the mikvah.

The only highlight of my evening at Temple Beth El was meeting Dr. Herschel Teich and Bezalel Folk. Bez was Israeli and didn't care what other people thought of me. Neither did Herschel. We quickly became staunch friends and talked until the wee hours about this strange ostracism happening.

"This is terrible what they are doing to you," said Bezalel while observing the rejection in action after the service. "In Israel, once you are converted, no one can bring up your past faith again. You are simply a Jew."

"That's true here too, but this is different," said Herschel. "Esther is like the matriarch of the entire community. She has worked her way into the hearts of every organization and community group.

Some people consider her to be irreplaceable. They even say she is the glue that holds us together. I disagree because anybody can be replaced, but nonetheless, that is what you are facing."

As soon as his wife turned away, Herschel snarfed down a brownie and piece of cake to appease his incredible sweet tooth. "It will take a long time for Esther to accept you, Pamela, if at all," he continued as he licked chocolate icing off his fingers. "She has been in constant tears since she met you, and definitely near hysterics whenever you speak to anyone. You're going to have to be patient."

"Or not return to this place," I said. "There are other synagogues."

"Or that." This diminutive man was smart and kind. He would never lie. Climbing Mount Everest was probably easier than winning Esther over. I watched her glance my way and she promptly burst into tears. Who was I kidding? Everest was definitely easier to overcome.

"What is she saying to make them hate me?" I wanted to know.

"You don't want to know."

Oh. Maybe he was right. I didn't want anything to take away the glow I felt inside. I resolved to ignore Esther just like I ignored certain doctors at work.

I decided to try the Orthodox synagogue the next Saturday morning. While listening to the traditional service with the cantorial music, my heart eased open and I felt a warm rush of serenity enter me. If I closed my eyes, I could hear Rabbi Dickerstein singing to Rochelle, his face radiant.

Much to my delight, I encountered Holocaust survivors and their families. Some of my former patients escorted me to the basement of the synagogue where a *Kiddush* had been laid out. The word Kiddush referred to a communal gathering held immediately following Shabbos morning services at synagogue. Tables groaned with a full spread of food and treats. Jews considered Shabbos a queen. This display was indeed fit for a queen.

I scanned the room, taking in the Tudor construction and the hundred or so people. One long wall of this giant room held ten stained glass windows made out of the richest gem colored glass. Rainbows danced on the opposite walls when the sun shone through.

I almost squealed with delight when I saw Mrs. Smith, my librarian, approaching me. "Here, Dollie," she said in motherly fashion. "Try the gefilte fish. It's divine." She tousled my hair. "I've missed you."

Rutie from the deli beamed with pride. I almost didn't recognize her without the flour on her cheeks. "Have one of my cinnamon buns, sweetheart."

So much welcoming and acceptance. So much happiness. I had found my home.

That happy thought was short-lived. I spied the Orthodox rabbi on the other side of the room. From the way his congregants greeted him and the men reverently shook his hand, he seemed to carry a lot of righteous power over these kind people. I gulped when I saw his face. He was the obnoxious rabbi from the hospital. The words misogynistic and sexist came to mind. We'd had words at the hospital a few times—actually a lot of words. My job as a nurse was to be responsible for the well-being of the patient and family and I took that very seriously. I never could figure out what this rabbi's job was because every time we fought—er, debated, it was about him trouncing on the rights of women. In short, he was no Rabbi Donin.

He stared at me the entire time I was there. His venomous brown eyes made pictures of Satan look saintly. After several minutes, he strode towards me. I could feel his anger from ten feet away. "You did not have an orthodox conversion. You cannot be in my *schul*. Go back to your temple."

I did not know how to respond. Well, that's not true exactly. I truly wished I didn't respond. However, instead of being silent, I squared my shoulders and summoned my newfound Jewish strength to surface. "And who died and left you king of the world?" It slipped out.

He stormed away. It didn't take a lot of brains to see he would return, prepared for war. I had seen his intolerance and hostility on display too many times in hospital, even in front of sick and dying patients, and I wouldn't give him the satisfaction of declaring war on me and distressing my survivors.

I didn't go back to either synagogue the next week, or in fact for months.

Luckily for me, I didn't need to go to synagogue to talk to God. I'd learned how to do that from my grandmother years ago, and I had perfected that skill quite well.

32

The death of a parent is rarely expected and never accepted.
(Anonymous)

Life continued. I lit Friday night candles, learned how to bake challah, and continued to see William. Mom was doing okay, but I still sensed something was horribly wrong. When July rolled around, she announced she had been invited to a wedding and needed a new outfit. She and I went shopping at Devonshire Mall, near the hospital.

Mom suddenly stopped walking. "Where am I?"

"What do you mean," I said, my heart hammering against my chest. She wasn't kidding. "We're at the mall, about to have lunch."

My mother cried harder. "Who are you? What are we doing here?"

I could barely breathe when I saw the panic on her face. Clearly the metastatic cancer had reached her brain. "Tell you what," I said in a calm nurse-like voice, "let's go visit Dr. Maus. You like him. He's the guy you think looks like the movie star, Jimmy Stewart. Let's see what he has to say."

"I'm not sure what's going on," he said after examining my mother. "We did her scans three months ago and they were clear. Unless it has metastasized to the base of the brain. That's the one spot where the image isn't clear sometimes. We'll do the scan again."

The repeat test showed a large metastatic area around the medulla oblongata. In the file of my nursing brain, I recalled the medulla played a critical role in transmitting signals between the spinal cord and the higher parts of the brain, and in controlling autonomic activities, such as heartbeat and respiration. In other words, people stop breathing when the cancer invades it.

When Dr. Maus suggested admitting my mother to hospital, she became hysterical. "No! I'm going home. My daughter will take care of me until I die." Her eyes pleaded with me. "Won't you, Pam? You'll do this for me."

I wanted to find a corner where no one could see me and weep. The past five years had been difficult with all her episodes, fits of tears and requests, but this was going to beat them all. Nothing was in place to help me care for her. What if she needed oxygen or an IV or a Foley catheter? I couldn't do this.

Mom's eyes brimmed with tears. If I was afraid, then how must she have felt? Beyond terrified. She needed me. She trusted me to help her. I sucked in a deep breath. "We'll figure it out, Mom," I assured her. At least she remembered who I was again.

My brain went into frenetic overdrive, trying to think about everything needed to pull this off, including how much money I had in my bank account (under fifty), how much credit was left on my charge card (up to 400), and what I could steal from the hospital to defray costs. The more I thought about what I was about to undertake, the more I panicked.

I moved back home for a few days to assess her condition and what her needs would be. By the end of the first week, she had declined so rapidly that I gave her sponge baths and spoon fed her.

I fell apart every time Will came over. "I don't know what to do to help you," said Will one night when I couldn't stop crying.

"I never did talk to my father. And I'm so angry. Why does he have to be so blind? He just hides from all of this."

And that was the truth. Dad couldn't face this at all. He had moved into my old room after Mom's surgery five years earlier and never moved back into their bedroom.

"Well, I'm here," said Will. "What do you need me to do?"

"I don't know. I have laundry, dishes, and housework, but—"

"Say no more. Go sit with your mom."

I watched my mom sleeping that night. Her sleep was so quiet, calm. "Okay, God, remember my prayer from five years ago? If You're going to take her now, make it fast and without pain." I swiped the tears from my cheeks. "And if You wouldn't mind, give me the strength to do this for her."

Will stopped by the house every day, always with takeout food or groceries. We didn't exchange a lot of words; we didn't have to at this point. He did simple things—took out the garbage, washed dishes, vacuumed.

By the end of the second week, Mom needed twenty-four-hour care. My days literally focused on Mom, work, and trying to figure out where the money would come from to pay for everything.

"Why don't you call your supervisor," said Will. "Maybe she can get supplies for you."

Will had made a great suggestion. My supervisor gave me secret permission to steal. "Take whatever you need," she said when I told her about my mother's decline. In an era when women seemed to have an "every girl for herself" attitude, she immediately became a pillar, a godsend for me. She even helped me pack IVs and tubing to keep up Mom's electrolytes and fluid intake, Foley catheter to prevent incontinence, blue pads to prevent messes in bed, and whatever else she thought I might need. She would have torn an OR room apart and given it to me if she thought that would have helped.

Money became a huge issue. Dad's minimum wage job covered

nothing. And Mom's sick pay ended three years prior to this. I couldn't discuss the financial situation with either of my parents, so I plugged along as best I could and went into major debt.

Because I couldn't afford to take any time off work, I called Evelyn for help. Despite our dire situation, Evelyn refused to come and stay with Mom. She thought Aunt Lenora in Florida should be the one to help keep watch over my mother. "She's between husbands and needs something to keep her occupied."

I had only ever met Lenora two or three times and, family or not, I wasn't sure I could handle a stranger hanging around while my mother was in the throes of dying. But I was desperate. The cancer had advanced even more and Mom's kidneys were shutting down.

Will and my father picked up Lenora at the Detroit airport the next day.

It was as if Lenora wasn't there. She mostly stayed in her room but made my mom lunch and kept her mouth moist while I was away. Which is all that I needed.

By the end of the second week of my mother's decline, I became a nurse and only a nurse—a robotic nurse. If I handled it any other way, I would never have been able to continue. I bathed Mom, changed her linens, did the laundry, and controlled her meds. William did everything else. My dad sat on the couch in the living room and stared straight ahead.

Tootsie arrived for a short visit. Evelyn decided to join her. They took turns caring for Mom while I went to work and did chores. It had been over a year since the sisters had been together. Unfortunately, my mom barely recognized them.

"She's going fast," said Tootsie while helping me fold laundry in the basement.

"Yes. She'll be gone before the end of August." I gave Tootsie a quick hug. "Don't come back for the funeral. It's okay, really."

"But you need people around you who love you, darling girl."

"I'll be okay."

In one of her few remaining moments of lucidity, Mom held my hand while I sat by her side. "I don't want to die."

Looking at my mom in the evening light, I couldn't see any difference in her face. Because she declined so quickly, there was no time for her to lose more weight, or develop a deathly pallor. Or for me to prepare myself or my dad for her death. I never thought she would take such a sudden turn for the worse.

"I know, Mom," I replied while stroking her cheek. "I don't want you to die either. But it's okay to let go. You certainly won't be alone up there. And I'll be okay down here." That was the second time I said that to someone I loved. "I'll be okay." I wasn't going to be okay, not for a long, long time.

And her one dying wish—that Esther and I would be friends— the one wish that mattered the most to her, I could not fulfill. That was a horrible failure for me I would never get over.

Tears coursed down her cheeks. "It's going to happen fast, isn't it?"

"Yes," I said. "But it will be painless. You won't even know it's happening." I squeezed her hand tighter. We both knew I was the only one she could have this conversation with. Apparently, so did God. "And I'll be right here with you. I love you."

"All I ever wanted was to have mattered. I never have."

"Sure you have." I spent the next hour reminding her about her job and how many people she had helped over the years at Blue Cross. "You hired that teller who is now your boss. And you made me."

She sighed. "My only achievement that was worth anything."

By morning, my mother was unconsciousness. After an hour of watching her breathing become more and more shallow, I knew what I had to do. It was what my mother would have expected from me if she had known about it. I called the chemo doctors for the prescription of Morphine, Gravol, and Valium, the death cocktail. Once administered every hour as always prescribed, she would be dead in only a few hours—peacefully, without pain, and in her sleep.

Sam Yoshida delivered the prescription. He gasped when he saw Mom lying in bed, unconscious. "Oh my God, Pam, you're doing this alone?"

I shrugged. "She wanted to die at home. I'm fine."

Sam gave me a huge hug, an unusual action for him. He was distraught. As a doctor, he should have called for an ambulance and sent my mom to the hospital. But as a friend, he didn't want to stop me from fulfilling my mother's last wish.

"This isn't right." He kept his arm around me. "You're correct; it's time for the morphine cocktail. Are you sure you can do this? I can stay and give the doses."

"Thanks," I said, "but I'm good."

In spite of my words, he gave my mother the first dose. He took her pulse. "It'll go quickly now."

I walked to the door, motioning for him to follow. "Go home to your kids, Sam. I'll be okay."

After talking to my father for a few minutes, Sam slipped a piece of paper in my hand. "This is my home number. I only live a few blocks away and can be here in a couple of minutes. We'll talk more when this is all done."

Lenora had listened in. She gripped my arm after Dr. Yoshida left. "When my sister dies, I want to be the one to call my family."

"They're my family too, you know." From the look on her face, Lenora clearly didn't think I was part of the Pilch clan. She eviscerated me with her attitude and words. I didn't need any more crap to deal with at this point, especially an aunt treating me like an outsider in my own family.

I felt more alone at that moment than I ever had before. The humiliation of thinking my family, the ones I grew up with and worshipped, did not consider me to be one of them was beyond the Pale.

"I'll tell my uncle and aunts."

Lenora turned away. "No. They're my family, not yours. They need to hear it from me."

I nearly fainted from the pain in my heart. Who the hell says that to someone who was about to lose her mother?

My father sat in the living room while all of this happened. "What's going on?" he said after Dr. Yoshida left and Lenora returned to her room.

I sat beside him and held his hand. "Mom's taken a turn for the worst." I winced when I heard such provincial words coming out of my mouth. It made me sound like a nurse instead of a daughter telling her father he was about to lose his wife. "She's not going to make it through the night." I placed a blanket around his shoulders. "Do you want to be by her side when she goes? If so, you should come into the room now."

Dad leaned away from me. "No. I'm good here. You do that if you want."

I headed back into the bedroom and injected the medicine into my mother's IV tubing. The house had become silent, as if waiting. The only real sound was my mother's shallow breaths.

I moved the two beds closer together so I was a hand's touch away from Mom. By midnight she was in a deep coma. I dozed off while holding her hand.

Very little time passed before I felt a whisper across my cheek. I opened my eyes and witnessed my mother taking her last quiet breath.

It was done. Swiftly. No pain. My prayer had been answered.

"Thank you, God," I said into the dark shadows of the room. As staff members on the chemotherapy ward would say, it was a good death.

Still feeling completely numb and acting as a nurse instead of a daughter, I padded into the living room. My dad slept soundly, contentedly. "It's over Dad. She's gone."

Dad sat up and rubbed his eyes. "What'll we do?" His voice sounded child-like.

I awkwardly pulled him close. "It's okay. I've got this under control. Why don't you make us some tea?"

I called Sam's home number. Then I called Willard. Lenora rushed into the room when she heard my voice.

"I told you I wanted to call him. He's my brother."

I handed her the phone. "So, talk to him. I'm done." This all seemed so petty. My mom was dead.

I called my own Will in the morning.

We buried Mom on August 23, 1978, on a beautiful, sunny, summer day. She would have been pleased with the sun. My mother hated the rain and being cold. More than two hundred people attended the funeral, including the former bank teller. Clearly Mom mattered more than she knew.

I gasped when I spotted several of my Holocaust survivors, Ben, and doctors I worked with in the crowd. They stood around me like sentinels, in strength, solidarity, and comfort. Every survivor looked at me with so much compassion and love, as if to assure me—you can make it through this, we're here for you. These people were my real family and they weren't going to let my mother's death defeat me. Their presence filled me with strength and resolve.

And there was William. He stood by my side during the funeral and gripped my hand tight. No words passed between us. He came back to the house afterwards and stood nearby, in case I needed him. He stayed there. Waiting for me. Knowing I would need him more at the end of that day than I ever needed anyone.

My poor dad was in a state of shock. It never occurred to him that Mom would die, especially so fast. Only four short weeks had passed since her first confused state and her death.

Several days after the funeral, I breathed easy. I had done the right thing by my mother, and I was relieved that her battle had ended. But feeling relief made me feel guilty.

"Relief is a normal response, Pam," said Sam when I told him how I felt. "You need to remember your mother's disease didn't change just her life. It changed yours and your dad's. Five years is a long time to not live normally. Now that her ordeal has ended, you and your dad need to find balance again. You can't do that without recognizing the battle is over and you can finally feel relief."

Sam made sense and my mind acknowledged he did. But not my heart. My mother was dead and instead of grieving, I felt relief. I didn't think I could ever get over that guilt. I owned it.

September flew by before I could catch my breath. I gave up trying to send out any more thank you cards when October rolled around. Enough was enough. I didn't care what people thought of me for not writing them a note. Instead, I made Canadian Thanksgiving dinner with my dad, carved pumpkins for Halloween and bought candies for him to give out.

When Mom's six-year-old Maltese dog suddenly died, Dad wept like a baby. That was the last living trace of Mom. All that remained of my mother was memories. I buried the dog in the back yard.

Dad slid into a major depression after that. Preparing for Christmas was really bad for him. As a practicing Jew, I no longer celebrated the holiday and I was content with that, but I needed to help my dad through his first Christmas alone.

I called him December the first. "You putting up the tree?"

"I've got it part way up. Can't get in the mood to do the rest."

"I'm on my way."

When I arrived, I found him sitting on the floor, holding a branch from the artificial tree. His forlorn look and a bottle of whiskey on the floor beside him, unnerved me. I sat on the floor, across from him trying to decide how to handle the situation. "Not into it, huh?"

He shook his head.

"Listen, I've been thinking about this. We don't have to celebrate the way Mom always wanted to do it. And we sure as hell don't have to make that fudge. We can do whatever we want. If this tree depresses you, then let's get rid of it."

"But, if we don't have a tree, what would we do? We have to do something."

"I don't know. Maybe we could do a movie then eat Chinese food with Will. He says he does that every year."

"What do we do with all these decorations? There are eight big boxes of them."

I thought a moment. "If you're sure you don't want them, I'll offer them to one of the units of the hospital. The patients will love the tree."

My dad wiped his eyes and blew his nose. "But are you okay with it?"

I gently slugged his arm. "Your daughter's a Jew now. I have no problem not celebrating Christmas. Let's meet Will at the local Chinese restaurant to discuss further." I could tell by the smile on Dad's face that a huge weight had been lifted from his shoulders.

After the three of us had filled our bellies, I pulled out a holiday stocking from my purse and slid it across the table to Dad. "It's a holiday present," I said. "Ballroom dancing lessons. I had to give you the gift early because there is a Meet and Greet for all of the beginners in three days."

"What a weird present," said my dad.

"I know, but try it out for me, okay?"

234

My father gave me a dubious look but agreed to go to the first event. He called the day after the Meet and Greet. His voice had a lilt to it from being so happy. He'd loved every minute of it and even met a woman named Norma who also square danced. She was taking him to one on Saturday. Did I mind?

"Dad, that's fantastic," I said. "Did you want me to go with you to buy some clothes for the dance?"

"Actually, Norma and I are at a store right now. I'm using their phone to check with you."

I had to hold back my laughter when I heard a woman calling him Freddie. My dad was going to be okay. When I really thought about it, my parents hadn't been happy in their marriage for a long time. In fact, I always thought they would have divorced if Mom had not become ill. By giving him dance lessons, I had also given Dad his freedom to do whatever he pleased with the rest of his life.

Another prayer answered. At this point in time, I was developing a big crush on God.

My best present that Christmas came from Sam Yoshida and the other cancer doctors. "I felt so helpless watching you by your mother's bedside that last night of her life, and there was nothing I could do to help you," said Sam. "So, if you're up to it, I want you to meet with me to discuss what you needed to care for your mom at home."

I agreed, but I was thinking this was going to be the most difficult conversation of my life. Luckily for me, I was still the OCD girl of making lists and taking notes. I brought them with me. I also brought William, my staunchest ally, security blanket, and bodyguard. After our initial meeting, Sam showed me pages and pages of a tentative plan for home care workers, visiting nurses, supplies delivery and home visits by all professionals. And a Hospice plan for dying patients. He reminded me of David Herzl; a man with serious meticulous attention to detail.

By making sure this happened, Sam became the one person who made my mother's life matter almost more than anyone else's, and I was grateful. He was definitely one of those good people my librarian had spoken about. Probably the best.

33

God did not create woman from man's head, that he should
command her; nor from his feet, that she should be his slave;
but from his side, that she should be nearest his heart.
(Talmud)

William officially asked me to marry him in February 1979.
He got on one knee on a floor strewn with red rose petals,
in a room laden with candles, and put a diamond ring on my finger.
We kissed, I swooned . . .

Well, that's how I had dreamed it would go. Instead, he tackled
me to the floor, sat on me, tickled me until I said yes, then put an
engagement ring on my finger. Ridiculous, I know, but typical of
William. I had figured out William did things for people to show
his love. He did what needed to be done in order to keep me safe
and happy.

"I never really thanked you for helping me when my mom died,"
I said later that night while gazing at the diamond on my finger and
marveling how it sparkled in the light, like a beacon of joy.

"Of course, I was going to be by your side, and I always will,
every step of the way, no matter what we face." He pulled me closer.
"You're my girl," he said. I was his girl. Such a simple but profound
thing to say. I looked into his eyes and felt humbled. I could see

right down into his soul. "I love you," he said, "and I'm giving you my all. Anything you need."

"I love you too, Will. I love you so much, it scares me."

"I know. It's why we're getting married quickly, before you can change your mind. Nobody else could understand me the way you do."

We spoke to the rabbi and decided on June the third as our wedding day. My first phone call was to my dad. Typically, he seemed more preoccupied with his new life than my announcement and that was just fine with me. A few weeks after that first Christmas alone, he and I talked about how painful it was for him to be around me so much because I reminded him of my mother. I gave him permission to call me only when he needed me.

My next call was to Ben Luborsky. "Mazel tov! You're going to be a beautiful June bride. I'll be in Israel then, but I'll be thinking of you every minute of the day."

My first solo step on my wedding to-do list was to visit Isaac at the bookstore. I asked him what I needed to make my wedding as *halakhically* correct as a Reform wedding could be. I may not have converted to Orthodox Judaism because of William, but by golly, my wedding was going to be as orthodox as I could make it.

"Okay, the first thing you need is a *chuppah*, the canopy you get married under," said Isaac. "I have one with poles so you can pick your four dearest friends to hold it up. I'll get it cleaned and you can borrow it. And a special Kiddush cup. It'll be my gift. *Kippahs* for all the men's heads. A special kippah for the groom. . ."

By the end of the visit, I had over twenty pages of notes, had ordered kippahs for the men and one special one for Will, candles for relatives to carry while walking down the aisle, and I made a visit to the Kosher baker next door.

Will still had not told his parents. But the rabbi did. I swear the screams of horror could be heard as far away as Florida.

While Will handled his mother, I dealt with everything else. We had a mere four months to plan it all. I asked Evelyn to help me shop for a dress. She refused, still upset that Aunt Lenora stayed with my mom during her last days. "But you're the one who suggested her," I pointed out. It didn't matter, her mind was made up. Clearly, craziness infested my family as well as Will's.

A work friend helped me pick out my gown. I could never afford the dress I truly wanted, and Evelyn had taken the joy out of the moment, so I bought the one my friend chose.

Esther announced she would not attend the service or reception if I invited any of the Jewish people who had become friends with me. She would be mortified if they showed up. Those friends she banned included Dr. Luborsky and Herschel Teich. Fortunately, Ben was going to be in Israel. Herschel assured me he was fine about not being a guest.

Because Bezalel and I had become great friends, I did insist he be one of the four men holding up the chuppah. We didn't tell Esther he was going to be there.

My wedding day was one of those gifts from God—bright blue sky studded with flimsy white clouds, as if a crown. The sun was the sky's largest jewel. The soft, summer breeze passed over me like a gentle, compassionate spirit that I immediately recognized and loved.

Will's sister, Ruth, stood as my maid of honor. Aubrey would be best man despite what he thought of me. He'd never let his brother down, a wonderful trait that the two brothers shared. That staunch support amongst the three siblings was as strong as any could be. Judith seemed to be on the outside of the ring, and I felt sorry for her to miss this loving bond.

We decided the ceremony would take place inside Will's mother's synagogue, a plain beige building with an ultra-modern interior which was beautiful in its own way, if you enjoyed modern art. And beige.

My bouquet consisted of tiger lilies and burnt orange tea roses, in honor of my Hebrew name, Shoshana. The simple white chuppah almost floated towards the *bima*, altar, while a string quartet played Pachabel's Canon in D. I stopped walking when I saw so many of my survivors in the shul, all of them smiling at me. Of course, they would be here to help me celebrate. My family.

When I saw Will waiting for me at the bima, any worries or fears I may have had, disappeared. His smile conveyed all the love and devotion he had for me and it would be all I would ever need. When I reached his side, he took my hand and kissed it. "Hi," he whispered. A simple word filled with the wonderful world we were about to explore together.

Cantor Mogill sang beautifully. *My Beloved is mine and I am his...*

Esther cried throughout the entire ceremony, punctuated by a couple of loud gasps of despair. Everyone knew they weren't tears of joy, consequently we stood in two receiving lines: one for guests who wished us a hearty mazel tov, and a second line who offered Esther their deepest condolences. In every picture of the wedding, Esther cried and stood as far away from me as possible. Our wedding was declared to be the saddest the Jewish community had ever seen. Sigh. At least she showed up.

There was one moment of huge pain for Will—when his sister Judith came to the service but refused to attend the reception. She chose her friend's reception over her brother's. Sadly, Judith was not in any of our wedding pictures.

Our little reception took place at TBQ's The Other Place. Their Grande room was in the Tudor style with rich dark woods and beams. The florist I had chosen had been a patient of mine and outdid himself with the flowers and center pieces. Candles standing in the middle of burnt orange roses, ivy, and tiger lilies adorned every table. In my mind, it was magical. Our wedding cake was the official dessert and the flowers on the cake matched the flowers in the center pieces, only they were better, way better—they were made of butter cream icing, my favorite.

Of course, Will had ordered a jazz quartet for the reception, one of Windsor's best. They did know a few Jewish ditties for a Hora. Unfortunately, we only danced one.

Will and I had the obligatory bride and groom dance and that was basically it as far as dancing went. The music was fabulous though and many people sat around enjoying the band.

Esther did not participate in any of it.

Remembering that we lived in a party-hearty city, Will and I had intended the reception to last until at least midnight as most receptions did in Windsor. Our festivities started at six. The Jewish people left the reception long before eight pm, right after cake cutting. Because my family lived in Detroit, they left before 9:00pm.

By 10:00pm the hall stood vacant except for the wedding party. Once again, I felt cut to the core. After watching me wallow in sadness, Will decided the night was way too young for our celebration to end. "Everyone to A&W," he shouted.

A tradition in Windsor was to adorn wedding cars with hundreds of tissue flowers, the more elaborate the design, the better. My workmates had made hundreds of multi-colored tissue flowers during their break times at work. Cans trailed behind the bride and groom's car and acted as noisemakers. Once the reception officially ended, we jumped into our still-decorated cars and took off for the drive-in restaurant, honking our horns all the way. It was quite a sight to see that night—a bride and groom and their wedding party sitting on the picnic tables at A&W, chowing down on burgers and fries. For dessert we dug into the top layer of the wedding cake that was supposed to be frozen and eaten by the couple on their first anniversary.

The loud roar of Harleys announced the arrival of the Lobos biker gang. The leader recognized me from high school. "Weird wedding reception," he said.

I took a bite of my burger. "Mother-in-law troubles."

"Oh, nasty mothers-in-law, those bitches. I know all about that." When he returned to his Harley, he cranked up the music loud enough for the entire parking lot to hear and asked me to dance. Everyone laughed at the sight of a bride dancing on a picnic table with the Lobos leader of Windsor dressed in his leather jacket and jeans.

Eventually the wedding party headed for our apartment. Will jubilantly made a toast to me and our new married life. "We have our entire lives to figure out our crazy families," he said with a laugh. "All we have to do is survive the brunch my mother has planned for the out-of-town guests, tomorrow."

Ruthie groaned. "Let's hope everyone behaves."

Esther did not invite my family to the brunch, not even my dad who lived a few blocks away. Another insult. "She's just going to keep on doing this," I said to Will before going into the house. "Maybe my uncle is right. Maybe I don't have the strength to put up with this."

"Yes, you do. I would never marry a girl who couldn't stand up to my family," said Will. "You'll get used to them. Hold on to my hand the entire time. And we'll only stay an hour, tops." He kissed me. "It's all we have to do, then we're on our honeymoon for three weeks."

I nearly panicked as we crossed over the threshold. My mind had gone back to that day when she denied my mother's dying wish. Will looked at me as if he understood. "Think of these folks as copies of the orthodox rabbi you've argued with so many times and defeated."

These folks? I almost whimpered when I finally looked around. The living room and dining room were packed with strangers. The only face I recognized was Ruthie's. She waved and smiled from the dining area.

Esther darted over to us when we entered the living room and she gave Will a huge hug. She gave me a hug as well, but a pained expression appeared on her face. Baby steps, I told myself. At least she acknowledged my existence. Baby steps.

Will moved over to the dining table filled with food. "Want something?" he said.

I shook my head no but gratefully took the tea Ruthie offered me.

About an hour into the brunch, Will's Uncle Phil arrived. He had refused to come to the wedding. I thought it was because Will had married a convert, but that wasn't true, I learned. Phil was mean-spirited towards Esther and her children and cruelly refused to attend any family gathering or event on the Goldstein side. That he appeared at the brunch was supposed to be some great honor.

Phil stopped in front of me, his gaze slowly roaming up and down my body with a look of loathing on his face. "I give this six-months," he sneered and walked away. I hated him.

Will protectively pulled me to his side. "Right, we're going now." Will said goodbye while I headed for the car.

"This isn't going to work," I sobbed when he got into the car next to me. "They hate me. And six months? Who does Phil think he is?"

William squeezed my hand. "If it helps, I can guarantee my mother will come around when we have our first baby."

"First baby?" I wailed. "I'm terrible with kids."

William gave me one of his drollest expressions as he pulled out of the driveway. "You'll be a great mom. It's me being a father that's a worry. The poor kid won't stand a chance of ever fitting in."

34

The traditional blessing thanks God for three things:
shehechiyanu (giving us life), v'kiyimanu (sustaining us),
vihigiyanu lazman hazeh (allowing us to arrive at this moment).
Implied in this blessing is a commitment to vitality,
to sustained presence and awareness.
(Rabbi Donin)

Our incredible month-long honeymoon took place in British Columbia and Alberta. Neither of us had ever seen mountains before and we both wanted to mark our special occasion with something monumental. Seeing the Rockies seemed pretty monumental, especially Roger's Pass. Earth's life rose through those mountains. They looked like great rocky declarations of hope and peace. They gave shelter to lush green forests and animals large and small. Everywhere we looked, we saw granite spires, rubble-strewn summits still peaked with snow, hardy flora at our feet, a million elk, towering gold thunderhead clouds above the peaks, and eagles soaring high and free. It was a perfect celebration.

Will and I fell back into our routine work life when we returned home. He remained a part-time tennis pro/mailman and a student in the university MBA program. I was still an OR nurse, where I saw Dr. Luborsky nearly every day.

Now that the conversion and wedding were over, Ben and I discussed Israeli politics.

It didn't take long before I found myself reading book after book about Israel. I instantly fell in love with David Ben Gurion's passion and courage. So many books were written about the man. Ben and I discussed what David Ben Gurion stood for, what his beliefs were, while we waited in between surgeries. We always seemed to be in the same rooms most days. It didn't occur to me that the Jewish surgeons requested me as their circulating nurse so they could protect me from any repercussions that might occur after Dornanalty's dismissal. Will had to point that out. The queen of obtuseness struck again.

"Ben Gurion wasn't that religious," said Ben one day. "And he denied being a Zionist. But he believed in the Jewish people and Israel. He made a quote, something about what our role on earth is. Suffering makes a people greater and we have suffered much." Ben nodded his head. "I remember it now. We had a message to give to the world, but we were overwhelmed, and the message was cut off in the middle. In time there will be millions of us—becoming stronger and stronger—and we will complete the message."

"He was talking about the Holocaust and so many Jews being killed," I said.

"Yes. And he was right. Your generation is going to realize and finish that message. *Tikkun Olam*—repair the world."

What a tremendous responsibility and I wasn't so sure I wanted it. But maybe that was the point of the Jews. Nobody wanted that responsibility and the world certainly needed help. God had made Jews as stubborn and defiant as they needed to be, strong enough to survive thousands of years of antisemitism and a Holocaust. With this kind of history, I quaked with fear at what might be arriving in the future.

A few weeks later, Ben encouraged me to try returning to Sha'ar Hashomayim, the Orthodox synagogue, again. Maybe Saturday?

Kiddush this time was in honor of me and my absent husband. Ben and his wife Anne attended, as did several of the Jewish doctors, the octogenarians, and Holocaust survivors. Schmuel, the hospital barber, and his family came as well.

It definitely was a different reception than my wedding. I was being mobbed by people who wanted to hug me and wish me well.

"Dollie, welcome to the tribe," said Rutie from the deli. "Come to the deli one day and I'll show you how to make those cinnamon buns."

"Sweetheart, may you have many, many children, and please, when you have a daughter, name her after my mother, Rachel," said a survivor I had cared for at the hospital.

These people were the Jews I had read about in books and loved. I could relate to them, adore them, and give them my respect.

One woman, Leone Schott, introduced herself. "Mazel tov, you brave girl," she said. "I converted as well, back in the thirties, when it was considered even more scandalous to do." She winked at me. "I'll call you next week and we'll have lunch at the deli."

With my self-confidence restored, I jumped in with both feet and joined all three of the major Jewish organizations—Hadassah, B'nai B'rith, and United Jewish Appeal. My regret was not joining Pioneer Women. My mother-in-law belonged to that one. As I attended meetings and tried to volunteer to committees, several members ostracized me. Either they were friends of Judith's or their moms were friends with Esther, or worse yet, they themselves did not approve of marriages between Jews and the *goyim*. My conversion meant nothing. It wasn't orthodox.

Fortunately, there was another group of women, a much larger group, who ignored this pettiness and immediately befriended me. They were women like me, social workers, nurses. Israelis who had moved here also welcomed me with open arms.

"It's fascinating, isn't it?" said my new friend/mentor, Leone Schott, at one of the meetings while observing the younger women who rejected me. "None of us can figure out how they got to be this way." She pointed at one girl. "Her parents are Holocaust survivors, and she does all the right things. She does it dressed to the nines with her makeup just so, and after she's gone to the gym. All the girls look up to her."

Two of the most respected women of the group walked over to meet me. They were fondly known as the two Sadies and were best friends.

Leone explained the situation to the women. "Oh, they're second-generation, most of them," said Sadie L. That I understood from Mr. C.'s son. "They're afraid of you, dear Pamela," she continued. "You dared to come to *shul* on Saturday, especially after the rabbi told you that you couldn't."

"And we've all heard how you told him off at the hospital because he rejected converts," said Sadie P. "We were especially impressed when you stepped in for Mary Spegleman. We all love her. When the rabbi wouldn't let her touch her dead husband because she had not converted, we thought it was such a *Shanda* and *Charpa.*"

Leone took my hand. "I thought it was so sweet how you took the body out of the morgue and placed it in a quiet room where they kept the flowers being delivered to the hospital. It meant so much to her to have that private time to say goodbye."

"Yes, we all cried about that one," said Sadie L. "You've had tongues wagging for months before you even got married. I've been so eager to meet you."

Leone chuckled. "You look a little *plotzed* Pamela. You didn't know you were the talk of the Jewish community?"

I could feel my cheeks burning with embarrassment. "I had no idea. That's some gossip group you've got going there."

Sadie L. laughed. "We're a small community and we need a quick way to reach everyone, especially for funerals. A person could die at nine in the morning and by lunch time everybody knows that person died and when the funeral is taking place. You could say we have perfected communicating. Now, getting the facts right is another story."

"Listen," said Leone. "You've converted which means you're Jewish. There's no doubt about that fact. So, here's how to start acting like a real Jew. We try to have moral courage and make our actions matter."

"Leone is right," said Sadie L. "We'll show you what to do so you feel like part of the *meshpukha*. Right now, we're trying to figure out what to do about the Ethiopian Jews and how to save them." She clucked and shook her head. "So much controversy."

"I'm in," I said. I sensed another trip to Isaac's because I had never heard of Ethiopian Jews.

"Knew you would be." Leone nudged me. "Let me introduce you to Anne. She sells hats for Orthodox women to wear in Shul. You're going to buy your first hat, tomorrow. I'll take you. It will make an incredible statement, especially to the rabbi."

I hesitated a moment. "In case you haven't noticed, he's not fond of me."

Leone sniffed with disgust. "I wouldn't like you if he did." She offered me a tuna fish sandwich. "Just a little by the way, Jews invented tuna fish sandwiches."

I laughed when she announced that.

"And deviled eggs," said Sadie L.

These women, so warm and loving, had accepted me just the way I was. "You'll all help me, right?" I said.

All three women held up their wine glasses. "You bet we will," said Leone. "God bless you, my dear woman, and welcome to the tribe. Here's to many an exciting adventure together."

According to Leone and the two Sadies, religious women in North America wore hats in Shul, technically to respect God and Shabbat, the bigger and fancier the better. "It was a tradition that was practiced in Europe before World War II," said Leone, becoming serious. "We Orthodox women have brought the tradition back now, out of respect and honor for those women who perished in the camps."

"Does everyone do this?" I said.

"We certainly do, and in New York. I've always assumed all of us do it. I also wear a hat every time I go outside to do business."

"She's known as the hat lady," said Sadie P.

"What a wonderful tradition," I said.

"Yes," said Leone. "Some of the younger women refuse to wear hats. They don't understand the meaning of the hat tradition, but even they will wear little lacy kippahs that are at the front door of the sanctuary."

I bought three hats the next day. I was ready for battle, er—shul.

35

Every time history repeats itself, the price goes up. Humanity needs to pay attention, now, for we can no longer afford the cost.
(George Santayana)

Here was the best kick in the *tuchus*. It had barely been a year since OMA (Ontario Medical Association) suspended Dr. Dornanalty but, because there was such a severe shortage of anaesthetists, surgeons pleaded to have him reinstated. Dornanalty was the best anaesthetist in the city. I requested a transfer back to ER. Nothing was going to change; it was better to leave.

"I'll miss you," said my supervisor on my last day in the OR, "but I completely understand."

I hauled my over-sized purse over my shoulder. "Thanks again for your help when my mom was so sick. I wouldn't have made it without you. I'll never forget you."

"No problem, kid. Someday, you'll return the favor. I can't believe your mom died a year ago already."

"Me neither," I said and left the OR without looking back. Onto the future with Will.

36

*In the beginning there was faith—which is childish; trust—
which is vain; and illusion—which is dangerous.*
(Elie Wiesel)

I couldn't have asked for a better husband than William. After being married for six months, I could extoll his virtues for hours. Oh, we fought, and a lot, especially about money.

And how I did the damn laundry.

We both used a towel only once, and wore shirts only once, so I put everything in the gentle cycle. With his very own special meticulous attention to detail, like David Herzl and Sam Yoshida, Will insisted that clothes had to be washed according to instructions. It was how his mother washed them.

I warned him. "Do not ever compare me to your mother, and if you say one more word about the laundry, you will do it for the rest of your life." I shoved another load in the washing machine.

He pulled the shirts out of the machine. "But it says permanent press. My mother says—"

I whipped the Bounce box at his head. We argued for an hour. Finally, I screamed, threw the laundry detergent at him, and walked to the doorway. "That's it. You're doing laundry, now. For the rest of this marriage."

"You are so damn stubborn."

I pointed out that he was even more stubborn than me, otherwise he would have realized the error of his ways and shut up in the first hour of the argument about laundry.

He growled. "I'm not stubborn at all. And I blame your stubbornness on your Irish side of the family."

I stormed back into the room. "And what does my Irish side have to do with this fight?"

He grabbed me by the waist and we fell on a nearby sofa. "Nothing, but it got you riled enough to come back in the room." After a long kiss, he put on a contrite face. He wasn't fooling me for a second. "If I say I'm sorry, do I get out of doing the laundry?"

"Never," I shouted and flounced away.

Another battle we had really should have made me sit up and take notice—when Will refused to allow a mezuzah on the front door of our apartment. "We don't own this place. So, no mezuzah," he said in that stubborn voice of his. This was going to be a major battle.

"But we live here, it's our home."

"No, drop it."

"But other people have them on their doors."

"I said no. That's final."

No mezuzah. "But when we own a house of our own, I'm having one on every single door post!" I shouted at his retreating back. I put one up in the middle of the night.

Other than the religion issue, there was only one other drawback in our happy lives. Will's mother. She announced she wanted us to be at her house every Friday night for Shabbos. She insisted all four of her children be present. Fortunately, I did shift work and worked several Fridays. I had to admit if I ignored her jabs and digs at me, Friday nights were fun.

Moishe ended up being a fine father-in-law during those tense months of adjusting to having a disapproving mother-in-law. He cracked ridiculously inane jokes at the Shabbos table while trying to get to know me. Clearly, Will developed his "skill" of delivering jokes from his dad.

Moishe liked that I was a conservative Jew. "It'll be interesting to see how you raise your kids," he said one day. "My biggest regret in life was not being orthodox enough. If I had it to do over again, I'd be kosher. I'm pretty sure my kids would have been different, more religious."

That simple statement led Will and I to a war that had no resolution.

"Did you hear what your father said at the table tonight," I started when we returned home. My anger had not settled after that conversation. And it wouldn't until Will and I came to an agreement of some sort about Judaism. Will had fought me every inch of the way when I tried to do anything Jewish that might involve him, like putting up a mezuzah on our door. Here I was, part of one of the most beautiful religions in the world with traditions that any sane person would be jealous of, and a Jewish husband who refused to let me practice my faith.

I braced for a major battle. "Your father would have done things differently. He would have been kosher, more orthodox. I don't understand you. Why do you hate being religious? It's not because you don't believe in God. I know it isn't."

Will said nothing—it was a very long, loud nothing that spoke volumes about his disdain for his religion.

"Will, talk to me! Is it because of your mother's obsession with the temple?"

Will looked out the living room window before answering. "All religions are based on what happened to dead people. Christianity is berserk about a guy named Jesus who supposedly died on a cross.

The Muslims are nuts about some man who told them to kill infidels, especially the Jews before he died."

He folded his arms across his chest and faced me. A shiver ran down my spine. He was also ready for battle and determined he was going to win. "And then there's us, the Jews. We've got more dead bodies under our feet who died for this religion than other religions combined. We're on a fricking mountain of dead Jews, probably a mountain range of them. Rabbis insist that it wasn't just our ancestors that Moses liberated from Egypt, but we, me, I was personally freed by God. Over three thousand years later."

He poured himself a drink. "Even receiving the laws of Torah were given not to just the ancestors, but to all of the future Jewish descendants, biological and spiritual. Jews don't think of anything being in the past; it's always in the present and moving into the future. Torah is never discussed like a history; we still think it's all in our present. Our ancient religious traditions are yolked around our necks and we are drowning because of them."

"That's not true," I spluttered.

"Yeah? You love your Shabbos candles so damn much, but what do they really represent? The recurrence of the creation of the world, and we remember that every damn week. Look at Passover. We eat the same damn matzah we've been eating for thousands of years. After all these years, you'd think we'd be able to have found time to let the bread rise while running for our freedom. At least we could find a better tasting recipe."

I plopped on the sofa, feeling nonplussed and having no idea how to debate any of that. And if I wanted to practise Judaism, I needed to find the argument to stop his anti-religious beliefs. "So, do you hate Israel as well?"

Will thought another long moment. "No. Everything there is physical. In Jerusalem, I'm told you can use a set of stairs and suddenly find yourself in the Roman era, or the times of the Maccabees, or Masada. But it's physical, you can walk away from it. My mother's religion is all in the mind, based on a book of guilt and shame."

He took off his shirt and headed for the bedroom but returned almost immediately with his toothbrush in hand. "And here's what else. Israel, when you think about it, has given us Jews a gift. It has shown us our past and where it should be—on the ground, not wrapped around our hearts, squeezing the life out of us. It's given us a Jewish identity, and a secular future, which you'd think would be great, right? Wrong. What do non-Jews think about us present day Jews and Israel? Nothing. We're nonentities. We're still the Other people, marginalized. Oh, and best of all, if we wouldn't mind, be fucking dead so Arabs and terrorists can take our land."

We stared at each other. Never had I ever felt more alienated from a person than I did from William at that moment.

"Do you know why I still identify as a Jew other than for my mother?"

I shook my head, not able to hazard a guess.

"Because of incidents like the one that happened with Dr. Dornanalty. Antisemitism. During the Holocaust, it didn't matter how many generations had passed since a Jew practised his faith. He was still destroyed. Israel gives us a ledge, a firm footing to stand on. A reason to fight back, and whether I'm religious or not just doesn't matter. Israel's my land, my history. It shows up with every archeological dig. I am part of a people whose history is 7,000 years old. I'm still part of a people 1,000 years ago. I was even part of a people in World War II while dying in those camps. I'll be damned before I let anyone put me down because I'm a Jew. Religion doesn't and shouldn't matter."

Will looked at the clock in the kitchen. "It's midnight. I have to be up early for work." He let out a deep breath. "Look. You want to practise Judaism, fine. I have no right to tell you no. Can we call a truce, because nothing you can say will change my mind about anything."

"Sure," I said. "Just don't be condescending to me like you just were." I wiped my cheeks when I realized I had been crying almost this entire time.

Will sat beside me. "I'm sorry. But you've met my mother and see how she is. The Holocaust didn't just affect the survivors. It affected every Jew in the world. Reactions varied. A lot of Jews made *Aliyah* to Israel. Others became like my mother, highly emotional, paranoid, and irrational about things like me falling in love with someone like you. She's the queen of the Other People club. My father won't let any of us watch the news because she gets worked up and sobs every time it's on. She can't help herself. None of that generation can. And if six million Jews were murdered today? I'm not sure how I'd react. Maybe I'd turn into my mother."

He rose to his feet. "I'm going to bed. Coming?"

I shook my head. "I'll join you later."

37

We cannot indefinitely avoid depressing subject matter, particularly
if it is true, and in the subsequent quarter century the world has
had to hear a story it would have preferred not to hear—the story
of how a cultured people turned to genocide, and how the rest
of the world, also composed of cultured people,
remained silent in the face of genocide.
(Elie Wiesel)

Simply put, Schmuel the barber and his wife, Leila, became friends of mine after I took care of their daughter in ER one night. I saw Schmuel every day at work. Leila said I had a calming effect on him and their daughter and she often asked me to dinner. When I began conversion lessons, she taught me how to set the table and cook for Passover. I taught her how to cook for Schmuel's diabetes. She showed me how to make a traditional honey cake, and a Shabbos brisket. I explained blood sugars and how to give her husband insulin injections. And how not to put so much sugar in the brisket and honey cake.

Leila made beef tongue. Eww, again with the tongue. She never sliced it or made it look appealing. She just plunked it on a serving platter with potatoes and carrots. Whole, as in unsliced. I grimaced every time I saw it on the table, nearly gagging.

Why? "Because when you're poor," Leila said, "nothing goes to waste. It's also why we eat chicken feet." She grinned at the face I made. "We pickle them too."

No!

Leila also taught me how to play cards. Euchre. We played every Wednesday night after supper while Schmuel worked late. Leila didn't like to be alone at night. I never asked why, just relished the time with her. She often became nostalgic and spoke about helping her mother in the kitchen and learning how to cook those "delectable" tongues and chicken feet.

Schmuel came in at the end of his day and joined us at the table, regaling us with stories about work. It seemed like an idyllic setting and time.

On one of those nights, Schmuel ran into the living room, screaming hysterically. His eyes bulged in terror; the veins on his neck looked as if they were about to pop. His face had completely drained of color.

He crawled into the coat closet and curled into a ball on the floor. A puddle of urine spread around him.

"Schmueli, Schmueli! What's happened?" cried Leila.

I followed him into the closet and felt his pulse. One-hundred-eighty-four. He stared straight ahead, his eyes wide, as if in a catatonic stupor.

"Schmuel, what's wrong?" I said in a low voice.

His entire body shivered. When I tried to touch him, he screamed.

"Ich bate az ses ich nicht emes," cried Schmuel. *"Dos kan zich nicht trephen noch a mol. Dos kan zich nicht trephen noch a mol . . ."*

I recognized the language as he cried on. Yiddish. "What's he saying Leila?"

"He's praying to Hashem to not let this be happening again."

Crap. This was like Jacob when he got hysterical in the hospital.

"We need help," I said. "Where's your son?"

The front door burst open just then and Schmuel screamed at the sound. "*Nein!*"

Leila sank to her knees when she heard his terror.

"I'm here," said Nate as he ran into the room. "I was walking down the road when I saw him pull into the driveway. He left the car running and just ran inside. What happened?"

"I'm not sure," I said while taking his pulse again. "Something at the hospital."

Leila explained to her son what Schmuel had been saying.

"I'll call the rabbi," said Nate. "He'll know what to do." I rolled my eyes with exasperation. The last thing any of us needed was that man.

I turned to Nate and motioned him to come to the closet. "We have to get your dad out of the closet and cleaned up before the rabbi arrives."

Nate wrinkled his nose at the odor. "He peed his pants?"

"Yup, and a bit more."

We eventually managed to pull Schmuel out of the closet and walked him to the bathroom.

"It's okay Schmuel," I soothed going into nurse mode while cleaning him up. "No one will ever harm you again. I promise you this. I can protect you."

Relief flooded over me when Schmuel acknowledged what I said. At least he wasn't completely catatonic. I gave him a reassuring smile even though I felt nothing like a calming, assuring nurse. There was a gnawing in my gut that warned me this was going to be yet another horrifying experience that would change the way I viewed the world.

It took a few minutes to clean him up and put him in his pajamas. Once I had him settled on the sofa, I gave Schmuel a shot of whiskey to help calm him. Then another. "You're safe, Schmuel," I kept saying. "I'm here. I'll protect you."

Schmuel had become almost catatonic again. "It doesn't matter anymore," he murmured. "They're here." I quickly gave him another shot of whiskey. There was no way I was going to lose Schmuel to his terror, no matter what it was.

When the rabbi arrived and saw me sitting with Schmuel, he glared. "Why are you here? Get out."

I rose to my feet and stood by Schmuel in a protective manner. I didn't budge when the rabbi moved closer, intending to move me away. There wasn't a chance in hell that would happen. I was definitely taller than him, and no doubt stronger. "I'm here because I'm a nurse and Schmuel's friend. We work at the hospital together."

I stared back at the rabbi's fierce eyes, daring him to cause a scene. If he did, I was going to punch his lights out. I really wanted to knock him flat. I think he sensed that because he backed away. Out of my reach.

"I'm staying, Rabbi," I said in a fiercely stern voice.

The rabbi knew when to back down in defeat and turned his attention to Schmuel. The two men talked for an hour in Yiddish.

"Do you know what they're saying?" I said to Nate.

"They're talking too fast."

Leila sat on the couch in between us, holding both of our hands as tight as she could. "He's telling the rabbi about Warsaw." Her jaw tightened. I could hear her teeth grind. "The dent in Schmuel's head comes from the war. A Nazi captain at Auschwitz bashed his head in with his boot. He has a plate there now. His hip is permanently displaced, too."

Her eyes never strayed from her husband's face. "My Schmuel came face to face with that monster today. The Nazi captain who did this to him was one of the patients on the fourth floor. Herr Schmidt."

As I watched her eyes, so intent on her husband's face, I wondered how I'd react if that were Will. I'd be raging mad, ready to pull someone's face off for terrifying my husband. It still wasn't clear to me whose face that would be.

Schmuel's eyes looked as if they were permanently bulged out with horror. He held the rabbi's hand to his heart, as if trying to gain some of the rabbi's strength.

Leila sucked in a deep breath and placed her head on my shoulder. "That Nazi is such an awful monster."

I rested my head on hers. "What is he saying?"

Leila squeezed my hand tighter. "When Schmuel's train pulled into Auschwitz that night, most of the soldiers were inside the camp already. Because he was so small and young, that awful man picked him to be his kicking ball. He kicked him so hard that Schmuel went flying and he kept kicking him until his body landed in a garbage heap that was going to be burned because of lice."

Leila pulled out a hankie and wiped her eyes. "They left him for dead. When he came to, the gates of Auschwitz were closed and he escaped into the woods. He joined a few other Jews and hid. Schmuel was only a little boy—twelve."

Leila cried out when Schmuel collapsed on the rabbi's shoulder. "That Nazi wanted Schmueli to cut his hair today. When Schmueli recognized him, he dropped everything and ran out of the hospital."

I looked over at Schmuel who still clutched the rabbi's hand to his heart. "So, he's looked the devil in the face for the second time," I said, wondering how such a heinous Nazi could still be living in Canada. "Schmuel's a hero to have survived the war the first time. What do we do now?"

"I'll call the president of B'nai B'rith," said Nate and headed for the phone.

I went to the tiny kitchen and made Leila a hot tea with whiskey. After making sure she drank most of it, I sat beside her. "Tell me again what he said when he was in the closet." I wanted to vomit, I felt so horrified.

"He begged God not to let the Holocaust happen again." She wrung her hands. "He would die if he had to face it again."

The rabbi walked over to us. "He's fine now. We prayed. He just needs a good night's sleep."

I looked over at Schmuel. He was anything but fine. His entire body quivered; his eyes still filled with terror. I knew, like I did with Sarah and Jacob, that I would never again see my friend the way he used to be. Something in him had snapped. The rabbi was a fool.

Leila said goodnight after Nate and I helped Schmuel to their bedroom. She turned back to me before shutting the door. "You'll let yourself out after talking to Nate?"

"Of course. I'll come by after work tomorrow, to make sure he's okay." I ran a shaky hand through my hair and sat down at the table. "Call me in the night if you need me."

Nate announced the president of B'nai B'rith would begin proceedings immediately to investigate the Nazi in question.

"So, justice will be served?" I said when Nate sat beside me.

"Except for the years he got to live Scot-free in Canada. In my books that means justice will never be meted out."

"But now that we know he's here, his happy days will be over."

"Maybe. It's a slow process."

I needed to clean myself from the filth and horror of the night and went into the kitchen. After making sure the water became so hot it steamed, I scrubbed my hands with a stainless-steel pad. Even the pad wasn't strong enough to clean away the filth of Auschwitz. Nothing was. Nothing ever would be. I scrubbed until my hands burned from the steel and the skin became raw.

"This is never-ending, isn't it?" I said when I returned to Nate. "There's always some shit that happens that brings the camps crashing down on them all over again."

Nate poured himself a shot of whiskey. "My mother and father go through the motions of living happy lives, but you know what? When I lived at home, both of them had nightmares so terrifying that they ended up taking turns falling asleep so the other one felt safe at night. It's why Mom is so tired. She takes the first watch so

Dad can get enough sleep to go to work."

He downed his second drink. "What kind of life is that?"

I had no answer. What kind of answer could there be?

I could barely breathe. My emotions were all over the place, the biggest one coming to the fore was anger. I wanted to hurt the bastard that had terrified my friend. He was so close. I could go to the hospital and . . . and . . .

"You spending the night?" I said, eventually gaining control of my temper.

"Yeah. I'll stay."

"See you tomorrow." It was going to be a tough ride home. I had to pass the hospital. As soon as I entered the apartment, I fell into Will's arms and sobbed.

38

Every act of forgiveness mends something broken in this fractured world. It is a step, however small, in the long, hard journey to redemption.
(Rabbi Jonathan Sacks)

Goldstein, you're subbing on the chemo unit for two weeks," said my head nurse. "One of the nurses had major surgery and can't return to work yet."

The chemo floor was not any place I ever wanted to work again, but I convinced myself that two weeks was tolerable.

The staff waved hello when they saw me. "Thank God," said the new head nurse. "It'll be like old home week for you. We are so swamped with this new chemo protocol. And so many of the patients are dying. Can you take the four private rooms as patients? They're all in final stages."

"I'm on it," I said.

I nearly fell on my face when I entered the first room. One of my patients was none other than Herr Schmidt, the Nazi that had beaten Schmuel to a pulp when he was a kid.

What the hell? I felt completely betrayed by God, stabbed in the back. "Are You kidding me with this shit?" I mumbled rudely.

The man was in terrible shape. The midnight shift had three deaths and a Code Blue. They had been so short-staffed. None of the other patients received care. Herr Schmidt had been incontinent of urine and feces. Vomit trailed over the bed rail. "Help me," he moaned. His lips were blue.

"Oh shit," I whispered.

After an hour, I had the man washed with sheets changed and teeth cleaned. I also had him heavily sedated and oxygen running. No one had given him any pain meds since the day before.

"Thank you, nurse," he whispered and kissed the back of my still raw hand.

"You're welcome," I said while wiping his kiss off on the bottom of my uniform.

I left him to sleep and attended to the other three patients. He still slept when I peeked in on him an hour later. He looked at peace.

After his wife and son arrived, I explained the status of his condition. "He's in a lot of pain," I said. "But I'm giving him as much sedation as was ordered. If it's not enough, I'll call the doctor for more."

The wife was grateful. The son had noticed my necklace with the Magen David on it. If looks could have killed . . . that young man hated me on sight because I was a Jew and he didn't even try to hide that fact.

I decided to continue to think of this patient as Herr Nazi instead of his real name. That way I could keep him tucked in that compartment of my mind filled with horror and Holocaust and not give him very much thought until this ordeal ended. There was going to come a time when I would have to deal with all that had happened in these past hours. I couldn't face it while working.

Two of my patients died before lunch. The third patient had gone into a coma and his family sat by his side with their priest. I focused my attention on Herr Nazi and the thrush growing in his mouth.

"You don't like me," he said near the end of my shift.

I gave him a brief smile. "I'm the barber's friend. I assume you remembered him from then? The little boy?"

He squeezed his eyes shut and a look of remorse crossed his face. "Yes, I remember. I think I scared him yesterday, but all I wanted to do was apologize."

Apologize? I couldn't go there with this-this-this man. He thought an apology was going to do good at this point in their lives. My anger was so fierce, so visceral. I had barely been able to catch my breath the entire day.

"How's your pain?" I finally managed to say. "Do you need more medication before I leave for the day?" I clenched my hands behind my back so Herr Nazi could not see how white my knuckles were. A base human urge to hurt him flowed through me.

"I'm good for now, dear, thank you. You've been very kind."

With a mechanical smile, I swallowed the bile rising in my throat. "Goodnight, then," I said and turned to leave.

"Nurse?" called Herr Nazi. "Thank you. You made me feel better today."

I let out a giant sigh of relief when I picked up my purse and sweater to head for home. I had made it through the day without screaming in rage or hurting someone.

Schmuel blocked my way from leaving. He had watched me the entire day attending to Herr Nazi and glared at me as if I had become a monster, just like the man.

"You were my friend. I trusted you. How could you? How could you even touch him?"

"I have to Schmuel. I took an oath to care for all people. If I don't keep my vow then I'm as bad as he is. I can't pass judgment."

"He's not people," he roared and walked away, his limp more pronounced than ever before.

I burst into tears as I watched him leave the unit. "What am I doing?"

I nearly fainted the next day when I learned Herr Nazi had requested me for his nurse. "Why?" I cried softly. "Dear God, why me taking care of him?" Of course, there was no answer.

Schmuel watched me from a distance every hour of that day, tears coursing down his cheeks. The few times I tried to talk to him, he shook his head and turned away.

By the end of the first week, Herr Nazi constantly cried in agony. "Help me, please."

I wanted to hate this man. I wanted him in pain. I wanted him to have the agonizing death the doctors predicted. However, when I looked in Herr Nazi's eyes, I no longer saw an evil Nazi. I saw a pitiful old dying man.

His wife explained Herr Nazi had been a good citizen and helped his friends and neighbors. A stellar human being since his arrival in Canada. Proof of that was in the bouquets of flowers in the room and hundreds of cards wishing him good health.

Except for this one thing back in World War II, he had been a good man.

Except for this one thing.

Dr. Dornanalty immediately came to my mind and all the times he called me kike-lover. Will's story about the Nazi sending the Jewish children to their deaths came to the fore as well.

Except for this one thing.

I felt so confused. What was the morally right thing to do? "Where are You when I really need You?" I asked the sky.

At that moment in time, Herr Nazi didn't care about me as a woman, as a human, as a Jew. He trusted me to do my job as a nurse, to help him. If I turned my back on him, if I didn't try to ease his pain, wouldn't that make me as bad as him?

Damn it all to Hell.

I remembered what Rabbi Donin said when we discussed the Holocaust. "We are all Hashem's children, Pamela. How can we expect Hashem to choose from his children? Us, the Nazis, the terrorists in Israel, a murderer? How does He choose? He created all of us with love, and no matter what we may do wrong, He forgives all of us, exactly like a loving parent does whenever their child has erred."

When I had asked about someone being inherently evil, he shook his head. "The sin may be evil but not the man. We are all created in the image of Hashem. It's why we have to forgive our enemies no matter what they do. It is the only way to be free of the pain our enemies caused. Forgiveness is the only way we rid the world from evil."

"I can't even begin to think about forgiving Herr Nazi," I cried to God. "And don't You expect me to."

There were times through the next few days, as the pain got worse, that Herr Nazi gripped my hand and clung to me. "I don't want my wife and children to see me cry. I don't want them to see me in pain. Give me something to put me out of my misery."

I looked down at the Magen David hanging from a chain around my neck and then I stared at Herr Nazi's pain-filled face. "There is a combination of medications we can give, but you'll be knocked out until the end. Is that what you want?"

"Yes. Please."

I asked one of the chemo doctors to talk to Herr Nazi. He returned to the nurse's desk and ordered us to give him the morphine "cocktail" to help him.

As his nurse, I stayed by Herr Nazi's side as much as I could. He clung to me every time.

His son went into a rage about that. He truly hated me. I was the symbol of all that had plagued his father's nightmares throughout his life—the filthy Jew. The scum of the earth. He accused me of withholding his father's pain medication. He made official complaints. Dr. Yoshida defended me, especially when he saw how often I was giving the medication.

"This must be torture for you," he murmured, "to care for this man, knowing what he was."

"It's not good."

"It won't be long now."

None of the pain medications worked on Herr Nazi. He still suffered horribly. Herr Nazi stared at me with those anguished, pleading eyes. "All I can see are dead Jews—skeletons," he cried.

I nearly fell to the floor. It wasn't the pain from the tumor giving him so much grief. His past had caused his mind to become a courtroom which forced him to be his own judge and jury regarding the horror of his ugly deeds as a Nazi.

Herr Nazi became more and more terrified as the never-ending scenes of his deeds in the camps played out in his mind. "They're pointing their fingers at me, accusing me, condemning me," he screamed at one point, clawing my arm. "Help me!"

I didn't have to say a word. His own conscience condemned him to Hell.

"I did terrible things, awful things, Pamela."

He wanted to confess to me everything he had done. I could feel the blood draining from my face. His own suffering completely blinded him to the pain he caused in my soul in this indecent, hideous moment. He was oblivious to the inhumane and depraved torture that this inflicted on me, a lone Jew.

I frantically tried to release his grip from me. "I'll get a priest for you. You can tell him."

"No! I need to tell you. I know I did wrong and I am begging you to forgive me. As a Jew."

God had just punched me in the gut.

Judaism taught me there are two types of sins, the first being humans against God. The second sin is committed by humans against other humans. If this man had wronged me personally, I reasoned, I could have forgiven him. It would have been a sin against only me.

But Herr Nazi asked me to forgive him for sins he committed against other Jews in a concentration camp. He singled me out to hear his confessions and shoulder all of his sins, and absolve him, pardon him. This I could never do. The Jews he sinned against were people I knew and loved. People like Schmuel.

"I ordered the murder of Jews from a small nearby town. I ordered them to be sent into the gas chamber. It was near the end of the war. I could have released them and told them to hide, but I was so intent to fulfill my orders." He vomited and groaned when he remembered even more. "There were even little children, no older than my own."

The pain in my heart crippled me.

The sin of killing another individual, or in this case, an untold number of Jews is a sin too big to be forgiven. Some people even believe that God cannot forgive that sin. I didn't know what to do.

Repentance in Hebrew comes from the word *Teshuvah*, meaning a turning away from evil, a turning toward Torah. It is a process not a single act. This man confessed that when he had the opportunity to display moral courage and let the Jews leave and hide until the end of the war, he chose not to do that. In that moment, I wondered if he was truly repentant or did his fear of what lay ahead of him make him quake and say anything to absolve himself.

But that was him and his *tsuris*, trouble.

I had to make my own decision.

There is Teshuvah, but I also knew something else called cheap grace—say you forgive someone, not meaning those words, and walk away. My grandmother taught me about that. If I said the words that forgave him, he would die in peace. His Nazi son would be gone from the unit forever once he died. I didn't have to mean the forgiving. I would be helping the man move on. My grandmother would have agreed with that thinking.

We are all created in the image of Hashem. It's why we have to forgive our enemies no matter what they do. It is the only way to be free of the pain our enemies caused. Forgiveness is the only way we rid the world from evil.

As much as I wanted to be the bigger person like Rabbi Donin and truly forgive Herr Nazi, I couldn't do it. All I could think of was Schmuel hiding in a closet, incontinent, and begging God for help because of something this schmuck did in Auschwitz. And Jacob screaming in terror from a smell . . .

But . . . I looked at Herr Nazi and gently touched his cheek with a trembling hand. "It's all right," I choked on the words, not meaning any of them. "You're forgiven. Close your eyes and let go now."

I had taken the cheap grace way out. I wondered if the man understood what I had done. It didn't matter. With my words, he felt free to die.

"Thank you," he whispered.

Herr Nazi died before the end of my shift.

I headed for my car after work ended. Schmuel waited for me there. His face streaked with tears, his hands balled into fists, his rage and hatred focused on me.

"You held his hand. You *forgave* him! You had no earthly right to do that. You're worse than he is!"

Trying to explain why I said those words wouldn't do any good. Schmuel had condemned me to hell. I said nothing and let him rage on in Yiddish. I didn't need to know the meaning of the words spewing from his mouth to understand him.

Schmuel finally stopped his tirade. "Did he suffer at least?"

"Yes," I said. "He spent his last moments of consciousness back in Auschwitz. Guilt tore him apart more than the cancer."

Schmuel closed his eyes. "Good." His eyes bore into me with so much hatred and hurt. I cried out at the sight of it. "You betrayed me. You betrayed all of us. You're just a *goyishe* pretending to be a Jew." He turned and started to walk away. "We are no more friends. You are my enemy now. Do not ever come to my house again."

I sank against my car and wept—such a long, ugly cry—and I couldn't stop myself while watching Schmuel hobble away. "Oh God. What have I done?" He thought I betrayed him. The worst pain in the world goes beyond the physical, even further beyond any other emotional pain that one can feel. It is the betrayal of a friend. And Schmuel said I had betrayed him.

Hours passed before I could get in my car and safely drive home. I never returned to Schmuel's home again. I never called. I stayed away as he demanded. I was an evil that died, not even good enough for a *shiva*.

I didn't discuss any of this with Will or Leila. Not even Ben. It had been too painful to endure let alone relive and examine. I wasn't sure if I did the right thing or not, but I do know I had not been able to find it in my heart to mean the words that I said. "You're forgiven."

And if I was any kind of loving, Jewish soul, I should have been able to do that. To make matters worse, even though I didn't mean the words, I now believed I had betrayed every one of my Holocaust survivors by just saying those words to my patient—*You're forgiven.*

If I had been wrong in my actions, who was going to forgive me? No one.

39

If the world will ever be redeemed, it will be
through the virtues of children.
(Talmud, Nedarim)

I was a different human being when I returned to ER after the
two-week stint on the Chemo unit. I doubted every encounter
I had with patients. I doubted my own sense of worth as a nurse.
My head nurse worried because I had been the one who was best
at calming irrational and hysterical people. After Herr Nazi and
Schmuel, I had no confidence left to do that. I lost my instincts.

Ben Luborsky sought me out a few weeks later. "We need to talk
about what happened with Schmuel," he said when he saw me. "Now."

Once we were in a room alone, I turned on him. "I know I didn't
handle the situation right," I started, "but I—"

"Stop right now. I will not allow you to feel bad over taking
care of a patient in desperate need of your nursing skills because a
Holocaust survivor doesn't want you to do your job. You did what
you thought was right. And you did what was best for your patient.
That is all there is to say."

"He thinks I betrayed him," I cried.

"I understand that. But you and I both know you did no such thing.
You took an oath my dear, a vow to care for anyone in need of your

nursing services. Just like I took an oath. We have higher standards to follow, and people like Schmuel will never understand them."

He placed his hands on his hips. "It pains me to say this, but it's the truth. Schmuel is a damaged soul. We will never be able to help him beyond what you have already done. You cannot fix people like Schmuel. Neither can I. We do the best we can, but sometimes it simply isn't good enough. Have I made myself clear? Do you understand what I'm saying?"

I felt as if he had thrown a bucket of ice-cold water on my face. David had said almost the exact same words to me on his boat. *You can't fix a goddamned thing, Nurse Pam. You can't fix the hate that Israel faces and you can't fix your Holocaust survivors. All you can do is what you're doing now. Love them and care for them.*

I sucked in a deep breath and exhaled. "You don't hate me then?"

"Hell no. Neither does anybody else who has heard what happened. Now, sharpen up and be the nurse you're supposed to be."

I smiled. "Yes, sir."

Ben smiled too. "When I heard him talking yesterday, I just knew you'd have taken every accusation he made to heart. I got here as soon as I could." He put his arm around me for a moment. "Be a little tougher. All right?"

"All right." He gently chucked my chin and left the room.

Our first wedding anniversary was spectacular and at the same time a little bit terrifying. It was the day I discovered that the abdominal tumor I had felt for three months and feared was malignant, was not a tumor at all. It was a baby.

Surprise! My gynecologist apparently was incorrect when he announced six months prior to our wedding that I would never have children because of my endometriosis. Ha! Take that my dear doctor. Apparently love and Jewish sperm can beat any odds, including diseases.

June 3, 1980 was also the day William discovered the University of Windsor accepted him into law school.

Oops.

"Well, now what are we going to do?" said Will that night.

I shoved a saltine cracker in my mouth. My morning sickness was a 24/7 kind of thing. Discovering I was pregnant at the same time my husband discovered he was accepted to law school made it so much worse.

"Well, there's one thing I've learned." I chomped on another cracker. "There is never a convenient time to have a baby. We just carry on until the baby is born and we figure things out from there. So, you'll go to school and I'll work until they kick me out of the hospital. I have six months leave after this baby is born to get everything settled before going back."

Much easier to say than do.

We left it until the last minute to move out of my apartment and into a townhouse on the east side of town, closer to the hospital. We had only one car. Will needed to be at school and I needed to be at work. At least the townhouse was on a bus route.

I brought up my biggest fear while unpacking boxes. "What if your mother rejects our baby? What if she hates the baby? What if —"

Will put his fingers over my lips. "Shh. My mother will love this baby the moment she sees him, I promise you."

I barely heard him as I continued to cry. "What if I hate the baby? I was an only child and have never been able to relate to kids. I hate them in the ER."

William pulled me to his chest and brushed my forehead with his lips. "Calm down. You are going to be the most awesome mother the world has ever seen."

I didn't believe him, but it was nice of him to say.

On January 21, 1981, Windsor was victim to the winter storm from Hell. The wind raged and blew waves of snow across the parking lot in front of our place, causing mountainous drifts to swirl and rise up against the trees and buildings. Eventually the wind softened and crooned as snow blanketed the window panes.

It seemed only fitting that Joshua Nathan Goldstein chose that time to come into the world, not with wails and cries like other babies, but quietly. Like a flake of snow.

Joshua turned to me with his blue eyes wide open and stared. He knew who I was.

"Hi, my sweet Joshua," I whispered.

"He's beautiful," said Will. "Just like you."

"And huge," said the nurse. "He's nine pounds fifteen ounces. No wonder you had such a hard time pushing him out."

Will made the necessary calls to let everyone know that both Joshua and I were fine. Within minutes of the call to his mother, we heard an announcement: "Security to nursery, third floor—"

Will heaved a knowing sigh. "That will be my mom causing all the commotion. I'll head over there and try to stop them from arresting her."

In her excitement to see her grandson, Esther had ignored all of the rules, rushed into the sterile nursery with her boots and winter coat still on, picked up Joshua and cried—tears of joy mind you, but she cried. The staff told me later she wouldn't let nurses near her or the baby. My hardhearted mother-in-law held her grandson close, unmindful how the snow from the shoulders of her coat and the brim of her hat fell on him. The nurses said they feared she was a crazy lady. Esther claimed she was just emotional.

My fears about Esther were unfounded. She did not reject my son that day. In fact, she and Joshua bonded on the spot and she immediately became one of the most devoted grandmothers a child could ever want or need. She loved him so much.

Esther still didn't like me and continued to make it a habit of tossing criticisms my way, but that was okay. She did not reject my son.

And on an even brighter note—after almost two years of marriage, I finally had a name I could call her—*Baba*.

"

40

Whenever men and women are persecuted because of their race, religion, or political views, that place must—at that moment— become the center of the universe.
(Elie Wiesel)

When I returned to work, I asked for a permanent afternoon shift. That way, I was home all day with Josh while Will did his postal route in the morning and went to school.

Meanwhile, in the rest of the world, antisemitism carried on and on, as did violence and racism. Now that I had my own child, my fears and worries rose exponentially. Gertie Smith, my librarian, telling me the hatred of Jews reached a peak of violence every seventy years or so haunted my thoughts every day. She was right. There have been numerous genocides of Jewish people throughout the centuries before the Holocaust. I decided that whoever it was who said history repeats itself must have been talking about the history of the Jews. And those who dare to belittle their immense suffering are not only heartless, they are also historically ignorant because, sad to say, the Holocaust and the twentieth century were not necessarily the worst century for Jews. Since Biblical times, there has been tumultuous and bloody bitter fights to simply survive against enemies that were intent on eradicating us.

Which is why when I watched the news in the seventies and eighties, I thought the world had gone mad yet again. Men like David Duke questioned how many Jews died in the Holocaust if any of them ever did! Had the Holocaust been a purge of any other race or group of people, everyone would have accepted those facts. Nobody disputed that at least 800,000 Rwandans died in the genocide that occurred during the Rwandan civil war. Or that 1.7 million Cambodians died in the Cambodian killing fields. My mind boggled at the vehement denials of the Holocaust and the increased antisemitism.

Russia's treatment of Jews was a prime example of this increased hatred towards Jews, and especially how the world ignored it. Before the 1960s, Europe and the Western countries were largely unaware of the extremity of degradation Jews in the Soviet Union faced on a daily basis. Or if they were aware, they didn't give a rat's ass.

Russia, Rwanda, Somalia—I am certain the Western countries only ever understood there was one commonality between those three countries—they all ended in the letter A.

Elie Wiesel published *The Jews of Silence*. His book became a call to action, directed at Jewry in the Diaspora whose silence regarding Russian Jews had been deafening. It wasn't a drop of silence on their part, it was a bloody ocean.

Because of Wiesel, Jews around the world snapped out of their complacency and staged rallies, wrote letters, and pleaded for Soviet Jews to be granted emigration rights.

Under Leone Schott's leadership, the Windsor Jews did their part as well, and I stood right next to her. She included fighting for the rights of Somalians and Rwandans. She and I went to marches in Detroit for the Rwandans. We went to fundraisers for Somalians. We wrote so many letters.

Leone was one fierce warrior.

"You don't need friends for approval when you follow Torah," Leone said in a voice that brooked no argument. She clutched my hand. "You and I are fighting for human dignity. This is how you become a devoted Jew, Pamela. You have to use that moral courage you already possess. Torah sets far more value on moral courage than physical courage. This courage, my sweet girl, is a demonstration of our confidence and trust in Hashem. If you don't believe me, read the Psalms. *Hope in Hashem, be strong, keep thy heart steadfast, yea, hope thou in Hashem. Through Hashem we shall do valiantly.*"

She put her arm around me. "I'm not always going to be here to keep this community on its moral path. You're going to have to step up when I'm gone."

"Just me?" I said with a smile tugging at the corners of my mouth. I found it endearing when Leone became so righteous. She never talked down to people when she did. Rather, she seemed to become more and more charming. I vowed to own that skill myself one day.

"Oh, there are others coming out of the woodwork. You'll find each other when you need to. Make sure you recognize them and become friends with them."

Leone and the B'nai B'rith women wrote thousands of letters. I felt so proud standing amongst the crowds of peaceful protesters with a placard in my hand, rallying for freedom. It was the right thing to do.

Not even one drop of silence existed anymore.

41

Mames farshteyen vos kinder zogen nisht.
"Mothers understand what their children cannot say."
(old Yiddish saying)

Either endometriosis was a load of poop or I needed a new obstetrician. I was pregnant again.

Will was still in law school but I didn't care. I adored my obstreperous son, Joshua, and to have a second child was the best thing that could happen. We moved to a bigger apartment on Victoria Avenue. It was huge with over 2200 square feet. I put up another mezuzah.

"What happened to that girl who announced she hated kids and never wanted children?" William teased when I told him of our coming bundle of joy.

He made me laugh. I remembered saying that to him. Funny how motherhood evolves a woman's opinions.

42

We are all flawed. It's part of growing up to realize
your parents are flawed as much as you.
(Anonymous)

We rarely saw my father after the ballroom lessons. He danced
every night of the week and on weekends he was off to square
dancing conventions—Kentucky, Ohio, Chicago, Minnesota—and
he attended each one with a new woman. I could not keep all of
them straight. Many called me, asking what they could do to get
him to marry them. After each distressed call like that, I recalled the
lines from a song in *Finian's Rainbow*: "When I'm not near the girl
I love, I love the girl I'm near." Ah, my dear father—his flirtatious
Irish roots were definitely showing.

Because of his lack of money, we ended up paying for a lot of
the dance trips. Dad enjoyed his new life so much, I mean he *really*
enjoyed his new life, and I was thrilled for him. I didn't care about
the money, nor the reputation he was gaining in Windsor as a true
ladies' man. After so many years of a sad marriage and watching my
mom die, he deserved to be happy.

Dad liked being a grandfather but didn't know what to do with
a baby. I was fine with that as well. He never did figure out how to

be a father, so I arranged for activities he could do with Josh, like going to breakfast at McDonald's.

Dad was never big on words or displays of affection towards me, not even when I was a kid. Since I moved out and got a job and married, our relationship boiled down to dinner every few weeks, or lunch. He did come over one day, in between his traveling, to ask if it was okay that he rarely saw me.

"I'm not much good with words. Never know what to say to you, now. Never did."

"It's okay, Dad," I said. He had such a hard time talking to me, and acted as if he had done something wrong. Was this guilt over Mom? "I understand," I said. "We're just on different paths, right now. So long as our paths keep meeting, we're good. Just remember that Josh does need a grandpa to look up to every now and then. I'm always here for you."

My dad gave me a genuine smile. He must have been a really good-looking guy back in his day with a smile like that. "You're a good kid, you know. I'll call you in a few weeks. The dance circuit is really busy this time of year."

43

True friendship never dies. Nurture it. Savor it.
Guard it well, deep in your heart.
(Anonymous)

A wonderful miracle happened the next summer. The horrid orthodox rabbi moved away to Israel. I felt bad for that poor country. In his stead, however, we lucked out and welcomed a young orthodox rabbi and his family to Windsor, just four houses away from us. They had a child Joshua's age. Rabbi Ira Grussgott and his wife, Miriam, quickly became our dearest friends.

I always wanted to be *Kosher* and practice being *Shomer Shabbos,* where after sunset on Friday one rests and does nothing until after sunset and *Havdallah* service on Saturday.

William adamantly refused to keep Kosher so Ira and Miriam could eat at our home. "No way in hell, Pamela Goldstein. I refuse to follow a bunch of ancient rules that should have been thrown away years ago."

"But we already don't mix milk with meat."

"No, and that's that."

Determined to win this battle, I relied on my fiery one-fifth Irish heritage to help me pursue this until I had victory. I brought it up nearly every time we spoke.

William found himself in a constant state of fury. I wasn't backing down. Unfortunately for him, I had also remembered Rabbi Donin's words about the woman being in charge of the home. I would win this time.

"None of this Kosher and Shomer Shabbos means anything to me," he shouted during one of these oh so many arguments.

I had tried reason, begging—anything I could think of to get William to change his mind. All that was left were the knock down shoot 'em out tactics.

"So, you like pork then?" I said.

William glared at me. "Pork is not the be all and end all to being Kosher and you know it. Let me put this another way so you understand. Being kosher means nothing to me."

A diabolical plan had come to mind. I dared not tell my friends about it, but I was desperate. If it worked, we'd be kosher in a few days.

"All right, then, William."

Will shot me a suspicious glance. "What does that mean?"

I shrugged and walked away. The next morning, he had bacon with eggs. Lunch consisted of a ham and cheese sandwich. Supper was pork chops.

William knew what I was doing. It had come down to a battle of wills. "Pork again?" he said with icy politeness.

"It was on sale."

A second week of pork three times a day passed. Our home now owned a wall of iced silence that was getting bigger by the day, hour, minute.

When the third week began, Will finally roared and threw a plate of cabbage rolls made from pork across the room. "All right! I give up. It might mean something."

I felt so relieved. It was an awful thing to do to William. And all that pork was making me sick.

With his acquiescence, the ice wall came down. "Thank you," I said.

William's glare softened only slightly. "You put pork in front of me again, and we're divorced." With that he walked out the door.

Whoooa, I had never seen Will so angry.

After he returned, I called him back to the dinner table for salmon, asparagus, and roasted potatoes. And his favorite—German chocolate cake.

He devoured everything in front of him. I snuggled up to him with another piece of cake. "I love you, you know."

Will glared at me. "Don't think for one second this makes up for three weeks of torture." After he downed another piece of cake he sighed. "Well, maybe a little."

The kosher battle ended and I was the victor. It was a bitter and angry fight and at one point I truly thought we were going to divorce. One thing was certain. It would be a very long time before Will would allow me another victory. I faced that fact. That's what really happened. I knew of no one who was smarter than William. Certainly not me. He just finally saw how important keeping kosher was for me. I suspected the battle would be on again if Ira and Miriam ever left town.

By the end of the week, my kitchen was *kashered* and ready for Shabbat. New plates, new utensils, new pots—new everything. Ira and Miriam were our first guests.

It was a whole new magnificent Jewish world for me. Miriam and I walked to shul every Saturday, took turns for Shabbos dinner and Saturday *Havdallah* service. I became *Shomer Shabbos*. All of this happened much to Will's and Esther's dismay.

I had one saving grace. William liked Ira. They were definitely matched intellectually, and he really enjoyed spending time with Ira and Miriam. Will was willing to put up with "all of this" for his friend's sake.

After several months passed, Ira encouraged me to have an orthodox conversion. Reform conversions were not recognized in Israel. "Trust me, you want your kids to have that right-to-return to Israel, if, God Forbid, another Hitler should appear," said Ira.

That right-of-return was a huge thing for Ira. His parents were Holocaust survivors and Ira desperately wanted to move to Israel. It didn't take rocket science to understand why he felt the incredible need to move.

I began classes immediately.

Ira was so wonderful and special in so many ways. He and Miriam were a joy to be around. He was also very progressive in his thinking about how to stop assimilation, using exciting new traditions in the community, to celebrate Judaism.

"We can't have stagnation, Pam. Nostalgia is very sweet, but we cannot recreate the old congregation," he said more than once. That statement sounded more like what William believed. "A lot of this Jewish community in Windsor is hung up on 'Do we move to the left or the right?' If I have anything to say about it, we're not going to move left or right, but forward and up, spiritually and with energy, true to Orthodox Jewish law, with veneration and respect."

Eventually, Ira's parents came for a visit. His mother made me a beautiful Shabbos apron out of lace. His father treated me like a long-lost daughter.

I adored Ira, but I was in awe of his father. It was like meeting a *tzaddik*. Technically, a tzaddik is one in whom we see our true selves. And by being in our presence, he connects us to God.

Ira's dad was a highly respected international speaker and teacher.

I remember the night Will and I sat glued to our seats as he escorted the host of a talk show through Mauthausen on TV. He described what life was like in the camps and mentioned how women gave birth there. Nearly all of them killed their babies to prevent the Nazis from torturing the little ones and using their skin for wallets and lamp shades.

Ira's dad walked over to an open area by the women's barracks and kicked around some dirt. "This is where they would bury them," he said and proceeded to explain details of the burials and barracks. He suddenly stopped talking, bent down, and picked up a bone—a tibia—from a baby. The man dropped to his knees and let out an unearthly, anguished cry that cut a soul asunder as he clutched the bone to his heart. Will and I cried along with him.

I ran into Joshua's bedroom and picked him up, making sure he still breathed. I stayed there all night, holding him, rocking him, singing lullabies, and crying. I couldn't seem to cope with anything about the Holocaust anymore. "God, help me understand. Give me strength to understand."

God wasn't answering that night either. It was as if He deserted me.

As loving and friendly as Ira's dad was towards me, I just couldn't bring myself to talk to him. It wasn't even a year since Herr Nazi and his death and I still felt demoralized and unworthy of any Jewish respect. I didn't think I was worthy of even being in the man's presence.

He seemed to understand my lack of confidence and confusion, and he also sensed something awful had happened. He left me to think on my own. But he made sure that I knew he accepted me, flaws and all.

After several visits, he asked me to walk with him after Saturday morning services. "You have a huge pain in your heart, Shoshana. A huge guilt." As soon as he had learned my Hebrew name, he only used that—Shoshana.

I cleared my throat which had started to close up. "I saw you talking to Schmuel today at Kiddush. Did he ever tell you about the Nazi patient I had at the hospital?"

"He made mention. I would like to hear what you have to say."

We sat on a bench in the nearby park and I poured my heart out, explaining my thoughts and why I had chosen cheap grace over refusing his request. Of course, I blubbered by the end and it wasn't a pretty, feminine cry either. I seemed forever doomed to be an embarrassment to myself when crying, but I managed to express my deepest fear. Had God deserted me because I chose cheap grace over true forgiveness, or worse yet, because I had taken care of this Nazi? That question had plagued me since the incident happened.

He handed me a handkerchief. "Well, that's some thought process," he said while lovingly patting my back.

"Was I wrong?"

He shook his head. "No. Not at all. You did exactly the right thing, not only as a Jew but as a decent human. You allowed him dignity in his dying. It wasn't up to you to judge. I had a similar experience several years ago when a Nazi asked my Jewish community for forgiveness. I actually didn't even have cheap grace as you call it. I said nothing. Prayed a lot and then walked away."

I took in a huge relaxing breath. If there was anyone I could believe, it was him. I had done the right thing.

He teasingly nudged me and grinned. "You're getting pretty close to becoming a tzaddik with this kind of tough decision making."

I wiped the tears off my cheeks. "I leave that holy stuff to you and Ira."

He chuckled. "Probably another good decision. I don't know of any tzaddik who would question Hashem like you did. You yelled at Him? The only other person who did that and got away with it was King David and the only reason he did was because he wrote all those Psalms. You better get writing."

We chatted for several more minutes. He was being kind and giving me time to calm down. I asked his thoughts on Holocaust deniers. Windsor had a plethora of them, and they held a rally in the downtown core the day before Shabbos.

"Yes, I saw that," he said. "You know what, Pamela? All of us, including the Jews and the world, have put the Holocaust high up on a mountain peak and in a cage, never to be touched or examined or questioned. We don't allow anyone to compare it to anything like the Armenian genocide or Somalia. We scream bloody murder when anyone wants to do that."

"But isn't that the way it should be?" I said. "It was so horrible."

"Yes, it was awful. But what about other atrocities? Don't they get to compare their pain to ours? Why is a Jewish baby's death worse than a Palestinian's? So, if we keep the Holocaust on that pedestal and it is untouchable, people will definitely forget about it. You know what I want the naysayers and other angry people to do? Bring it on. Tell me what is worse than the Holocaust and I will prove them wrong. Any survivor can do that. The Holocaust should be in a fishbowl for everyone to see, everyone able to compare it to something else, everyone to examine through a magnifying glass, and they'll find there is no comparison."

I closed my eyes, suddenly feeling exhausted.

Ira's dad rose to his feet. "Let's go home. I can't miss my afternoon *Shabbos* nap, but I need a little nosh before I do that. Maybe some of Miriam's pie."

44

You gain strength, courage, and confidence by every
experience in which you stop to look fear in the face.
You are able to say to yourself, 'I lived through this horror.
I can take the next thing that comes along.' The danger lies in
refusing to face the fear, in not daring to come to grips with it.
(Eleanor Roosevelt)

Because William had two more years of law school to go, I still worked. My nursing interests leaned more and more towards psychiatry. I had long ago transferred to the Psych unit. Ironically, they had closed the Two East Isolation wing and turned it into the new Psych unit. Old home week, just different staff and head nurse.

One woman arrived on the unit in the autumn—a Holocaust survivor that the doctor diagnosed as suffering from Involutional Melancholia, paranoid depression. Ellie. She had survived Auschwitz and Mauthausen.

Ellie refused to eat. She believed that our lovely hospital dietician was a Nazi spy and poisoning her food. Well, I certainly knew how to handle that, thanks to caring for knife-wielding Bayla earlier in my nursing career.

Because of the Magen David I wore around my neck, Ellie trusted me. We talked about our community, but she had never been a part of it. She barely spoke and was reclusive, even with me.

In the evenings, after visiting hours, Ellie disappeared and none of us knew where she went. One night I spotted the skirt of her nightie flutter around the corner, and I chased after her. I found her just as she turned into the nursery.

"Oh no," I whispered. Ellie leaned against the windowed wall of the nursery and sobbed.

"She comes every night," said one of the nursery nurses. "It's heartbreaking. None of us know what to do. We would have called you guys, but we didn't know what floor she was on and she won't let any of us near her."

I walked over to Ellie and put my arm around her.

"He's dead," whispered Ellie. "See the blood?"

I looked at the newborn she stared at. The babe had not been bathed yet and still bore smudges of red from the delivery. "No, Ellie, this baby is alive. See? He's crying. The nurse is about to give him a bath."

Ellie finally focused on her surroundings. "Pamela?"

"Yes, Ellie. It's me."

Her tears increased into hysterical hiccoughs that expressed a grief too deep, too profound to put into words—such a broken, splintering sound.

"Ellie, what is it?"

She clung to my arm as if it were a lifeline. "I was born in Tunisia," she said. "Dov, my husband, said I was the most beautiful girl in all of our country. He lied of course. We were married when I was fifteen and moved to a little town outside of Krakow, in Poland, where Dov took on an apprenticeship, learning how to scribe and bind books. I worked as a maid." Ellie stared straight ahead of her, reliving those days. "I had a son, Aaron. He was the most beautiful little baby."

Her eyes became unfocused as she continued to remember. She spoke as an automaton. "The next day the Germans attacked our town and herded us Jews like cattle. We were going on a trip, they said, and they laughed at us. The women had to strip naked immediately, for 'inspection.' My baby started to cry. He was so cold. I was so cold. One of the soldiers heard little Aaron crying and grabbed him from my arms."

Ellie clutched me to her as if I could protect her from the anguish. "He threw him in the air and stuck his bayonet right through him. Aaron stopped crying but the soldier threw him in the air again and another soldier caught him on his bayonet." Ellie suddenly punched her fist onto the window as if it were the infant landing on the soldiers' knives.

I had become almost as distraught as Ellie, and had no idea how to help her. Several of the nursery staff watched on, all of them in tears.

"One soldier after another joined in 'the game' . . . another, and another. I screamed. Dov went crazy. He ran in the middle of them to save his son and they shot him so many times. His face was gone. And then the soldier who killed my baby turned back to me. He pulled me by the hair and threw me on the ground, next to my husband and son."

"Ellie." I clutched my own baby bump as I suffered along with her.

Ellie shuddered and groaned, her teeth clenched, her eyes wide. "He undid his pants and shoved himself inside of me. Over and over again. I thought I would die. I was still sore from having my little Aaron. And then the next soldier did it to me. By the fourth soldier, I felt no more pain. And no matter how many times they did that to me, I felt nothing. My Dov and little Aaron were dead. I had nothing to live for. They sent me to Auschwitz. After a few days I got sick . . . an infection. They sent me to Mauthausen so the 'doctor' could fix me. Well, he fixed me. He took out my womb. For the first time since they killed my baby, I screamed."

She raised her hands and clawed at her eyes. "I can't look anymore," she moaned. "I have to stop seeing it."

I stopped her before she could do any damage to herself. Her face was an unearthly white. "God, Ellie, please stop."

Like Sarah Masinsky, she couldn't stop once she had unlocked those emotions. Her teeth chattered with the shock of reliving her son's death. "I met Haim in the Cyprus camps. We married and came to Canada; he had a brother who lived here and he sponsored us. Hymie took care of me and never demanded anything from me except my company. I didn't love Hymie. I couldn't. There was nothing left inside of me to give anyone. Hashem wouldn't give me that."

She dropped her head on my shoulder and sobbed even more. "Haim died after only a year. He had consumption from the camps and it never got better." I grabbed her as she fell to her knees and screamed with the emotional pain.

"Oh, Ellie," I whispered. "I'm so sorry."

"I never told a soul about Dov and my baby. It hurts so much."

I had no words, nothing to say. I just knelt on my knees beside her and cried with her. So much for compartmentalization. It would have been better to have learned how to show true compassion for patients while in nursing school instead of being stoic.

Finally, I managed to pull myself together. "Let's go back to your room."

Ellie slept soundly that night—the first good night's sleep she'd had in years, probably since the war, but she needed someone to stay by her side until she fell asleep. I didn't leave her.

After I found her that night, Ellie felt safe in our care. She had told her story and by doing that she could breathe again. Her personality eventually started to glimmer a bit during the following weeks. There was even a sense of humor that surfaced every now and then.

After Dr. N. read my notes on what happened that night in the nursery, he announced it would be cruel to leave her to fend on her own. Ellie needed people around her that she could trust. Plans were made for her to go to a rest home as soon as possible. Because of the long list of people needing to be "placed" in homes, it would be months before Ellie would leave us.

45

The very best moments in a book are when you read a feeling,
a way of looking at things, or experience—which you had thought
only special and specific to you. Then there it is, written by a person
you never met, sharing your imagination.
It is as if a hand comes out of a different world
and takes yours to share the adventure.
(excerpt from the play, *The History Boys*)

Even though I worked psychiatry, I still hosted afternoon teas on the chemotherapy unit and read Harlequin romances to patients. I found it amazing how Jewish patients from other hospital units heard about the gathering and joined me every day. Eventually, volunteers from the cancer clinic delivered cookies for us. My patients promptly announced they weren't nearly as good as mine. "They weren't made with love," announced one survivor.

I brought Ellie with me whenever I went to visit the fourth floor. She even helped me set up the tea and cookies.

"I used to keep one of those journals," said Ellie at one of the Harlequin Romance Club gatherings. I had been writing while waiting for people to show up. "What do you write about?"

"I just wrote about one of my patients dying. I'd love to read your journals, Ellie."

Ellie waved her hand dismissively. "I tossed them away when I moved into my apartment. Every memory I owned went into the garbage with them." She looked over my shoulder and read the last paragraph. "Ah, Pamela, you have talent."

"Hardly. I'm certainly no Jane Austen or F. Scott Fitzgerald." I felt embarrassed. I never told anyone that I wrote, let alone allowed them to read my work.

The Harlequin Romance Club members showed up one by one, like clockwork, and took their seats after picking up a cookie and a cup of tea. Ben Luborsky showed up too and chatted with his patients.

Ellie suddenly clutched my hand. "Pamela, I've got it. You should write about all of us . . . our stories. It would be wonderful to have it all down on paper for people to read."

The patients became excited when Ellie told them that I wrote.

"Yes," said Mrs. P., another survivor, "you do need to write our stories. Only mix the truth with a little fiction so people actually read it. I don't think anybody ever reads those dreary testimonial documents. I know I don't and I was there." She suddenly became excited. "I know, write it like a Harlequin romance novel. Like the ones you read to us."

My patients all laughed. So did Ben. "Another adventure for you, Pamela. Good luck," he said as he got up to leave.

Schmuel joined the group when he heard everyone. He was never very far away from us when he was on the unit. He needed the camaraderie. Apparently, when Ben defended me and took my side, Schmuel was taken aback by that. He was in the process of slowly understanding, but he would never trust me again. A little socializing with tea and cookies though, he could handle.

"Not romance," Schmuel said. "Romance is for you women." He turned to me. "I got it, write a James Bond novel. You could make me a spy for the United States of America."

Those were the most words Schmuel had spoken to me since the day Herr Nazi died. And he looked at me. Before I could catch a glimmer of hope from that, he turned away. No, that was all he was going to allow.

"The Jewish hero would have to be virile and very masterful at sex," said Mrs. P. She was really getting into the idea of this book. "You could write exciting sexual scenes."

"Mrs. P.," I gasped. When I blushed, there was even more laughter.

"You would have to put in Israel and the Independence War," announced Schmuel. "Dat is very important, yes?"

Everyone eagerly agreed. I scribbled down notes. "So, let me get this straight," I said. "I have to write all of your personal stories down, but somehow you want me to put them in a romance-spy-thriller-epic-historical novel."

"Yes," they said simultaneously and laughed again.

I took in a deep breath. "Okay, then."

They spent the next few minutes giving me pointers on what to put in this masterful work of fiction I was to write, and it had to be completed before Ellie left the unit.

"A new war," shouted Schmuel. "Where Jews fight and win and it has to be much bigger den 1948. Dose Jewish soldiers got to be brave and mighty."

"I know," said Ellie. "One of those soldiers could fall in love—"

"With a young Jewish nurse from Canada," said Mrs. P.

I laughed when Ellie pointed at her. "Whose plane gets hijacked on its way to—?"

"Israel," cried Mrs. P. "And the soldier recites *Shir ha Shirim* to her." She clasped her hands together. "I love that poem. You are the Rose of Sharon and the Lily of the valleys. By night on my bed I seek you whom my soul loveth. My beloved is mine and I am hers." Mrs. P. had a look of rapture on her face. "That would be the most romantic thing. Oooooooh, and he has big green eyes and a dazzling smile!"

"Green? Okay, but wait," I said. I gulped. Hearing Shir Ha Shirim all of a sudden and an Israeli soldier with green eyes had put me into a spin. "I'm still confused. Where does James Bond fit into all of this?"

"I got it," said Schmuel jubilantly. "The Israel soldier is a spy. He works for Mossad of Israel. And Nursie has to have a big, bad stalker."

"Ooooh, yes," cried Mrs. P. "And he has to be over six feet tall. He has to do terrible things to her –"

"But she saves herself from him," said Ellie.

They all adamantly agreed on this point.

"A stalker?" I said. "Why a stalker? And why does he have to do terrible things to her? And how does he fit into a hijacking and a war?"

Mrs. P. laughed at the look on my face. "Who knows? But he has to be there. He could be the hijacker, maybe."

"No," said Ellie with determination. "He has to go after her in Canada, of that I am certain."

"Ah, yes, I see," said Mrs. P. "He invades her home and she beats him at his own game. She shoots him in the face and blows his head off."

"Ewwwwww," I cried. "Couldn't she just shoot him in the chest?"

"No, she has to destroy him," said Schmuel.

"I know," said Ellie. "He nearly kills her at least once, maybe twice. Then the third time she rises victoriously—"

"And then she shoots him in the face and blows his head off," said Mrs. P. triumphantly. "Did you get it all, Pamela?"

"Yes, I think so."

Ellie winked at me. "And maybe we could hear the first chapter tomorrow?"

When I saw Dr. N. the next day, I told him about the request for a novel. He roared with laughter. "So, Nursie Goldstein is writing the Great American Novel." He chuckled even more. "A stalker, huh?"

"Yup, well over six feet tall."

"Well, that's easy to figure out from a psychiatric point of view. He's the Nazis. That's why the little Jewish heroine has to beat him at his own game—to prove to the world that Jews can't be destroyed, no matter what." He tilted his head in a thoughtful manner. "Really interesting how the mind works to ease fear." He went back to writing in his chart. "You better get cracking. We just got notified that she leaves in two months. That's a lot of writing."

Two months!

Miracle of miracles, six weeks later, I had a finished first draft of the Great American Novel—Jewish style. All 287,865 words of it, approximately three times the size of the average novel. I called it "A Matter of Principles." It desperately needed an editor with gigantic skills, but there it was, a manuscript in all of its glory.

I went in on a day off and read the parts I thought worthy enough for them to hear.

They *loved* it.

"It's brilliant, Dollie," cried Ellie.

Oyyyyyyy…….

At their insistence I left the manuscript with them to read again at their leisure.

46

How much is one human life worth? How do you measure or prove degrees of fear, or pain, or suffering? Such questions are not in Harvard law books, or in any book on humanity. They need to be.
(Anonymous)

Work went on a steep downward spiral after I found Ellie in the nursery. A bipolar/anger management patient came into the unit. He was a Christian and a schoolteacher from Lebanon. Moe was very eloquent in his rage, but he didn't know how to explain himself, even in a fundamental way. As with most bi-polars, he was unable to articulate what drove him to such extremes. Moe was all wound, all rage against the world, and what he thought was an absent God.

Moe hated Jews and Israel—his main obsession for the rage.

His erratic behavior embarrassed his family. They were especially horrified by his temper tantrums, his hatred of Jews, and what he spewed about Israel. Israeli soldiers had saved their lives from Hezbollah. They could never hate the people who saved them.

There were protocols followed on Psychiatry. Dr. N. believed it was better for a patient to choose the staff member they related to the most and that staff would then become the patient's primary care giver.

Moe chose me. He made me listen to all of his confessions about his nefarious deeds. This was deja vu for me. First Herr Nazi confessing to me and now this angry little man. The bizarre thought that went through my mind was both men were under five foot six inches. Napoleon Bonaparte syndrome? Come to think of it, even Dr. N. was under five foot six. And so was Dr. Dornanalty! Oyyyyy. Maybe I was going crazy.

I explained to Moe that I was Jewish and this was not a good idea.

"I know you are a fucking *Yahudit*, that's why I pick you."

Feeling more than a little concerned, I tried to explain that by calling me a "fucking Yahudit" all the time did not make me feel very friendly, that I thought of him as my enemy.

"We *are* enemies," he snorted. "I know who you Jews are and what you stand for. I know what you believe." He spat on the ground. "I don't know who any of these other assholes are and what they think. You, I trust."

Um, thanks?

I talked to Dr. N., his doctor in charge, who was also Lebanese, and I asked if he could maybe convince Moe to talk to another staff member. Listening to Moe made me feel uncomfortable, on edge. I didn't want to go through another Herr Nazi experience.

"Look, Goldstein, what are you going to do? Refuse to treat every patient you don't like, or who hates Jews? That's not you. Never has been you. So, deal with this nut bar. You always have to accept a patient for who he is before you can figure out how to help him."

Dr. N. was right, and I knew it. That certainly didn't mean I had to like it or even accept what he said, but it would have been the mature thing to do.

After I left the unit that night, I stopped at the river to think things through. The Detroit River was wide and powerful, known for its mighty current. It was always there. A river is a river is a river, always there. But that wasn't true. The water flowing was never the same water and it was never still, always changing, always on the move. I was like the river. I was the same person by name, but different, always changing, growing. Always learning how to see a situation from a different light.

Of course, I had to care for this patient, Moe, and give him my best. He wasn't threatening me or my family, wasn't even threatening to do harm to Israel. I thought about the rest of the staff, wondering if there was anyone else who could understand him and help him, and the answer was no. Nobody understood anything about Jews and Judaism, let alone how the other Middle Eastern countries thought about us and Israel. No, it was going to be me. Another challenge from God. Dang. Besides, I'd already made my decision with Herr Nazi on how to handle people who hated Jews. If I was any kind of Jew, I had to care for him.

I had another little chat with God. "Are You reinforcing this point, because if You think You need to, I can guarantee it isn't necessary. I got the point the first time with the Nazi."

God didn't listen to me again.

Moe was on the unit for over three months. And for over three months I got called "fucking Yahudit" every shift I worked. I was pregnant, frustrated, and a basket case. However, after observing him in action and listening to him, I began to recognize the triggers that set off his temper tantrums. He lost his temper several times a day. I figured out how to manage him by pacing alongside him and slow his rage by walking slower and slower until he calmed down. In those first weeks, we did a lot of pacing. I think we could have broken records on a lot of marathons.

Psychiatric medications generally take two to three weeks to kick in. Those dang meds the doctor ordered couldn't kick in fast enough.

A huge revelation came when Moe met my son. He loved kids. I could tell from the way his normally angry face softened while watching me with Joshua. He enjoyed it when Will brought my son in for a bedtime story and hug.

Here was another kicker. Joshua liked my patient. I'm a firm believer that there has to be some good in a person if dogs and kids like him. So, I concluded that somewhere, deep inside, this man had once been a good guy, with a soft heart. Unfortunately, Moe had that side of him locked up tight and didn't let anyone near him. How could I reach him? How could I appeal to his sensibilities to let that good side out? For the life of me, I couldn't find the answers.

Moe loved it when I paid attention to him. He was charming, gentle, kind, then. He helped Ellie walk to the end of the hall to watch TV. I think he was so kind to her because he sensed she was as wounded on the inside as he was—kindred spirits. But what had wounded him so deeply?

Moe became more and more depressed as the weeks passed. "I don't understand why I have to control my temper when I get mad." Apparently, he never had to control his temper in Lebanon. He was the baby in the family—no responsibilities, no one to answer to for his actions. His mother confirmed that for me when she came to visit him one day. The father had given up on him and beat him. He never spoke to Moe once he had been admitted.

"Nobody loves me," Moe said with remorse. "I don't understand how I'm supposed to behave anymore. I want to go home."

"Your family doesn't want you around anymore," said his doctor none too kindly. "You scare them."

If Moe didn't understand the basics of good human behavior, how was he ever going to fit into Western society? I wondered how much of his aberrant behavior was actually caused by mental illness, or was it he had been thrown into a culture not his own that was the key trigger. Nobody ever seems to take into consideration that people from other cultures need to learn how to fit in. They need to learn how to go to a bank, go grocery shopping—how to behave during altercations—knives and guns weren't accepted over here in Canada. What could be done to help immigrants adapt to such foreign cultures, new norms, drastically different from their own?

A jarring moment for me during all of this was when I realized Moe was just an example of how so many refugees and immigrants react to their frightening new world. They were nothing but a conglomeration of other individuals struggling to survive, forgetting who they were in the past and trying to recreate themselves. Well, didn't that just sound too familiar?

Seeing the way Moe sat in a corner and hung his head after yet another temper tantrum subsided made me suspect he might try suicide. I knew he needed more attention than he would receive on the short-staffed shift. I stayed after work and played cards with him until nearly dawn.

Interesting thing about a friendly game of cards—people talk during the game. Moe talked about being a teacher back home and how he enjoyed watching me with my son Josh. He talked about how many kinds of bombs he knew how to make, how he learned this skill from his cousin, and how his mercenary cousin used to blow things up in Lebanon and Israel.

Moe re-emphasized how he feared he would never fit in "over here." He was the other people. He especially didn't understand why his family only came to visit him on Sunday. However, he understood he needed to learn how to fit in. He couldn't.

Moe was a perfect target for his cousin to recruit for Hezbollah. His cousin was being paid to fight for them and said he could get Moe a job. Those words chilled me to my bones. I tried to explain to the doctor about Moe's skills at making bombs. He didn't believe me, even though I had Moe draw pictures of all the bombs he knew how to make.

"He's giving me nightmares," I said.

"If you're so worried about this, think about the absolute worst thing that could happen with crazies like this around. You get killed? Your family gets killed? World War Three? Israel is nuked?"

When he sensed my genuine fear, he sighed. "Look, you think these freaks don't scare the shit out of me? They do. Put it into perspective."

I couldn't.

Eventually, Moe's temper tantrums subsided. The medications had finally kicked in. As the days turned into weeks, this depressed, violent soul refused to comply to society's rules. Nothing worked. I went back to the doctor.

"Goldstein, you're just not getting it. Moe and his family are immigrants. It's nothing new to be unable to fit in. Some adapt but most don't, so they end up living in poverty or on the streets for the rest of their lives. There's nothing you can do. Moe is lost. Irretrievable."

My hackles went up immediately. He had thrown the gauntlet down in my face. For the next two weeks I tried every tactic I could think of to help Moe learn how to follow the rules of Western society. Nothing worked.

I approached Dr. N. with another idea. A halfway house where they teach people . . . .

"Stop kid. I'm discharging him to a nursing home with a locked mental unit. Sometimes, Goldstein, we have to accept that there are bad eggs out there that we can never fix and then our responsibility is to try and protect society from them. Like Moe. You think I haven't watched you trying to get him to fit in? He just can't. So, we make sure he takes his meds and he doesn't have outbursts of destructive rage." He sighed. "And we make sure he doesn't join his cousin in Hezbollah by keeping him locked up. That's it."

That's it? A soul no one wants, gets locked up. Damn, I'd really lost the battle for Moe.

47

The loss of a friend is like that of a limb; time may heal the anguish of the wound, but the loss cannot be repaired.
(Robert Southey)

My OR supervisor called. "Hey kiddo, just got word. Strathman died yesterday. She committed suicide."

The news of Strathman's suicide struck me hard. I tried to rationalize her death, saying it was the result of a severe depression that she already had here, but for the life of me, I could not shake away her words on that night in OR. *My biggest fear is that nothing has changed. That people are still the same disgusting animals they were back then. And I couldn't bear to see that. I'd kill myself if I did.* Surely to God the people of Germany had changed. I read books that claimed they had. I'd also read books that said the Nazi party was rising in Germany again. I also had to admit that despite every effort by Jews and Jewish organizations around the world, antisemitism and violence against Jews was high, really high. Israel was being attacked on a regular basis. I found myself not knowing what to do yet again. And with one baby and a second on the way, I desperately needed to ensure my kids would have an Israel to turn to for safety.

My worries and fears were put on hold on May 9th. As the sun rose that day, Benjamin Jacob came into the world. No muss, no fuss. Nine pounds, fourteen ounces. My Benjamin. "Hello, sweetie," I whispered. "Welcome to the world."

With Will's law degree completed, and articling with a firm for another year to go, I returned to the psych unit before Ben was five months old. I worked the afternoon shift so we didn't have to pay babysitters. They were a luxury. Will brought both boys to see me before bedtime every night so I could breastfeed Ben. He brought them in a wagon with bottles of milk and snacks galore at the ready because we still only had one car which I took to work. The buses stopped at midnight and Will didn't want me walking home alone.

Three months after Benjamin was born, I completed my ortho- dox studies. It had only taken me six months to have an Orthodox conversion as opposed to the two years for the Reform version. How ridiculous was that? According to rabbinic law in Israel, I was officially a real Jew, and so were my boys. Just had to get through another mikvah. Oy. I'm not sure how it was possible, but this pool was filthier than the first one. Miriam was my attendant.

"Does nobody ever clean this thing?" I said to Miriam.

"I just close my eyes and do it really fast," she replied. "If you don't look, it's easier."

Not only did I have to be in the water, so did my boys. Josh thought it was great fun and eagerly dove in. When he was out of the water, I brought Ben in. After I submerged him three times and said the prayers, he lifted his head and smiled. And pooped.

Miriam handed me some paper towels in a panic. "Just scoop it up real quick and I'll throw it away. We'll use the five second rule. No one will ever know."

I burst out laughing. "Miriam, we have to drain the pool."

She started to laugh at the absurdity of the situation as well.

Together we drained and sterilized that pool. "This is good," said Miriam. "*Gam zu l'tova*. I have to use it in a few days. It'll be nice."

My heart swelled with pride after my orthodox conversion. After we returned home, I called Tootsie.

"So, are you and Will moving to Israel now?"

"Aunt Tootsie, I can barely get him to want to raise our kids as Jews."

"But they will be," she said with a chuckle when she heard the stubborn pride in my voice. "You wouldn't be my niece if they weren't." After a moment she added. "I'm beginning to believe that story about your great-grandmother being Jewish. She was really stubborn, too."

My stubborn pride aside, life seemed to be going well, albeit very busy and intense. I loved my life. Nothing could possibly could wrong.

Ha!

Ira announced he had accepted a job in Montreal. They would move within the month. Miriam and I wept long hours together as I helped her pack all of the children's toys. "We'll call each other," I said.

"And we can visit too. Montreal isn't that far, is it?"

"It's far enough."

My heart sank even deeper. I was never going to Montreal to see my dear friend. There was too much pain in that city for me.

Because we shared so much together including the birth of our new babies, Shabbos, and all the holidays, Miriam had become my sounding board, my confidante, and my dearest friend.

Being Shomer Shabbos was going to be next to impossible to continue. Even keeping kosher was in the balance. With Ira not around to defend kosher, Will would definitely try to end all things Jewish. As happy as I was, he had felt as if he had been in a Jewish prison. We were never going to agree on this issue and this broke my heart.

Leone, dear soul, decided I needed to sit on the board of directors at the community center to take my mind off of Miriam and Ira's departure. Within a few months, she had me sitting on the UJA committee as well. It wasn't much, but it did help a bit.

48

Somehow heaven and earth met in the Jewish heart, lifting people to do what otherwise seemed impossible. Descartes said: I think, therefore I am. The Jewish axiom is different. Ani maamin. I believe, therefore I am. This has never changed in 7,000 years.
(Rabbi Jonathan Sacks)

I continued to bring Joshua and Benjamin to synagogue every Saturday after the Grussgotts left town. Joshua had started going to *Morah,* teacher, Parnes' day school at the synagogue and knew all of the kids in attendance. He loved it and even announced to his Baba that one day he was going to be a rabbi just like Rabbi Ira. Hehehehehe.

I cannot describe the feeling of contentment I felt while sitting in shul. I wish I could. Everywhere I looked, I saw friendly faces—Morah Parnes with a smile that lit the entire synagogue, Leone Schott donning another glorious hat, the survivors praying—the cantor who now led services in the absence of a new rabbi. Saturday services always felt like a downy comforter embracing me, making me feel warm and loved.

One of the regular "traditions" of Saturday made all of us laugh—when the little kids saw Harry Weinstein, the butcher. They made a mad rush, scrambling over him, searching for the hidden candy he always had just for them. His eyes sparkled with joy and love at their antics. Somehow, he always seemed to have enough candies to go around.

During Kiddush I discovered more Holocaust survivors living in the local Jewish community. Fifty-one women in all. Leone explained that over one hundred survivors had been sponsored by our community post-war. A lot of the men had already died.

When I read the chronicles of our Jewish Center a few days later, that was the exact time when this community changed, going from a strong and vibrant people, leaders of the bigger community, to retrospective, insular, and protective. The Jewish community did everything they could to help the survivors recover, but in the end, there was nothing to be done but protect them.

Many of the women I met at Shul were lonely and widowed. My dear friend, Debbie Smeltzer, a social worker, discussed this with me at length. At last, we came up with a plan to organize the Caring Committee. We created a calling tree. Once a month we called each woman to see how they were doing. If they had a problem, we tried to fix it. Oyyy, fixing again.

One day, I sat down with a cup of tea and began the calls. "Hi Sarah, it's Pam. How are you today? Everything okay?"

"Ah, sweetheart. It's so nice to hear a human voice for a change. It gets lonely talking to the television every day. It doesn't talk back."

"Surely, you've spoken to someone since I called you?"

"No, I wasn't feeling well enough to go to shul this month."

When our conversation ended, I called Debbie. "Hey kiddo, these calls aren't enough anymore. These women need more."

"I'm getting the same sense," said Deb.

After much deliberation, Debbie and I progressed to having a call once a week, plus one afternoon tea with lunch and readings once a month. I made sure Ellie and other rest home residents joined us at these outings. She had progressed in her recovery to enjoying being in small Jewish social groups.

The topics of discussion varied. One day we discussed who was the most handsome actor in Hollywood. Gregory Peck won, hands down, although Paul Newman was right up there, plus he was Jewish and had starred in Exodus. The women lamented that Charlton Heston wasn't Jewish. He made a great Moses and a stellar Judah Ben Hur.

The topic of being the Other People came up on a regular basis. None of the survivors felt accepted into any city's society, including Windsor's. "It's like there is a big wall built around me," said one survivor. "There are some folks who talk to me besides you—Leone Schott, Helen Glaser—but they're both busy with tikkun olam and protecting Israel."

"But why do you care?" said Millie. I adored this woman. She had so much gumption. "I know who I am. And I know what I went through. I don't care what anybody thinks about me."

What shocked Debbie and me was how many of these women barely felt accepted by the Jewish community itself. They all agreed something needed to be done to change that attitude of the Jewish Community Center.

Their heads swiveled as one and they all looked at me.

"Why are you looking at me?" I said. "Wow, I hope this isn't going to involve another 300,000-word Romance novel I have to write."

The women all laughed. "Oh, Pamela," said Ellie. "You're so funny. But seriously, Dollie, you know us. You know what we're trying to say. You talk to them for us." Her head bobbed with each word.

"But this Jewish community thinks I'm one of the Other People. They don't listen to me about anything. What am I supposed to do?"

Ellie rested her head on my shoulder in a loving manner. "Oh, sweetheart, you'll come up with an idea. And I know it will be epic like the book. You always do."

At one of our gatherings the women brought up the subject of death and burials. I'm not sure how it happened or when, but Ellie had become the de facto leader of the group over the months, and she approached the issues they wanted to discuss. "Dollie, dear," she said in a matter-of-fact voice, "we want you and Debbie to perform our taharas when we die."

"Taharas," I said and looked over at Debbie. She shrugged her shoulders, not knowing what Ellie was getting at either.

"Yes. You know, when the body dies, people bathe it and put it in shrouds. We want you and Debbie. We want you should be the ones to do this for us."

"*Oy vez mir,*" muttered Debbie. There was a deer-in-the-headlights look on her face. She had never done any kind of nursing care before, let alone bathing a dead body. "Well, who does this now?"

Ellie sniffed indignantly. "Two strangers from Detroit. They don't know us at all."

She looked around at the other women and they all nodded their heads. "And you're our friend. You're my friend, Pamela, and I've never had one before. I want you should do this for me. We want it should be a loving friend who sees us naked and washes us and dresses us in our shrouds. Too many strangers have touched my body without my consent. For the final time, I want my friend to wash me."

"We all want you to be the one, Pamela," said Mrs. P. "Please."

"I will have to look into it." I chose my words carefully. "I'm not sure what this entails."

"But you'll think about it," said Ellie.

"Yes, I will think about it," I said while looking at Debbie. Her eyes were enormous.

When Will came home from work that night, I told him about the request. He snorted. "You've just been Jewish mama guilted. Welcome to my world with my mother. I always thought she was the queen of inflicting Jewish mama guilt, but these ladies have really finessed it. They've got you and Debbie wrapped around their little fingers."

Not helpful.

On my next day off, I went back to the bookstore in Detroit and explained what request had been made.

Isaac handed me a cookie. I suddenly realized that whenever something like this happened, a Jewish person handed me food. I think William was right when he jokingly said that Jewish history could be summed up in one sentence—the enemy attacked us, we won, let's eat.

"That's a very great honor they've given you," said Isaac. "It is the only mitzvah a Jew can do that is never repaid. I always knew I liked you." He handed me three books and another cookie. "This will cover everything you need to know."

When I bought all three books he laughed. "Ah, life must be good. You can afford more than one book."

It turned out nobody in the community would listen to me about beginning our own Chevra Kadisha and performing taharas for these women. The highest authority, the executive director of the Jewish Community Centre, refused to let a shiksa (ME!) tell him how to run his community. Me, with a Reform and an Orthodox conversion, I was still considered a shiksa. Good one.

I have to admit, I did not handle the situation well. "If you were any kind of a mensch, you'd pay more attention to your job rather than condemn me because you don't think I'm Jewish enough." I sounded like a dang queen. Whoa! Maybe the rumor about being from the German royals was true? "This place is a pigsty."

It was the highest insult I could give him. With those words out of my mouth, the battle began. I certainly wasn't proud of my approach, but tact and grace were never my forte when it comes to heated discussions. I swore the director looked as if he suffered from apoplexy by the time I finished arguing, and I argued with him on this topic at least once a month, at the Board of Directors meetings. I still sat on the board.

He decided to recruit the new Orthodox rabbi to be on his side. He announced he didn't think I was Jewish enough either. They were seriously stubborn, sexist men and hated the fact that I stood up to them.

I had to catch myself from smiling when arguing with them. They got red in the face when they realized that I made sense, and they didn't know what to do with a woman who made sense. At one point I felt like Jack be Nimble, Jack be quick. I had to dance and jump and twirl my way through obstacle after obstacle the director and his buddy put in front of me. For ten long years.

All at once the finish line was in sight and I burst over it. I wish I could say it was because of my great debating skills. It wasn't. This success happened for one reason only—the next Orthodox rabbi in line (our community seemed to go through a plethora of rabbis,) just happened to be the son of one of my survivors, and his mother wanted this to happen.

Of course, we could organize and run the Chevra Kadisha.

Of course, we could perform the taharas.

Of course, we can follow the Halachic procedure like they do in Israel.

And by the way, *Baruch Hashem*, you want to do this.

There was a lesson here: the power of strong-minded women should never be underestimated. Or maybe the lesson was you can catch more flies with honey than vinegar.

The rabbi notified the rest of the Jewish community about the new Chevra Kadisha. My survivors were thrilled. The rest of the community, not so much. They either liked the executive director of the center, or they quaked in their boots when he passed by.

A lot of battles happened that Debbie and I managed to avoid thanks to both the Orthodox and Reform rabbis fighting for us. The big question of the day was whether or not Debbie and I were worthy of such an important task, me being a shiksa and all.

I never understood what people expected me to do or say before I would be considered "worthy" of anything. At this point, I no longer cared. Like my survivor, Millie, I knew who I was and what I stood for, and what I had survived in my life.

Will explained. "It's not that you're unworthy. You have the temerity to tell people in high places, like the director of the Jewish community center, the truth. People don't want to know the truth, sweetie," he said. "Just ignore them. And yes, the center is a pig stye. It's why nobody goes there."

One month after the announcement, Debbie and I were cleared to begin. Joe ceremoniously announced to the community we had a new Chevra Kadisha. Oh, he told us, two more women wanted to be part of the team. So that was his game.

Criticism immediately came out of their mouths. "This orthodox method is so antiquated. We found a copy of this new ceremony done in Reform shuls and it makes it so much more modern —"

"No," I practically shouted. "It's being done according to Jewish law. Most of the women we're preparing for burial are Orthodox."

"But, what about the Reform and what they want?"

"No."

"And there's so much Hebrew. Nobody reads that stuff."

Really? I realized if I didn't stand up for Ellie and the other survivors, this would just be a watered-down Reform ceremony done with whatever amendments these two ladies wanted and only when they felt like it. No Hebrew?

"Please understand this," I said. "We have one Chevra Kadisha and we're going to be halachically correct. We're performing taharas just like they're done in Israel, Montreal, and New York. If this ceremony is good enough for all of those millions of Jews, then it is most certainly good enough for us."

"But I'm allergic to eggs," one of them said. "We have to skip that part."

"No," I said. I folded my arms across my chest. "No. Now listen to me. We are not changing any of this. If you're allergic don't touch the body once the egg is on it. And wear a mask."

Once again, my responses were no way to make friends, and Debbie and I acknowledged that. However, we had made a promise to our survivors, and we intended to keep it.

Within a few weeks, we were asked to perform our first tahara. The deceased was a Holocaust survivor. The Chevra Kadisha was in business and in spite of our initial differences, we women worked well together.

After I completed the first tahara, I went directly to Ellie's rest home to tell her the news. She grabbed me and hugged me tight before I could say anything.

"I heard," she cried. "*Todah raba*, thank you so much." She sat back in her chair, dabbed the tears from her eyes and gave me a beatific smile. "Now I can die."

Wait. What? Ellie was too young to be thinking about dying. It was going to take all of my strength and patience to fulfill the vow we took.

49

When life is involved, all laws may be suspended to safeguard the health of the individual, the principle being pikkuah nefesh doheh—*rescuing a life in danger takes precedence over everything.* (Halakha)

Over the years, my participation in all things Israel became non-stop. Not only did I have Leone leading me, I had my Israeli friends Bezalel, Devorah, and Rachel discussing what happened in Israel during every one of our visits. Letters to the UN became a weekly task because of their amoral discrimination against Israel.

Many of my survivors worked alongside us with diligence and determination. Letter writing reached a feverish pitch. They were determined that a sub-human existence would never happen to anyone else while they still lived. Antisemitism and racism needed to be fought even harder now. As Leone put it, "The world is looking more and more like Germany in 1938."

Meanwhile, terrorist groups, Hamas and Hezbollah, had taken over Gaza and the Palestinian Authority, torturing and killing innocent Gazans and Palestinians and blaming it on Israel. Over 40,000 girls were flogged one year for not "covering themselves" in public. These terrorists also exploded bombs all over Israel and various parts of the Middle East. They wanted to destroy Israel. They wanted war.

A new decade of terror had begun and we Jews had newer and more dangerous battles to fight.

50

When you are hurt, God feels your pain.
You are His most prized possession. You are His child.
(Rabbi Donin)

The Middle East aside, in March of 1986, things were going well. Will's brother Aubrey had become an ER doctor in town and Will was a practising lawyer. Life was good.

On Erev Pesach, I received a frantic call from Hotel Dieu hospital. Will's father had been rushed into the ER with vital signs absent. They weren't sure if he had fallen off a ladder or if he'd had a coronary. They had searched for Esther, Will, and Aubrey for over an hour and none of them could be found.

I called William's office and explained the situation, asked my neighbor to watch Ben and Joshua, then rushed to the ER. I saw Dr. Jina and the staff working on a patient in Resus I. Paddles to the chest, nurses pushing meds through an IV. They worked feverishly for at least another hour, and I stood at the doorway of the room, knowing it was my father-in-law.

Dr. Jina announced the time of death after I entered the room. "Pam, he is a relative?"

"My father-in-law." Not knowing what else to do, I collected his belongings and put them in a plastic bag while the staff cleaned away the debris of empty med boxes, broken containers, and the intubation tube. I stayed by Moishe's side. I didn't think it was right to leave him alone before Esther saw him. I was in a state of panic. What if I ended up being the one to tell Esther her husband was dead? I bit my lips together and nearly drew blood. This just couldn't be happening.

No one could find Esther. She was grocery shopping for that night's seder dinner. I called the Jewish Community Center right after the hospital contacted me and they had sent out a search party to find her. So far, no luck.

One of the ER doctors remembered Aubrey telling him he was going to a medical conference in Hamilton. He managed to track Aubrey down and told him to come home. Hamilton was four hours away.

By the time Esther charged into the ER, Moishe had been dead for almost three hours. She stopped in her tracks when she saw me. A look of abject horror crossed her face. "Why are you here? What's wrong?"

Dr. Jina walked over and told Esther that Moshe was dead. She sagged against the ER wall. I tried to put my arm around her but she moved away and stared at the door to the room where Moishe's body lay. She wouldn't go in.

"We found Aubrey and he's on his way home," I said. "Will's staff are trying to locate him. Is there someone else you'd like me to call?" Clearly, she didn't want me, but she needed someone.

"No," she replied with quiet dignity.

We stood there, an awkward trio, in the middle of the ER hall. "I'm so sorry, Pam," said Dr. Jina.

"Thank you. I know you did everything you could. We'll wait here for my husband." I turned to Esther. "Come and sit in here until William gets here."

She shook her head no. At last, my nursing instincts kicked in. I gently forced her into the private room and ordered her to sit. She surprised me when she obeyed.

When Will arrived ten minutes later, she hysterically rushed into his arms. He went into the Resus room with her so she could see her husband. "Moishe," she wailed. "No! It's too soon!"

Will looked over at me when she flung herself onto her husband's chest. "It's okay," I said. "Let her grieve. She has that right."

Eventually, she calmed enough to sign the papers for release of body to a funeral home and Will drove her home. He called me an hour later. "She still wants to do seder," he said on a sob.

"We're on the way." I picked up my boys and headed for Esther's. The meat was in the oven and I finished preparing the seder meal. The boys seemed to understand that something awful had happened and behaved well.

Will called the Chevra Kadisha and rabbi to make funeral arrangements. Then he notified his sisters. It wasn't until Aubrey arrived five hours later that Esther lost complete control and collapsed.

Food began arriving the next morning before dawn. I was glad I had decided to get to Esther's before 0800 hours. Trays and trays, casseroles and other platters bedecked the sidewalk to the front door. I felt overwhelmed by all of it—chickens, briskets, short ribs—Esther had two refrigerators and an enormous freezer. They were completely full within an hour. I lost count of the number of fruit baskets and cakes that arrived.

"Leave this for us to do, dear," said Belle Walman, one of the early arrivals. She and several other members of the community had come to make the meal for the mourning, post funeral. "You get ready for the funeral."

The funeral was huge. Over 400 people attended. Esther stood between her sons, not moving an inch, not blinking an eye. She would not weep at the funeral. There was only one time in the days of Shiva where she displayed any emotion towards me. She clutched my hand to her heart when I brought her tea and a sandwich. "Thank you," she whispered. I kissed her cheek.

Three months after the funeral and on a beautiful, warm spring day, I discovered I was pregnant again. Esther was still in a state of shock from Moshe's death. All she could do was cry.

Maybe 1987 would be a better year.

Just before I delivered in March of 1987, Leone called me from a hospital in London. "Listen sweetheart, I know you've got pneumonia. I just called to say goodbye."

"What do you mean?" I said.

"I'm having heart surgery tomorrow and I'm not going to make it. I just needed to say goodbye."

"Leone!" I cried while coughing. "Are you in London alone? I'll come up and be with you,"

"No, Pamela. You're ill. I'm all right with this. Get better. I love you."

Leone's surgery was booked for 0800, the first surgery of the day. She died on the table at 0835.

This death of my friend just wasn't right. The Jews of Windsor still needed this magnificent woman. We were a mess without her. I was a mess without her.

Herschel Teich had once said Esther was the matriarch of the community but he was wrong. Leone had always been the brave guiding light who showed this community how to move forward into the future by her actions. From fighting the sexism of the directors, to reprimanding misbehaving rabbis, to ensuring everyone in the community was alright. Leone's shimmering soul led the way.

"You want to be a Jew?" she had asked me when we first met. "This is how you do it."

"I'll remember, Leone," I whispered that night.

Jewish tradition says children should be named in honor of a deceased family member. If the name was disliked or too strange for modern western society, then it was okay to just use the first initial. Miriam was born on March 19, 1987—named after her Zaida, Moishe. Another little Goldstein eager to charge into the world.

Miriam wasn't like the boys at all. She came into the world screaming and howling and ready for a fight. I laughed at her angry, red face and tightly balled fists. "You're just like your father," I whispered and kissed her nose. I decided I was meant to be a mother of a girl. Together we could become a powerhouse and change things for the better.

William's panic began. "Oh God, the VISA bills are going to be atrocious."

I gave him a serene smile of satisfaction. "I promise, sweetie, I won't let you down on that. After dressing two boys for so long this will be so much fun. I hope the next one is a girl too."

"I have a news flash for you. We are done. I almost lost you this time and I am never going through these last nine months again. So, get it in your head. If you want sex with me, there will be no more babies."

"You're such a party pooper," I grumbled.

Esther's face shone with delight when she met her granddaughter for the first time. "Oh! She has Rachel's eyes."

"Who's Rachel?" I said.

"Rachel was the only one of our family to survive the Holocaust. No one knows for sure how the others died, but Rachel was sent to Auschwitz and survived. We know this because she registered in Israel when she made aliyah and became a doctor there. She just died a few years ago. A friend went to Auschwitz and took a picture of the thousands of suitcases that were there in a pile. The picture focused on a suitcase that had Rachel's name on it. We had assumed the worst."

Oh my God. William's family had a Holocaust survivor. I wondered how many other family members had perished. Esther was a second-generation Jew.

That explained everything.

Despite all we had gone through together, all the guilt, sarcastic remarks, her thoughts about me, including making me feel worthless, my heart was with her in that moment. "Well, Will wants Miriam as a first name, so she is named after Moishe, but we can certainly have her middle name as Rachel."

Esther hugged me. "Thank you."

51

Let the doors of your home be wide open,
and may the needy be often in your home.
(Avot 1:5)

For the first time in a long time, I felt happy. Miriam was a year old and adorable. The boys were in Orthodox religious school and knew the prayers for Shabbos and the holidays. They even wore tzitzit under their shirts. They knew the traditions and Hebrew. And during this time, Esther had decided she no longer wanted to have Shabbos and the holidays at her house. This was great!

My sons knew about the Holocaust in a much gentler way than I did. They met the survivors at synagogue. It always amazed me how children and survivors got along so well together. They sensed a kindred spirit. The survivors delighted in their every move, whether it was naughty or nice.

Going to shul on Saturdays had become a tradition that the kids adored. For me, it was home for battered hearts needing respite. This was unconditional love for one another. This was being Jewish at its most tender time. Will refused to attend and never experienced this wonderful side of being Jewish. I wish he had. The music called to my soul and the prayers whispering around the room captured my attention every time. I didn't care that William was offended because these words were from the mountain of dead Jews he envisioned. I loved them.

When I went to the synagogue on Saturday, I wore the most outrageous, wide-brimmed, beautiful hats I could find, in memory of Leone. She had been known as the hat lady in town and was never seen without one, always saving her best ones for the synagogue. I missed her so much. Wearing outlandish hats to shul became my way of paying tribute to my friend. It seemed only fitting to continue the tradition.

Will claimed he still didn't believe in any of the Jewish "stuff." This religious chasm between us was the biggest regret I had in our marriage. I feared we would never come to any agreement. But the need in me to practice traditions and make sure my kids knew them as well was all consuming.

Will and I invited, or rather I invited people over every Friday night and for every holiday. Esther was not happy at all about that, and Will took her side. The chasm became an irreparable gulf. She attended dinner at our home on Friday night, but left immediately afterwards to go to the Reform temple. Eventually she began skipping dinners.

When Joshua was eight, he had to do a family tree for his Religious School. The point of this exercise was to see how far back we could go as a family because most of the people in our community lost track after the Holocaust.

I called my mother's family in Texas and spoke to octogenarian Great Uncle Leonard. "Well, we were all sworn to secrecy as kids," he said when we spoke. "But I guess it don't make no never mind now."

I anxiously held my breath with expectation. Had Evelyn and Tootsie been right this entire time?

"There is talk that your great grandmother, Victoria Augusta, came from a long line of Jewish rabbis, from Holstein County in

Germany. She married my father, a noble Dutchman, and turned her back on her past." He chuckled. "Lord, if she's hearing me tell you this, she's rolling in her grave and getting ready to haunt me."

"I remember Grandma Alvina used to light candles on Friday and listen to Al Jolson singing Hebrew and Yiddish songs. Am I mistaken about the significance of that?"

"Probably not. Alvina was the stubborn one in the family. I don't doubt she continued that tradition stuff. She loved it. Her stubbornness served her no good purpose in the end, though. She suffered a lot in life because of who she married. And we all tried to warn her too." He sniffed. "There's a lesson there in your grandmother's life. Pay attention to it."

"So, let me make this clear," I said. "You're telling me then that we're Jewish, on my grandmother's side of the family. Right Uncle Leonard?"

"It was always the great family skeleton. That is, if you believed it. I never had reason not to believe it."

"On my grandmother's side, right?" I wanted to make sure that I was hearing correctly.

"Right. Can you imagine the problems that would have caused?"

And there it was . . . two complicated conversions later, one Reform and one Orthodox, only to learn my lineage was Jewish. Oh, the bitter irony of it all.

I was not a shiksa after all, had never been a shiksa. Not even for a second.

Ira laughed when I called him in Montreal to tell him the news. "Well, just think; you are the most Jewish person Windsor has ever seen. Mazel tov! Maybe all of our survivor friends sensed that in you. It could be why you all bonded so deeply."

52

Whenever we reach that point when we think we don't have it in us, maybe it's for that moment that we've been created.
(Rabbi Jonathan Sacks)

Throughout all of the excitement, joy, and turmoil in our lives, Dr. Luborsky and I remained good friends. I considered him my Jewish father and he was pleased with that. Ben's second wife, Anne became a huge part of my children's lives. She was an artist and once had her own art studio in San Diego before marrying Ben, and she eagerly taught my kids how to draw.

About six months after I retired from nursing in 1994, Ben called to tell me he had cancer of the lung, stage four with widespread metastases, and asked me to come to his home. He needed to discuss a few things with me.

I knew he was going to ask me to nurse him at home like I did for my mom. Dear God, give me strength. Another prayer. I suddenly realized that I had perpetually talked to God throughout my entire life, like my grandmother had taught me. Somehow, I am certain she never intended for me to talk so much! At this point, I fully expected God to respond and tell me to find my own darn strength.

I knocked on the door and entered. Anne and Ben waited for me. She had made three kinds of cookies and tea. We discussed many things in that time, as if nothing at all was about to happen.

After an hour passed, Ben got to the point. "You know how you took care of your mother at home when she died?"

I nodded, terrified of what he was about to ask me to do.

"Can you do that for me? I'm not very good at demonstrating my emotions, but after all these years, you must know I love you like a daughter. I want you to be there when I die and give me a peaceful passage into the next world, like I've seen you do for so many of my patients."

I looked at my hands, again praying for strength. God listened this time. I looked at Ben who stared so intently at me. "It would be my greatest honor, sir."

Ben sighed with relief. We spent the next hour discussing what we would need for supplies. He didn't want hospice to be part of his dying. He had me.

I arrived every day, helped him bathe, and urged him to eat. He was in a lot of pain and couldn't walk from his hospital bed to the kitchen twenty feet away. I insisted he take medication, but he didn't want Anne to see that. "It would destroy her if she knew I was in pain."

Ben became confused by the end of the second week. I arrived one morning to find him shouting at Anne about stealing his cookies. Poor Annie looked completely frazzled while trying to apologize to calm him. I quickly stepped between her and Ben, put my hand on his arm, and treated him as he had treated his patients when they reached this stage of their cancer.

"Ben," I said quietly but forcefully, taking charge of the situation. "The cancer has just spread to your brain and you're confused now. You asked me to be here for you and I think it was for just this kind of behavior. I love you, but you must calm down and get back to bed."

Ben frowned and stared at me as if trying to figure out who I was. Slowly his confused face lightened with acknowledgment. "Yes, Pamela. I remember." He collapsed in my arms.

I struggled to get him back to bed. Once I had him comfortable, I turned to Anne. "It won't be long now, Anne. You should call your children to come home." Two of her kids lived in Israel. They needed time to make travel plans.

When she burst into tears, I escorted her to the living room and sat beside her. "Is he in pain?" she said.

"No, I'm making sure his pain is under control. Tell you what. I'll stay until one of them gets here."

"Thank you," she whispered and let out a huge sigh of relief. Being alone with him was too much for her. She looked at her watch, an attempt to dissociate so she could cope. "My goodness. Look at the time. I'll make us some lunch."

While she did that, I called Will at work and told him about Ben. "Okay, it's Thursday, I can take tomorrow off," he said. "How's Anne?"

"Relieved I'm staying here."

Anne's two children from Israel would be arriving Sunday. I assured myself I could handle Ben, soothing him and keeping him pain-free until then. I prayed I could. By Sunday morning, Ben was in a full coma.

Anne's son, Moshe, arrived at noon and immediately began shouting orders. "Why isn't he in the hospital? This is barbaric!"

There was nothing I could say to make him understand. His sister, Miriam, agreed with him. They called Ben's doctor and had him transferred to Metropolitan Hospital immediately. I told myself it was okay because he was in a coma and only going to live a few more hours.

As I prepared to leave, Anne pulled me aside. "He's not going to make it until tomorrow, is he?"

I gave her a hug. "No."

"Will you come and see me at the hospital tonight? Ben wanted a quiet and simple death. My son won't let him have that. He'll make it all religious."

"I'll be there, then."

I arrived at the hospital at nine that evening. Ben was barely breathing. Anne was nowhere to be seen. "Where's Anne? She should be here, Moshe."

"She's tired. She needs her sleep more."

I looked up at the ceiling trying hard to control my temper. "He's going to be dead before midnight. Get her back."

"No, he's not. His eyes fluttered a few minutes ago."

"Call her back now."

He refused. I ignored Moshe after that. He stared at me as if I was a lowlife because I didn't practice Judaism the way he did. He had always looked at Will and me like that during every one of his visits. He treated Will with disdain as well, always making him feel worthless. Will had no tolerance for him.

I sat by Ben's side and quietly did what he had asked me to do—help him pass peacefully. I told him what a wonderful human being he had been, that he should have no fears of dying. That I would take care of Anne for him. "You can let go now, Ben. It's all right."

I kissed his cheek. "Let go, Ben. I promise it's all right."

Ben's countenance suddenly became serene. His soul had just passed. Within minutes he stopped breathing. My sweet mensch of a friend, the man who had taken me under his wing so many times, guided me through every ordeal of my Jewish life, and taught me how to be a good Jew, was gone.

After saying the Shema, I rose to my feet. "I'm leaving, now, Moshe," I said.

I observed Ben's funeral from a distance—apart from the people in the Rachel Kaplan funeral home—further apart from the throng at the cemetery. Will and I said kaddish alone, where no one could hear us. Anne glanced my way when the service ended and her son escorted her to the funeral car. I nodded at her. When everyone had gone, I went to the grave and shoveled dirt over Ben's casket, fulfilling the mitzvah of burying my brethren, my father.

Will did the same. "He was a great man," he said with a catch in his throat. "One of the best I've ever met."

I didn't go to the meal of the mourning or attend shiva. Rather, I waited until Anne's children left for home again before visiting her. We discussed all that happened while we sat in her house and sipped tea. She wasn't nearly as religious as her children and they had made her feel uncomfortable. I took her to the cemetery that day.

"Well, that's that," she said with tears. "He was so wonderful. I'm not sure where to begin again."

I gave her a hug for support. "So, you'll come for Shabbos tomorrow?"

Anne rested her forehead on mine and cried harder. "Yes, you're right. I'll come for Shabbos. A good place to start."

53

The mitzvah is a candle on Shabbat and the Torah light, meaning:
Because of the candles will come the light of the Torah.
(Proverbs 6:23)

Every summer Ira and Miriam led a Jewish sleepover camp for Orthodox children in the Catskills. They always invited my kids to attend. We couldn't afford it, but I decided one summer I would take the kids camping at nearby Willowemuk, just down the road.

The kids were excited because they loved camping with their mother, and they'd be seeing their friends again. I was excited because I'd be seeing Miriam and Ira. After Ben's death, I needed a morale boost.

We arrived during a horrible summer storm—howling winds and a sheet of rain that put Niagara Falls to shame. We slept in the car and ate frozen Hebrew National hot dogs for supper—my kids' favorite way to eat a hot dog. Vicious little carnivores.

During our visit, Ira and his family took us to see his father at a resort he stayed at with his friends. Ira's mother had passed on years ago.

"The residents love seeing the kids," announced Ira.

All the residents were Holocaust survivors. Everywhere I looked, I saw tattooed numbers on forearms. My kids had a blast in the pool with their friends and playing shuffleboard and cards with the residents. However, the longer we stayed there the more I felt like an outsider.

"I feel that way too," said Ira when I told him how I felt. "And I feel so guilty."

"Exactly," I said. "Why do we get to live in relative ease and they didn't?"

"Because that is what Hashem wanted," said Ira's dad as he joined us. He sat beside Ira and me. "Ira, I had no idea you felt that way around my friends. Don't you understand how much joy we get from watching you and your children leading wonderful lives?"

He turned to me. "And you, Pamela. I am so proud of all you do. You and Ira are doing exactly what you should be doing. You are being Jewish without fear and raising your children to be Jews. When we see you two speaking your minds in public, we know that regimes like the Nazis can never win again. You're both so strong and diligent defending civil rights. Because of you, Jews and Israel will do great things in the future."

He chucked my chin. "Do you know what's the most exciting and heart-warming thing you and Ira do?"

I couldn't speak. My eyes hurt from unshed tears. He knew me well, this wonderful man, this tzaddick. In fact, he knew me better than my relatives. He understood I could not respond without blubbering. "You both keep Shabbos. And because you still do, in spite of all the societal pressures around you to just ignore it, I hold you in the highest esteem."

"Why, Papa?" said Ira. "Keeping Shabbos is one thing."

"But it is one big thing. Many scholars think lighting Shabbos candles is the most important mitzvah we can do because it is the longest-living mitzvah that Hashem gave us to follow."

He watched his grandchildren playing with my kids. "If you think about it, Shabbos is the single most important representation of the Jewish people. So long as that tradition lives on, we survive."

He rose to his feet. "Pamela, there is nothing you can do for my generation. We are lost and broken souls. You have spent your entire nursing career trying to treat the untreatable. And even now you are performing the survivors' taharas. There is nothing more to be done. You and Ira have, by far, fulfilled every obligation your generation has had towards us."

He laughed when Joshua announced he was Judah Maccabee about to destroy the enemy army before he dove into the pool. "All the two of you need to do for us now, in our last days, is live as Jews and light candles on the Sabbath. *Dayeinu*. It would be enough."

54

Promises are just words unless they are fulfilled.
(Irene Hunt, Across Five Aprils)

The day after I returned from my vacation with Ira and Miriam, I received a phone call. Ellie Lieber was in hospital and asking for me.

I rushed to the hospital and found Ellie barely conscious. I sat at her bedside, held her hand tight, and gently brushed a wayward curl from her face. I was about to face the one tahara I feared performing the most. Her eyes fluttered open when she felt my hand.

"Hi, Ellie. I'm here," I said.

"Oh Dollie, *Baruch Hashem*, you made it. I so wanted to see you one last time. You'll be doing the tahara, right?"

"Right." I smiled when I saw a lone tear trail down her cheek. "Hey, my friend. I'm here, right where you need me."

"Yes. I've always needed you, right beside me like this. You know why I waited to die?"

I shook my head. "No."

She gave me a last impish smile. "To give you time to practice. I didn't want for you to make any mistakes on my tahara."

Ellie gazed in my eyes with such fondness. "You were a good friend, the best. I love you," she said and closed her eyes.

"I love you too, Ellie," I whispered.

Ellie never roused after that; her hand stayed linked with mine. Her eyes would never open again. She needed me to perform her tahara so she had closure on this life.

Debbie and I went through the motions of the tahara, just as we had done so many times before. "Ellie Lieber . . ." My voice caught in my throat and I paused until I could steady myself. "Forgive us for any indignity you may have suffered at our hands in our efforts to usher you from this world to the next. We acted in good faith and did this for the sake of all that is Holy."

"*Amein*," whispered Debbie. She impulsively hugged me while bursting into tears. "That's it. It's over. She was the first one that asked, and ended up being almost the very last to die. It's over."

None of the other members knew what she meant. We had never told anyone about our vow to these wonderful women. It was between Debbie and me and my survivors.

Epilogue

"I am bent but not broken.
I am the power of the thunderstorm.
I am the beauty in the beast. I am the strength in weakness.
I am the confidence in the midst of doubt.
I am Her. I am me, the woman I need to be."
(Kierra C.T. Banks)

In the year 2000, we traveled to Israel for the first time, for my daughter Miriam's bat mitzvah. I was a nervous wreck on the flight across that Atlantic Ocean. I have an abnormal fear of flying, not that it ever stops me from getting on a plane, but nonetheless I sit there white-knuckled for the duration of the flight. My biggest illogical fear on that trip, however, was that Israel really would summarily reject me. Old fears never die, I guess.

Dawn had just begun to show its beauty when we approached Israel. The horizon had bathed itself in a soft, pink ethereal glow. The entire area below hid in a lavender shroud of mist and clouds, but the gold peaks of the Judean mountains glistened under the rising sun.

An IDF jet appeared and seemed to escort us into Israeli territory. I gasped at the sight of it, shimmering in the sun's bright light like a star. I called one of the hostesses over. "What kind of jet is that?"

"It's one of our old fighter jets, the Nesher. Afula is having an air show today with all of our old fighters flying. Escorting flights into the Ben Gurion airport is part of their practice run. They do it every year."

"A Nesher," I whispered. "I know that plane."

She put her arm around my shoulders when she saw my face become wet with tears. "*Barucheem habayeem*, Welcome home," she whispered.

Barucheem Habayeem. My people. My country. My home. I am home.

THE END

Author's Note

The first time a Holocaust survivor told me how the Nazis tortured him in Mauthausen, I left the room and promptly threw up. I was twenty-one and a first-year nurse. Only moments passed while he took my hand and quietly described Dr. Aribert Heim performing genital mutilation on him as an "experiment," but his story altered my own point of no return to life as I knew it. Days no longer had any sense, nor any ordinary scale of hours. I was no longer innocent.

The survivors' determination to live as Jews in this post-war world of evil and madness resonated deep within me to my core. My own family held the same beliefs as they did—that we had a moral obligation to stand up against the wrongs of society, to make our voices heard. My grandmother had ingrained that responsibility into my soul and I have never forgotten it.

These amazing souls I had cared for had faced the Devil and survived. They believed people like Einstein who said, "The world is a dangerous place to live; not because of the people who are evil, but because of the people who don't do anything about it." Every survivor I knew chose to make the world safer by their battles against antisemitism, racism, violations against civil rights, and caste systems. They fought with a fierce hyper-vigilance, attended peace rallies, wrote hundreds of letters, made phone calls to government agencies, and marched with oppressed people. This was their norm, what good people do.

For the most part, my survivors told me their stories just once and never wanted to discuss it again. They lived what looked like normal lives but they never forgot their past. Neither did I. No more tears were shed in front of me once they told me about the war. There were too many battles for them to fight. But their history and pain were the impetus of how they lived. In the end, it was the impetus for how I lived as well.

In the year 2000, my family went to Israel for the first time, for my daughter Miriam's Bat Mitzvah. On the tour was a visit to Yad Vashem. At the center of the Warsaw Ghetto display is a photograph of Mordechai Anielewicz, leader of the Jewish Fighting Organization during the Warsaw Ghetto Uprising, and some of the children who lived there. In the bottom right-hand corner, Schmuel, the barber in my memoir, sits smiling radiantly at Anielewicz. He could not have been more than ten or twelve. I sank to the floor while I touched his face in the picture.

In that moment, the Holocaust was no longer the past. It was real, it was still here and still tangible in the present. And I could never escape from it. Not then, not now, not ever.

My husband, William, found me a few minutes later while I still sat on the floor with my hand on Schmuel's innocent face. He had the same reaction I did when he saw Schmuel and we wept together.

When we reached the building of testimonies and histories, I registered for another survivor from my book, Ellie. I also registered her husband and baby as two more Jews who died in Krakow, Poland. Because of the babe's age, they assured me his name would be written in the giant memorial dedicated to children who had been murdered. That memorial was a simple spectacular site—one lone candle reflected from 1.5 million mirrors—the number of children slaughtered by Nazis. For me it demonstrated that the loss of even one child is felt for all infinity.

Every new display at Yad Vashem became more and more painful to bear. One picture in the archives displayed a mountain of suitcases that had been removed from Jews at Auschwitz. The one that caught Will's eye had the name Rebecca Goldstein scribbled on it.

His mother had an aunt with that name and she had been killed.

Yad Vashem completely shattered me. I realized the Holocaust was a permanent part of every Jewish soul. We had survived the most heinous of crimes against humanity and had become fiercely strong. Theodore Herzl's Zionist movement raised enough money to literally buy back most of our homeland, Israel, one plot of land at a time, and rebuild it. Hebrew became the official language of Israel once more.

Since World War II, Jews have fought every battle in the world against antisemitism. But in the end, no matter how brave, no matter how strong we become or how many great inventions and cures we may discover, the hatred that caused the Holocaust against Jews is still rampant, and getting worse every day. For thousands of years this has been so. Many Jews wonder if Dana Horn was correct when she announced people only love dead Jews. Because of my survivors, I still have hope that this is not so. I still have faith that friendships can be made, understanding of one another can be found, and peace between nations can happen—so long as none of us forget what man has done in the past.

When I think of the Holocaust survivors who have since died, Maya Angelou's words come to mind...

And when great souls die,
after a period peace blooms,
slowly and always
irregularly.
Our senses, restored, never
to be the same, whisper to us.
They existed. They existed.
We can be. Be and be
better. For they existed.

Pamela Goldstein

Acknowledgments

I am a firm believer that writers are only as good as the people who helped them reach the goal of getting a book published—their publishing company, their editor, beta readers, writers critique groups, the quality of the local library, and of course their families.

I would like to acknowledge my fabulous team at the Steve Harrison Publishing House, Christina Smith, Valerie Costa, Christy Day, Steve Scholl, and Maggie McLaughlin. A very special heartfelt thanks to my publicist, Debra Englander for taking me under her protective wing and giving me the courage to follow through with publishing *Still The Soul Survives*. Her kindness and generosity have made her a best friend for life.

I must acknowledge my friends who voluntarily read the first rough drafts more than a few times. I appreciate each and every one of you, especially my dear friend and best beta reader ever—eagle-eyed Hedy Halpern. She read the manuscript almost as much as I did!

I owe an enormous debt of gratitude to my Ann Arbor Writers Critique Group, led by the gifted writer Karen Simpson. They spent over a year repeatedly reading, editing, and critiquing *Still The Soul Survives* until we were all happy with the end product.

There are no words to describe my deep gratitude and love I have for my editor and dearest friend, Carol Rehme. She possessed the patience of Job while teaching me nearly everything I now know about writing. It took hours, days, months, and two years for Carol's patient hand to guide me to this final version of *Still The Soul Survives*.

And of course, I need to thank my children Joshua, Benjamin, and Miriam, who read *Still The Soul Survives* for family and historical accuracy, ensuring every detail was in chronological order. Thank you to my grandchildren Savannah and Xavier for reminding me how important it is to future children that *Still The Soul Survives* be available for everyone to read.

Last but not least, thank you to my husband, the love of my life, William, for buying me the computer, tolerating my lengthy affair with said computer, and sitting alone all those long hours while I wrote and edited this book. My life with you was worth writing about.

Pamela Goldstein

About the Author

PAMELA GOLDSTEIN, retired nurse and author of Still The Soul Survives, has had short stories published, including several in the Chicken Soup for the Soul series. From 1996 to 2015 she produced and hosted the international Jewish radio show, "Boker Tov." She founded and chaired the Windsor International Writers Conference and its outreach programs (Canada) from 2013 until 2020. Pam is a member of several organizations including the National Columnists and Bloggers Association, American Authors Guild, RLS Literary Guild in England, and Writer's Union of Canada. A mother of three, safta of two, Pam resides in Canada with her husband, William.

Manufactured by Amazon.ca
Bolton, ON